Peter Moser

Lucas Cranach

His Life, his World and his Art

Babenberg Verlag

Peter Moser

Lucas Cranach

His Life, his World and his Art

Babenberg Verlag

Front cover:
Self-portrait, 1550.

Back cover:
Study of Dead Waxwings Hanging on a Nail, approx. 1525–30.

Endpaper (front):
Lucas Cranach the Elder's insignia around 1510–14.

Endpaper (back):
Lucas Cranach the Elder's insignia after 1537.

1. edition 2005
Babenberg Verlag GmbH, Bamberg

Graphic design: Dr Peter Moser

Translated by: Kenneth Wynne

Printed and technically processed by:
creo Druck & Medienservice GmbH, Bamberg

ISBN 3-933469-15-5

Table of Contents

Indeed, if I exclude the inimitable Albrecht Dürer – my country-man, this indubitable genius – then, in my opinion, this century must accord you the highest rank as far the long neglected and now newly awakened art of painting is concerned.

Christoph Scheurl (1481–1542), Humanist

Introduction

At the turn of the 16th century, Thuringian-Saxon central eastern Germany began to develop, alongside Nuremberg, into a significant centre of art and culture due to the circle which had established itself around Lucas Cranach the Elder.

The foundation of its university in 1502 made Wittenberg into an intellectual centre. People inspired by the spirit of Humanism gathered at the Elector's court and shaped the cultural life of this royal seat.

In 1505, it was to Wittenberg that Lucas Cranach, who had been born in Kronach close to Coburg in 1478, came after years of travel, which had taken him as far as Vienna. His first well-known works, with a high degree of expressiveness and idyllic charm, have their roots in this period in Vienna, in which he also had contact to the Humanists at the University of Vienna.

It was also in 1505 that Frederick the Wise, Elector of Saxony, appointed Cranach to be his court painter, as the successor to Jacopo de Barbari. Under Frederick and, from 1525 onwards, under his brother and successor, John the Steadfast, and later, from 1532 onwards, under John Frederick the Magnanimous, Cranach predominantly became the painter of the Saxon and Northern German duchies. The numerous portraits which Cranach painted of these dukes and their families contributed to him enjoying a reputation which transcended the regional boundaries of that time. His importance as one of the great painters of the 16th century, which he achieved, amongst other reasons, due to his close contact to the Electors, is also the reason why such a large proportion of this book has been devoted to the Wettin dynasty.

As early as in 1508, Frederick III the Wise granted his court painter the right to bear a coat of arms: a black serpent, with the wings of a bat, placed on a yellow background. Cranach was to remain in the position of court painter to the Saxon Electors for the rest of his life.

The close connection which Cranach enjoyed with Martin Luther is a second aspect in his life which deserves closer attention. After the Diet (assembly) of Worms (1521), Luther sent a personal letter from Frankfurt to Cranach which reveals the close friendship and particularly trusting relationship between them. Later, Cranach was to become Martin Luther's best man at his wedding and the godfather to his first son.

In September 1522, Luther's German translation of the New Testament was published with 21 full-page woodcuts by Cranach. By 1546, 200,000 copies of this book and its reprints had been produced in Wittenberg. Later writings by Luther, too, profited from Cranach's art, who helped to spread the message of the Reformation by means of his woodcuts.

On the one hand, Cranach's art and in particular the new technology of book-printing enabled the wider dissemination of Luther's writings in the German-speaking countries; on the other hand, Cranach profited from the interest in Luther's critical publications. The contact which Luther made to the House of Wettin through Lucas Cranach is particularly visible in Cranach's painting *Elector John Frederick I of Saxony with the Reformers* from around 1532–1539. Lucas Cranach created a picture around 1526 that became the portrait of Martin Luther which has become known throughout the world.

Cranach was, without doubt, a determined and multifaceted man with business acumen and a keen sense of the intellectual movements of his time. He produced works of the highest artistic quality and, at the same time, was a successful businessman. His style with short, definite, yet fluid lines reflects his inner emotions. He did not create his works in a relaxed and calm manner with his focus on achieving the best results possible; rather, he concentrated on achieving rapid results. Cranach must have been a man who was constantly in a hurry, who, at the latest after settling in Wittenberg, created a selection of compositions, head and figure types that he constantly varied and composed into ever new and innovative pictures.

The wealth of commissions which Cranach received from the 1520s onwards, not only from the Protestant side, but also, amongst others, from Cardinal Albrecht of Brandenburg, the growing amount of work carried out in his workshop and his particular business acumen made him into one of the richest men in Wittenberg. In addition to his workshop, he owned a bookshop and paper merchant's and, in 1520, bought an apothecary's and a wine merchant's. From 1520 onwards, he also took on political offices. He was firstly a councillor, then later mayor of Wittenberg for several years. After opening his workshop, Cranach was not primarily a master working on his own, but rather a producer who had several assistants. His sons, Hans and Lucas, were also employed in this artist's workshop.

Today, approximately 1,000 works have been preserved which carry the mark of Lucas Cranach or which can be attributed to him. These works are likely to be only a fraction of the total amount of his creations. A significant amount of his works, including the largely unknown woodcuts from the vaults of the *Stiftung Schloß Friedenstein* in Gotha are presented in this book and incorporated into his extremely interesting biography.

1472

□ Lucas Maler (Cranach) was born in Kronach, 24 kilometres east of Coburg in the Franconian Forest. His father was known as Hans Maler and was probably 24 years old at the time of his son's birth. Cranach's mother, who was possibly called Barbara, is thought to have been aged 21 when she gave birth to him. Lucas was the first-born child and his parents had probably married in 1471.

The oldest biographical source for Lucas Cranach is a document from the year 1556. It comes from his cousin Matthias Gunderam and reports that Cranach was born on 04.10.1472 in Kronach and that he had received training in the *ars graphica* from his father Hans, a wealthy painter and respected citizen. The document states that Lucas had four siblings (Margarethe, Ennlein, Mathias and Anna) and it was said that Lucas was able to read Latin.

According to the most recent research, Lucas Cranach had seven siblings, three of whom died in childhood. Other sources speak of up to eight siblings. Lucas received his training in his father's workshop.

1477

□ Barbara Brengbier, who was later to become Lucas Cranach's wife, was born as the daughter of the Gotha alderman Jobst Brengbier and his wife Katharina, née Jahn. Her father owned the house at Hauptmarkt 17 in Gotha, which is today the Lucas Cranach House.

1483

☐ Martin Luther was born on 10.11.1483 in Eisleben, a small town with less than 4,000 inhabitants in the centre of the county of Mansfeld. His 24-year-old father, Hans, was a miner. His mother, Margarethe, gave birth to nine children in all.

Shortly after Martin's birth, the family moved to the smaller village of Mansfeld (2,000 inhabitants), which is ten kilometres northwest of Eisleben. His father worked as a master smelter in the copper mines there.

1485

☐ Frederick II the Gentle, Elector of Saxony, died on 07.09.1464 at the age of 52 in Leipzig. His two sons, the 23-year-old Duke Ernst of Saxony and the 21-year-old Albert III the Courageous, took over the Electorate.

☐ The partition of the Wettin territories by Ernst in 1485 into the Ernestine and Albertine lines created a fateful weakening of the House of Wettin. As a result of the Leipzig partition, Ernst (*24.03.1441, Meissen, +24.08.1486, Colditz) received the area around Wittenberg, which meant that he retained the title of Elector, the south Thuringian part, the Vogtland and parts of the Pleissnerland around Altenburg. He chose Wittenberg as his residence.

☐ Albert III the Courageous (*31.07.1443, Grimma, +12.09.1500, Emden) received the northern part of Thuringia, the margraviate of Meissen and the area around Leipzig. He was accorded with the title of Duke and he established his residence in Dresden.

1486

□ Elector Ernst of Saxony, founder of the Ernestine line of the Wettin dynasty, died on 26.08.1486 at the age of 45 in Colditz as the result of falling from his horse.

The 23-year-old Friedrich III the Wise (*17.01.1463, Torgau) succeeded his father as the Elector of Saxony, the territory that had been granted to the Ernestine line as a result of the Leipzig partition of 1485. His 18-year-old brother, John the Steadfast (+30.06.1468, Meissen), became his co-regent.

Frederick the Wise was born as the first son of the Elector Ernst (1441–86) from the House of Wettin.

1498

□ From court records in Kronach, it is apparent that the 26-year-old Lucas Cranach was occasionally absent from his hometown in this year for reasons that were not registered.

1499

□ It is apparent that Lucas Cranach had permanently left Kronach before 1500. Unrecorded years of travel followed until, in 1502, he was registered as being in Vienna.

□ Joachim I (*21.02.1484, perhaps in Cölln, +02.07.1535, Stendal), at the age of 15, became the Elector of Brandenburg although it had been decreed by the Golden Bull of Emperor Charles IV that this office be only taken by a person over the age of eighteen.

His father, Elector Johann Cicero of Brandenburg, died on 09.01.1499 at the age of 44 in Arneburg/Stendal. He was born in Ansbach and was the first of the Hohenzollern dynasty to reside permanently in Berlin.

Joachim was the first son of the Elector. He took the oath of allegiance from the estates of the Empire with his brother Albert (*28.06.1490). Albert II was appointed cardinal in 1518.

1500

☐ On 01.03.1500, the 32-year-old co-regent John the Steadfast married the 19-year-old Sophie, daughter of Duke Magnus II of Mecklenburg. The marriage produced one child (John Frederick I, 1503).

☐ Albert III the Courageous, Duke of Saxony and founder of the Albertine line of the House of Wettin, died on 12.09.1500 at the age of 57 in Emden. His successor was his eldest son, the 29-year-old George the Bearded (*27.08.1471, Meissen, +17.04.1539, Dresden).

1502

☐ Still today, the reasons remain unclear as to what prompted Lucas Cranach to go to Vienna. There he came into contact with the Humanists at the university, amongst others, with the Professor of Poetry and Rhetoric, Conrad Celtis.

The young Cranach ranks amongst both the pioneers as well as the main representatives of the Danube School, as it is known. His early works are characterised by a high degree of expressiveness and idyllic charm. In the works from his time in Vienna, he already displays a 'Renaissance-like' mastery of space, whereby only indirect connections to Italian art may be discerned. In these years, his creativity with paintings, drawings and woodcuts reached its first peak.

☐ The 30-year-old painted the double portrait *Dr Cuspinian and His Wife* on the occasion of the marriage of the 29-

year-old Viennese Humanist Johannes Cuspinian to his 18-year-old wife Anna, the daughter of an imperial official.

Cuspinian's real name was Spießheimer and he came from Schweinfurt in Germany. He studied in Leipzig and was crowned Poet Laureate in 1493 by the 77-year-old Emperor Frederick III in Nuremberg. He became the Rector of the University of Vienna at the age of 27. He subsequently took on numerous other offices, such as that of the Superintendent of the University from 1501 onwards and, in 1501/02, that of the Dean of the Faculty of Medicine. He also served Emperor Maximilian I, the son of Frederick III (+1493), as his privy councillor and court historian.

□ On 10.04.1502, the 18-year-old Joachim I, Elector of Brandenburg since 1499, married the 17-year-old Elisabeth, daughter of King John I of Denmark. The marriage produced four children: Joachim II (1505), Anna (1507), Elisabeth (1510) and John (1513).

□ The University of Wittenberg was founded by the Elector Frederick the Wise. The city had been handed over to the House of Wettin in 1422, a year after the demise of the Ascanian dukes, and came to the Ernestine line in 1485 as their official residence.

The Saxon State University of Leipzig had come to the Albertine line in 1485.

The Crucifixion, before 1502.
Oil on beech wood, 59 x 45 cm.
Vienna, Kunsthistorisches Museum.

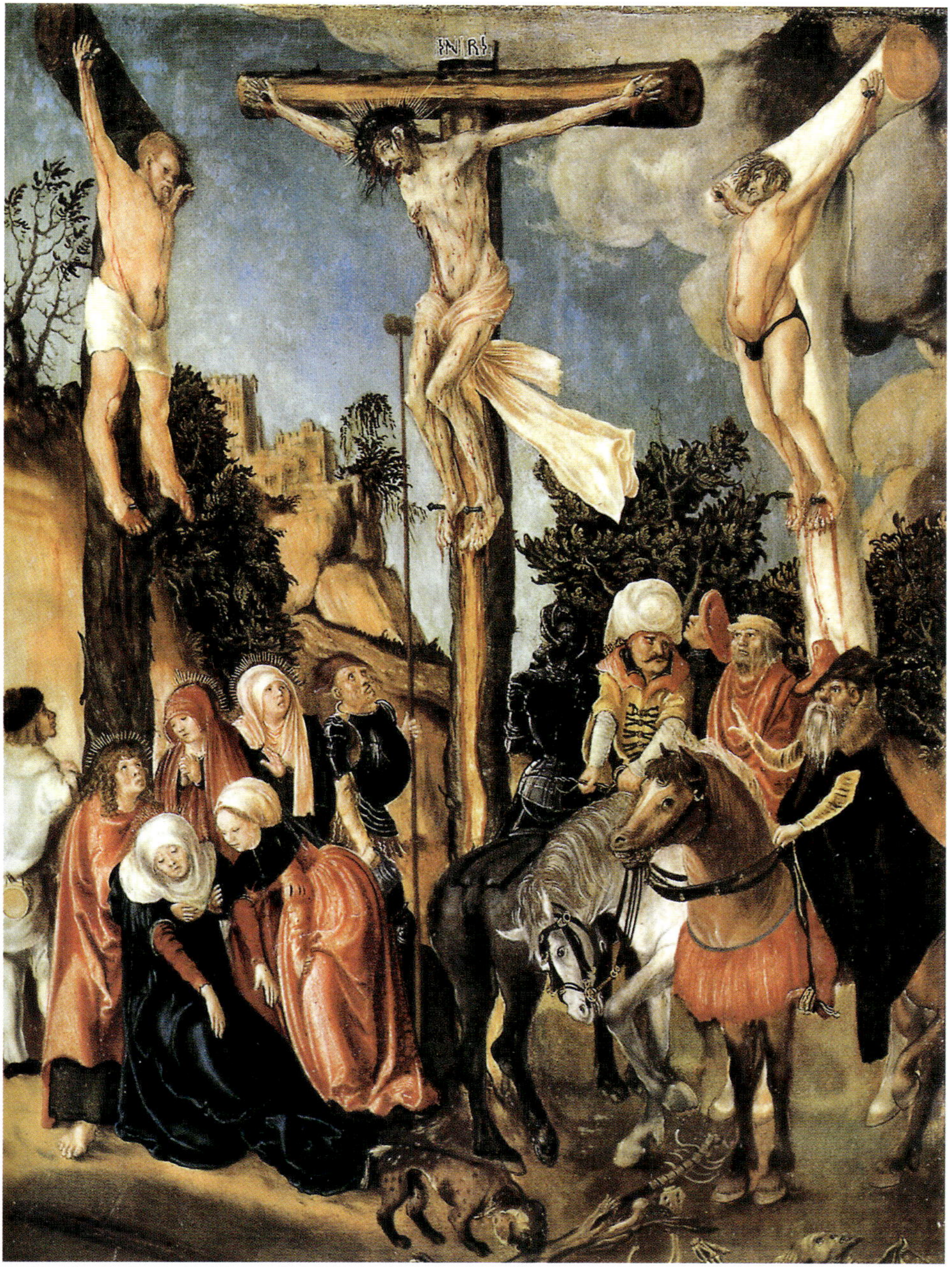
INRI

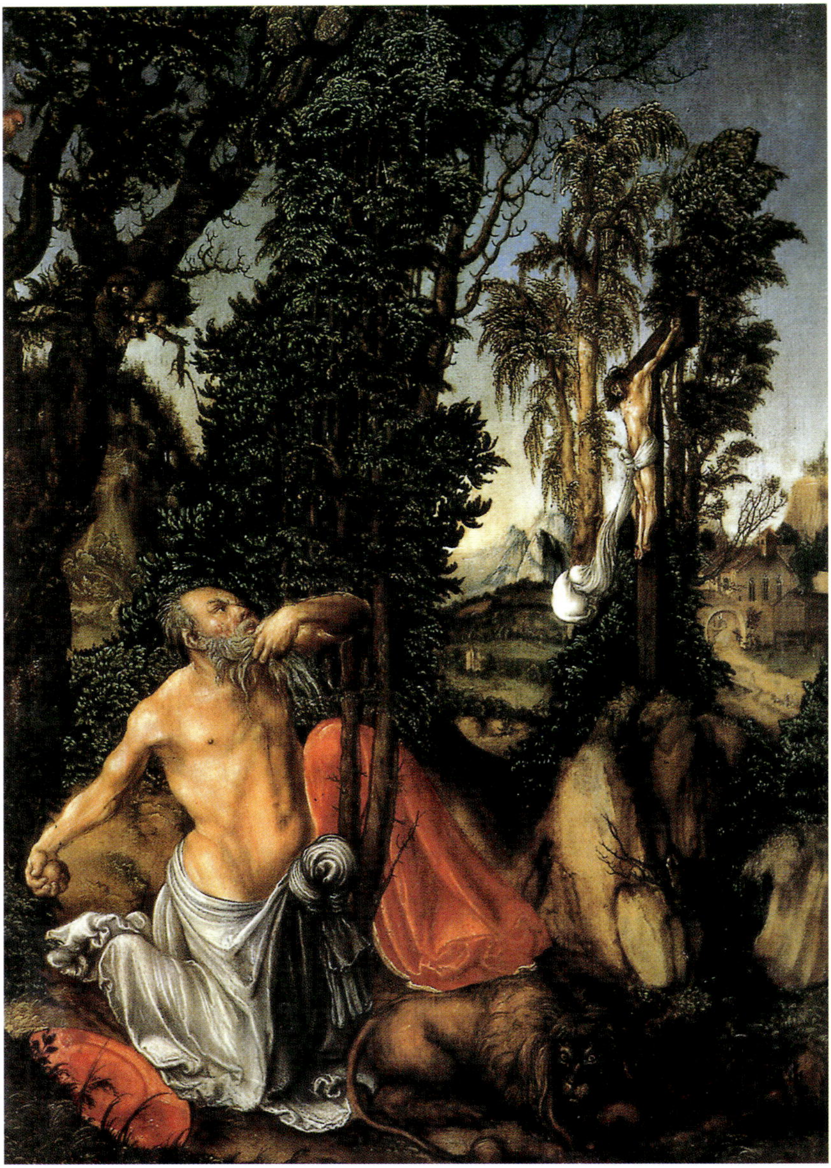

The Penance of St Jerome, 1502.
Oil on lime wood, 56 x 42 cm.
Vienna, Kunsthistorisches Museum.

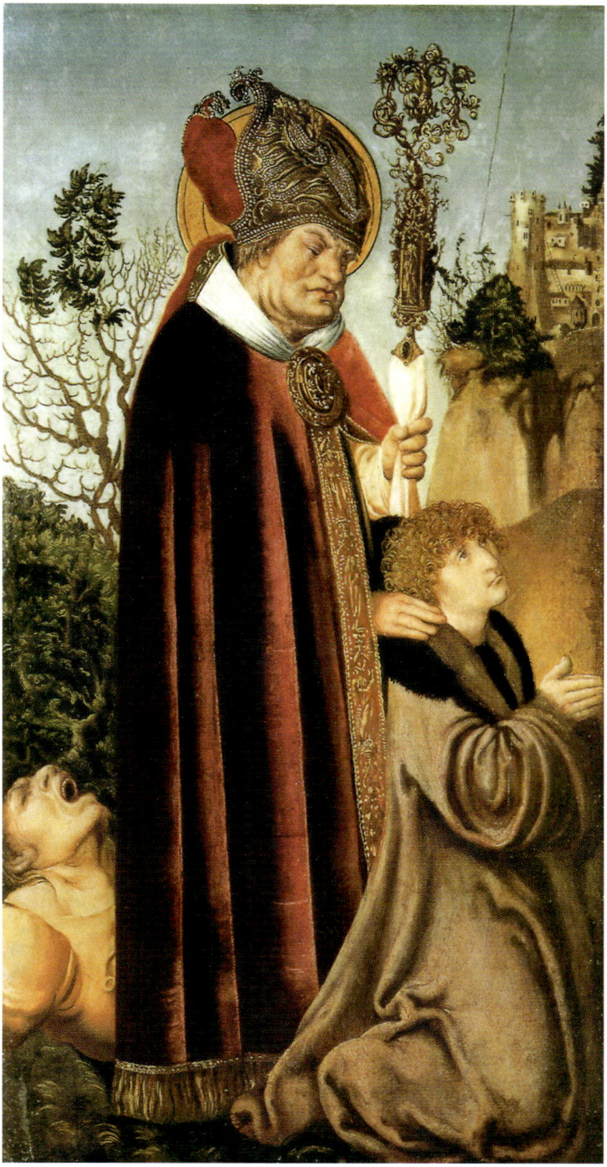

St Valentine and a Kneeling Donor, around 1502.
Oil on spruce wood, 91 x 49 cm.
Vienna, Akademie der bildenden Künste.

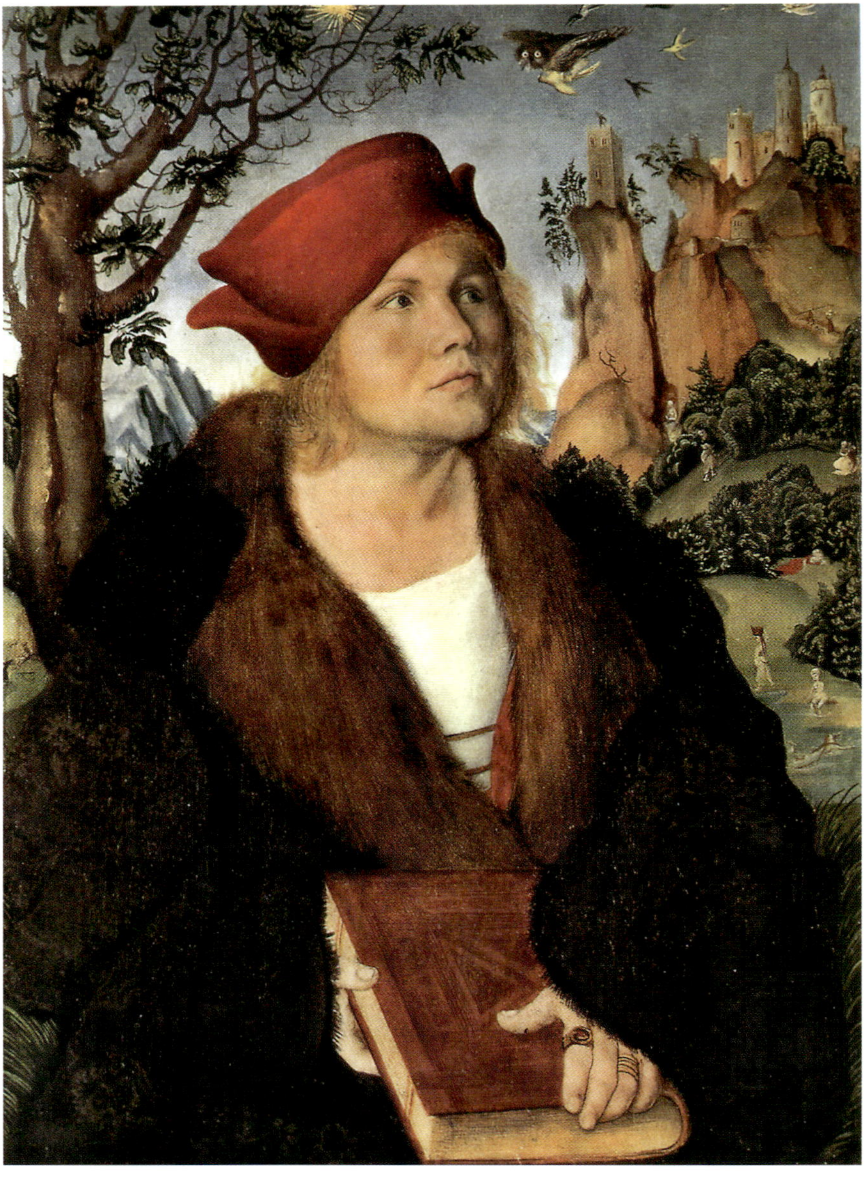

Dr Johannes Cuspinian and his Wife Anna Putsch, 1502–03.
Oil on panel, each 59 x 45 cm.
Winterthur, Oskar Reinhart collection.

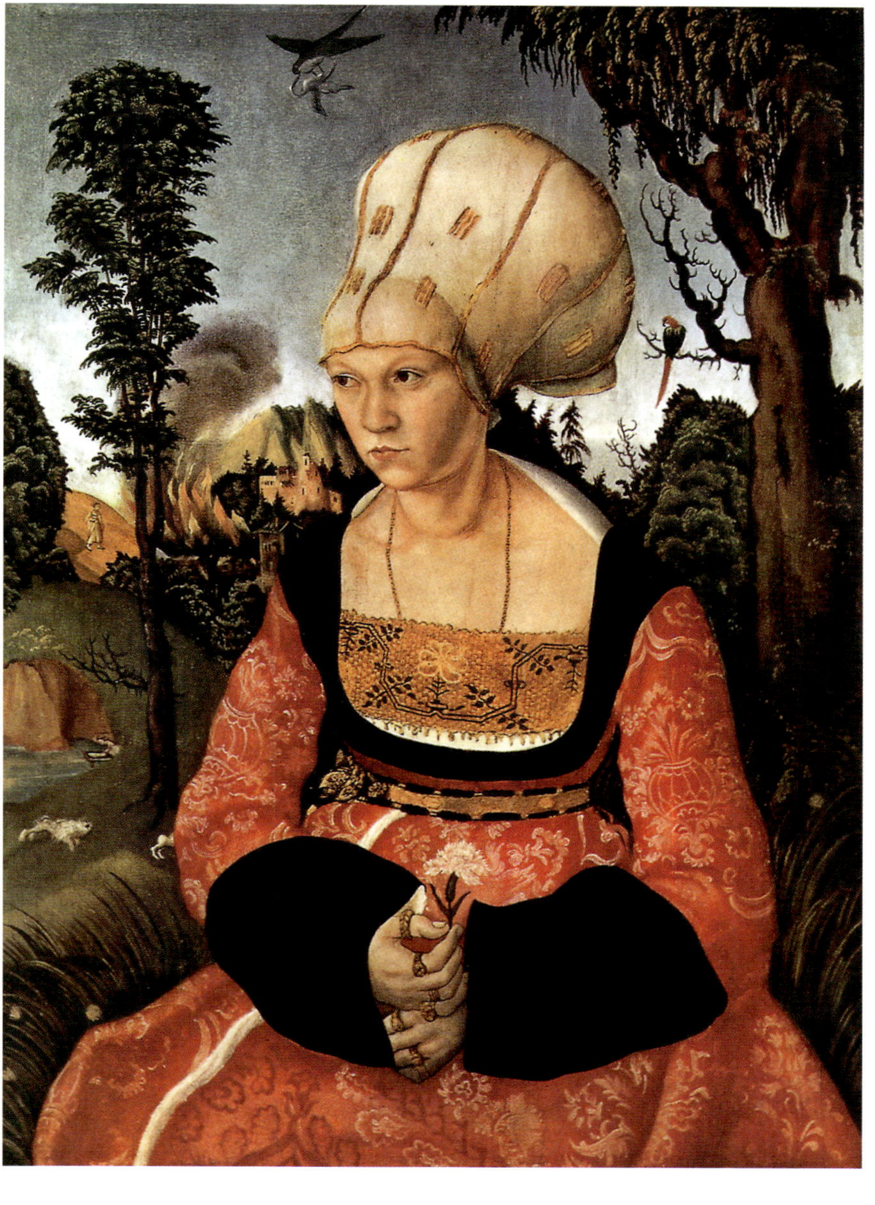

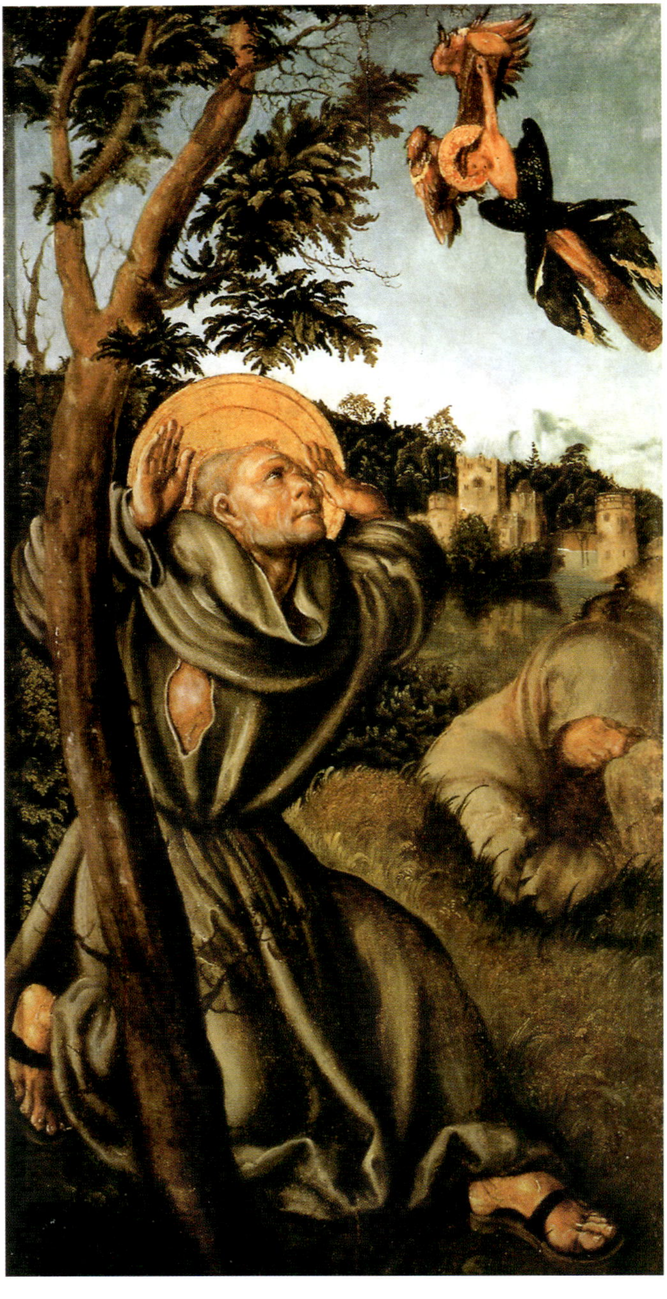

St Francis Receiving the Stigmata, around 1502. Oil on spruce wood, 87 x 48 cm. Vienna, Akademie der bildenden Künste.

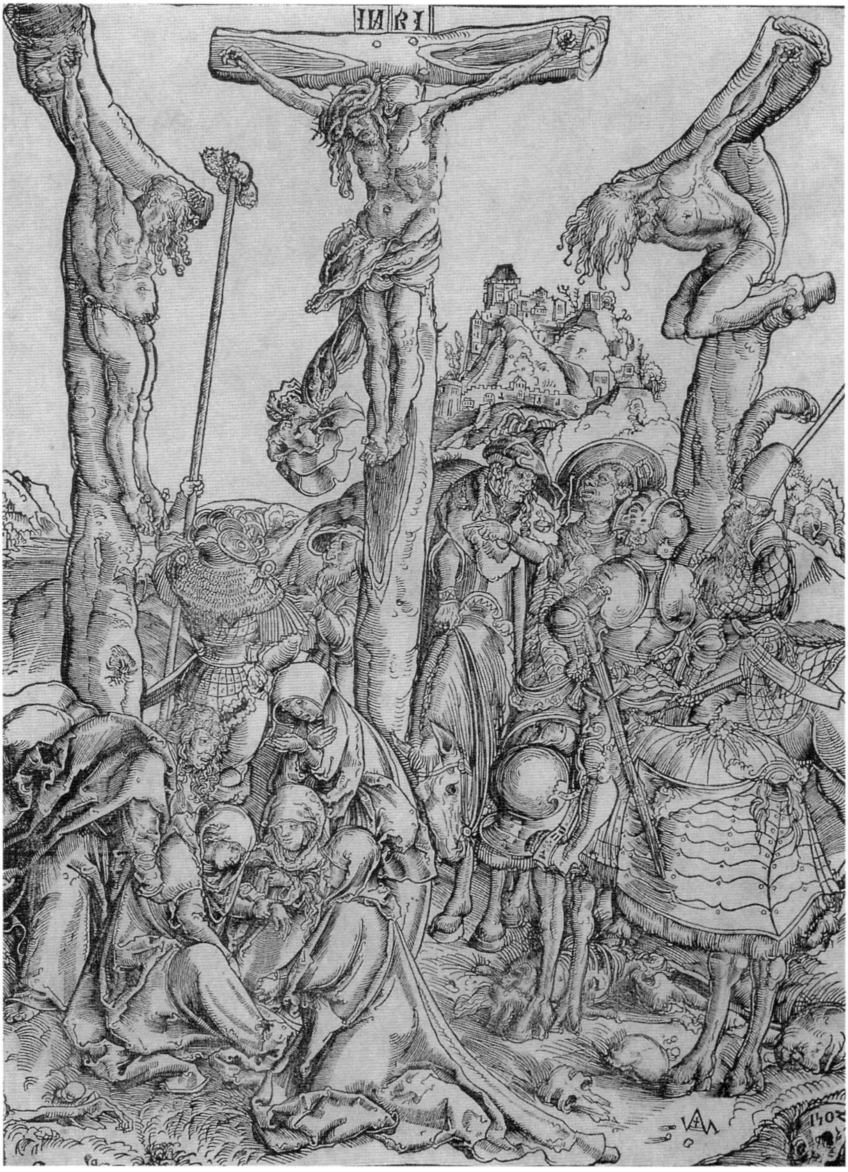

The Crucifixion (Calvary), 1502.
Woodcut, 40.5 x 29.2 cm.
Berlin, Staatliche Museen.

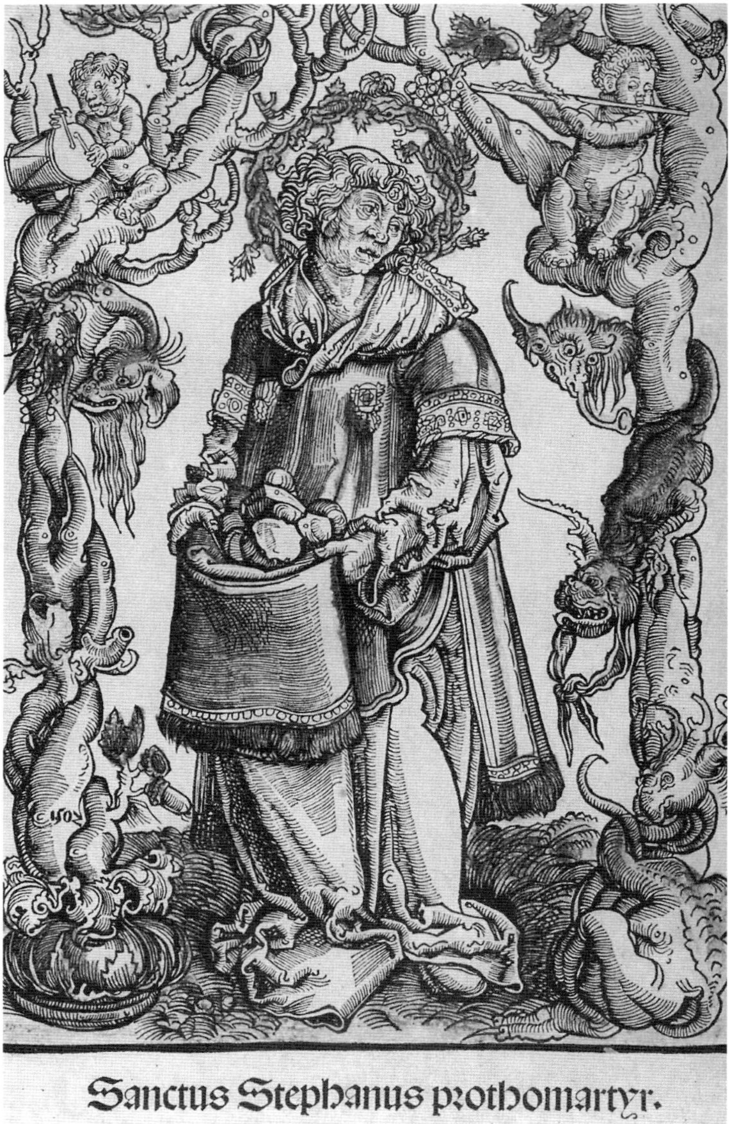

St Stephen, 1502.
Woodcut, 21.5 x 14.9 cm.
Berlin, Staatliche Museen.

1503

☐ Lucas Cranach produced woodcuts for the Viennese printer and publisher Johannes Winterburger. Paintings were also produced, such as the *Crucifixion* and the *Rest on the Flight into Egypt*.

☐ John Frederick I, the son of the 35-year-old co-regent John the Steadfast and his wife Sophie of Mecklenburg, was born on 30.06.1503 in Torgau. Sophie of Mecklenburg died on 12.07.1503, aged 22, in Torgau. Her grave can be found in the Church of St. Mary.

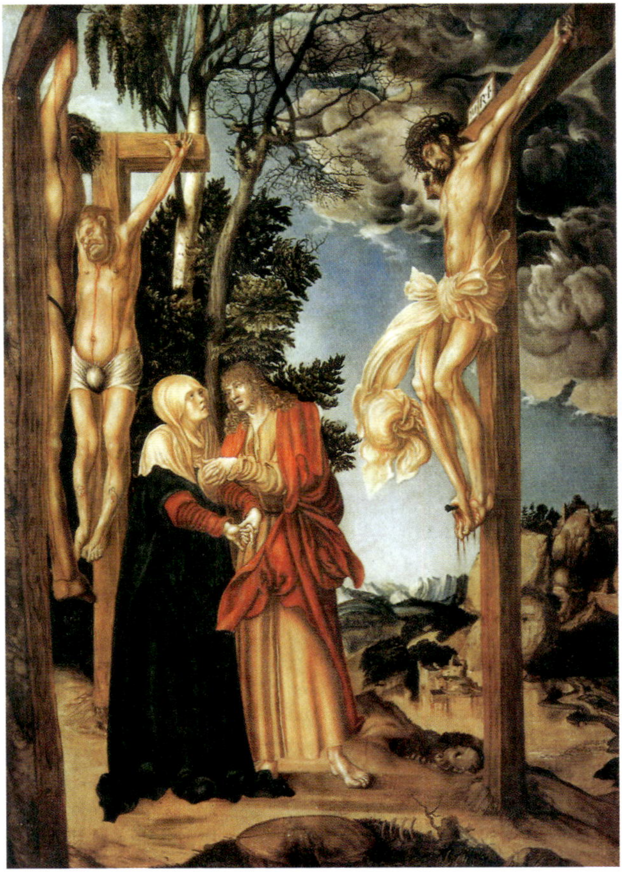

The Crucifixion, 1503.
Oil on conifer wood,
138 x 99 cm.
Munich, Alte Pinakothek.

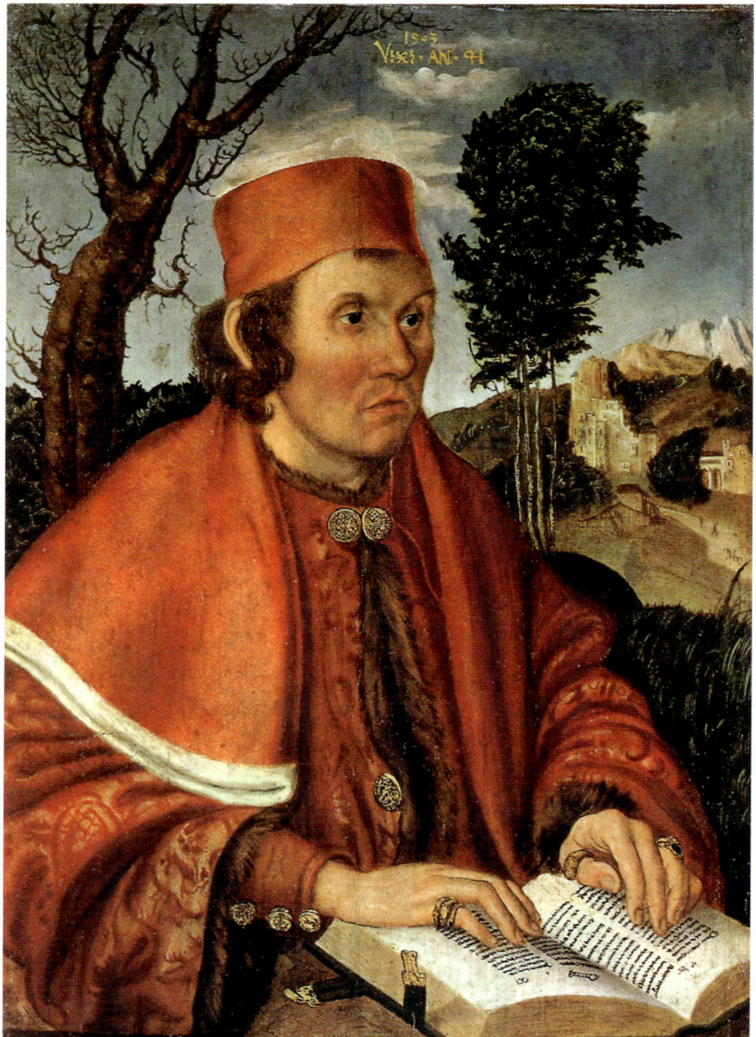

Dr Johann Stephan Reuss (?), 1503.
Oil on pinewood, 54.1 x 39 cm.
Nuremberg, Germanisches Nationalmuseum.

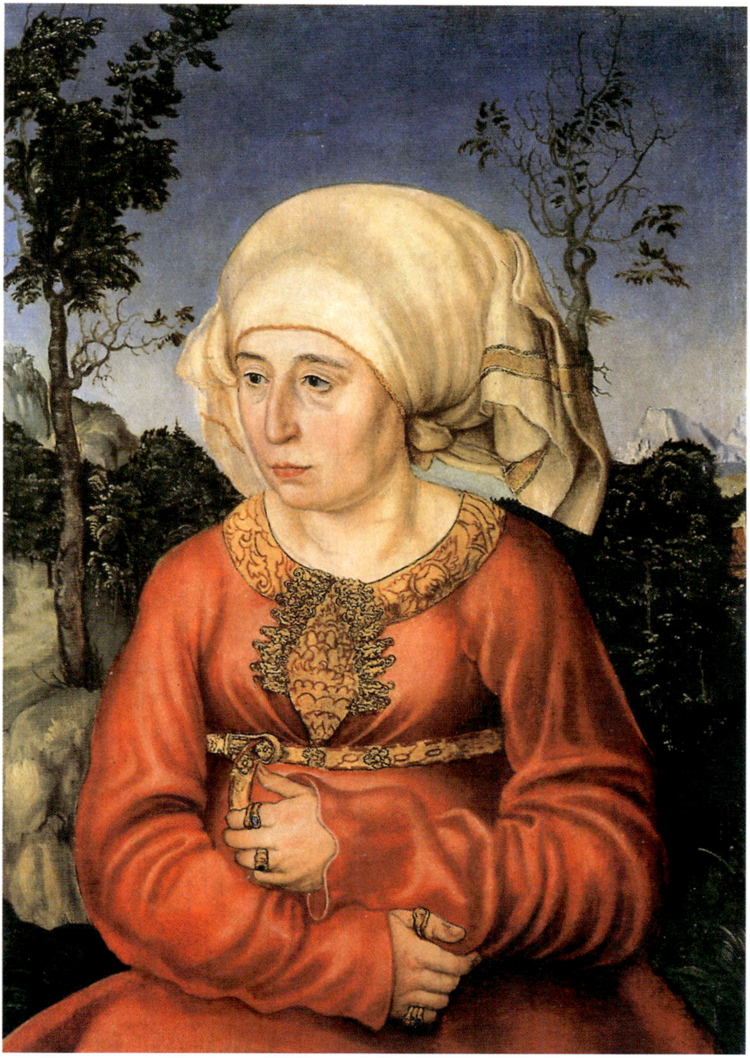

Wife of Dr Johann Stephan Reuss (?), around 1503.
Oil on pinewood, 52.5 x 36.2 cm.
Berlin, Staatliche Museen.

1504

□ In two monograms of 1504, the first evidence was found of the new insignia used by Lucas Cranach: *LC*. It remains unclear why the artist chose to use this short form from this point on.

In 1507, in the accounts of the Wittenberg treasury, he was referred to as *pictor Lucas Moller*, in 1510 as *Lucas moler* and, in 1513, as *maler Moller*.

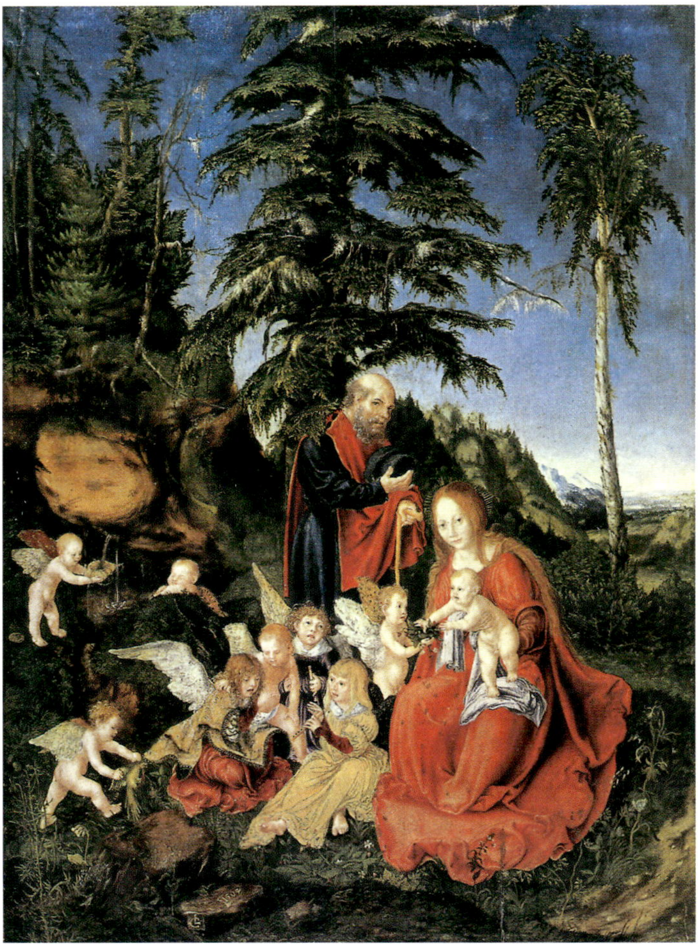

The Rest on the Flight into Egypt, 1504.
Oil on beech wood, 69 x 51 cm.
Berlin, Staatliche Museen.

1505

☐ In this year, a new era began in the 33-year-old Lucas Cranach's life. The 42-year-old Elector of Saxony Frederick the Wise summoned him to his residence in Wittenberg as his court painter, thus furnishing evidence that Cranach was by no means unknown any more at this point in his life.

He was the successor to the Italian painter Jacopo de Barbari. The well-paid position linked the 34-year-old painter to the Elector's court in a unique manner: in Wittenberg (2,000 inhabitants, 400 houses) his style changed completely. He had to live and work in Wittenberg, not only supplying paintings and works of art, but also furnishing castles (for example, in Coburg, Heldburg, Lochau, Torgau), designing decorations for festivals and hunts, caparisons (horsecloths) for tournaments, creating court vestments, costumes and carnival masks and designing coats of arms, medals and coins. In addition, however, he was also responsible for painting the exteriors of houses, fences, sleighs and wagons.

Occasionally he also was called upon to fulfil diplomatic missions. As a reward for his extensive labours, Cranach enjoyed a form of monopoly on art in Saxony. His large and well-organised workshop was thus to dominate the creation of art in the entire region. In but a few years, the painter rose to be the major landowner and one of the richest men in Wittenberg. His payment of 100 florins per annum corresponded to the remuneration received by a professor at the University of Wittenberg.

☐ Cranach was supplied with food by the Wittenberg court kitchens. There is first mention of a journeyman also being supplied with food by the court kitchens. The main focus of his work seems to have been in Lochau.

☐ Martin Luther, who had been a student at the Faculty of Liberal Arts at the University of Erfurt since 1501, passed his Master's examination and started his studies of law. On 02.07.1505, he was caught in a sudden severe storm close to

Stotternheim, eight kilometres north of Erfurt, and, in fear of his life, vowed to St Anna that he would become a monk. On 17.07.1505, the 21-year-old entered the monastery of the Order of Augustinian Hermits in Erfurt.

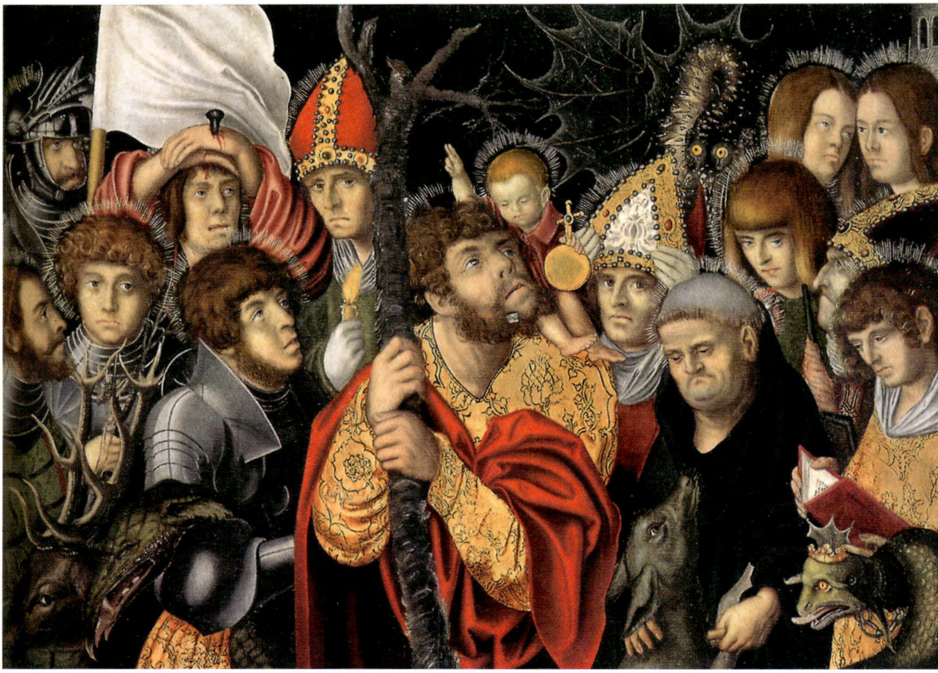

The Fourteen Helpers in Need, around 1505.
Oil on lime wood, 85 x 128 cm.
Torgau, Marienkirche.

Veneration of the Cross, 1505.
Woodcut, 38 x 28.4 cm.
Berlin, Staatliche Museen.

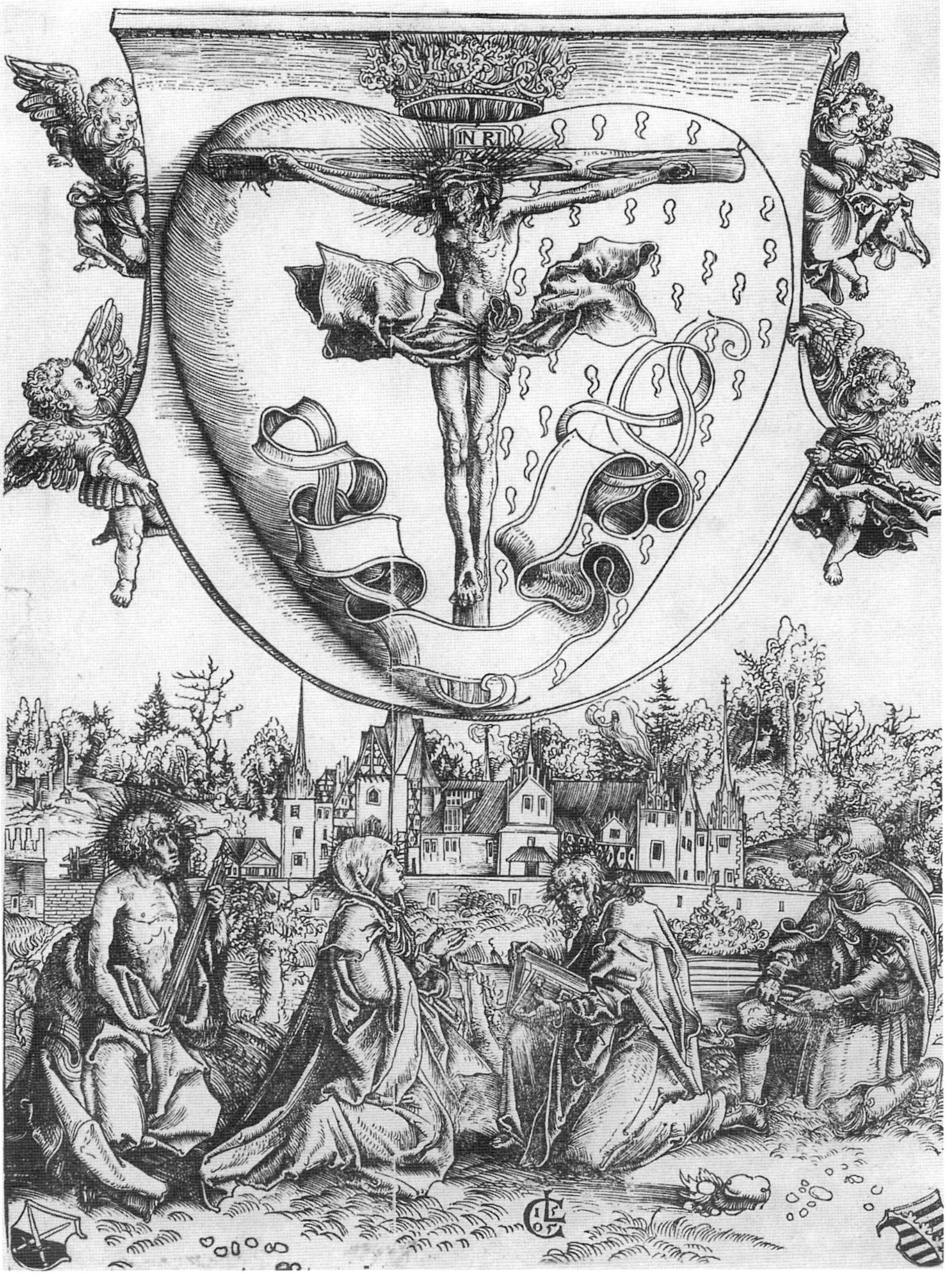
INRI

1506

□ Lucas Cranach worked with his journeymen in the hunting castle in Lochau until the beginning of September. There is the first mention of the artist possessing a horse, with the yearly fodder being supplied by the Elector's court.

□ The small town of Annaburg, 20 kilometres north of Torgau in the Annaburg Heath, which bore the name Lochau until 1573, had developed from being an early settlement of farmers from the Rhine area and from the Netherlands who had been summoned to the country from the mid-12th century onwards by Archbishop Wichmann of Magdeburg (1152–92) to drain the area between the rivers Elbe and Elster, which was marshy, but at the same time extremely full of game.

The Ascanian dukes, a ruling dynasty that was divided into four branches, Anhalt, Brandenburg, Lauenberg and Wittenberg, had built an earlier hunting seat in Lochau in the 13th century, but it had burnt down in a fire in 1422. The last surviving member of the dynasty, the childless Albert II, who was in the castle when the fire broke out, was able to rescue himself, but died shortly afterwards from the serious injuries he had sustained. Thus, the Wittenberg line died out and the Electorate of Saxony became vacant.

In 1423, Emperor Sigismund granted the Electorate as a fief to the Margrave of Meissen, Frederick the Warlike. His grandsons, Ernst and Albert, firstly reigned as joint rulers from 1464 onwards, then, in 1485, they divided the Wettin territories between them. The title of Elector remained with Ernst and his heirs, which was then known as the Ernestine line; these were Frederick III the Wise, John the Steadfast and John Frederick I the Magnanimous.

The territory of Lochau was taken over by the House of Wettin who had the hunting castle rebuilt or restored and who added a large deer park in 1498. Frederick the Wise had the wooden building of his predecessor demolished at the beginning of the 16th century and a huge new building built, comprising a front and rear castle. Cranach, amongst others, was involved in the fitting of the complex. In addition to the castle, spacious service quarters (stables, a brewery) were also built and a water supply system that was revolutionary for the time was installed. After the estate had been completed, the Elector chose the hunting castle with its gardens, ponds and canals to be his favourite residence. After his death in 1525, Lochau castle became forgotten.

☐ Evidence can be found for Cranach having stayed in Coburg. In January, he had paint, amongst other things, brought to Coburg in preparation for his work there. However, it seems likely that he himself only arrived there as part of the entourage of Frederick the Wise and Duke John the Steadfast at the beginning of August as the household – ranging from the most senior court officials, councillors, the treasury personnel, down to the band with the court choir, and the hunters – came to spend a six-month hunting trip there.

In Coburg, the costs were calculated for the summer and winter attire of the painter and his apprentices. In contrast to many servants who had to be found rented accommodation in the town, Cranach lived in the castle, the Veste, as it is known. The court painters accompanied the Elector's party on its hunts. Nothing remains today of the main work carried out at this time: the mural paintings in the Veste.

At the end of the hunting trip, Cranach most likely left Coburg on 12.02.1507, too. Where he went is not recorded; however, there is some evidence that the court painters were given the task of decorating the castle in Heldburg, 18 kilometres west of Coburg.

☐ The foundation stone was laid for the St Peter's Basilica in Rome.

☐ Erasmus, one of the 14 helpers in need, had lived around 300 B.C. as the Bishop of Antioch. In his woodcut, Cranach depicted the martyrdom of this saint against the background of a landscape that was very well known to him: the Veste in Coburg. In doing so, Cranach created one of the earliest depictions of this, the Elector's castle. The same was true in the case of the woodcut *Saxon Prince on Horseback before the North Side of the Veste in Coburg*.

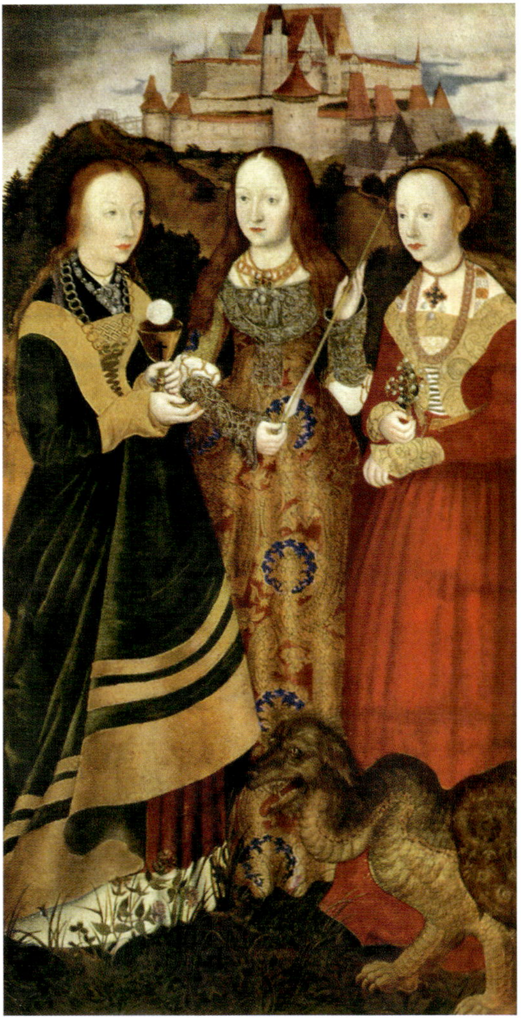

The Martyrdom of St Catherine (right wing of altarpiece): Sts Barbara, Ursula and Margaret, 1506.
Oil on lime wood, 124 x 67 cm.
Dresden, Gemäldegalerie.

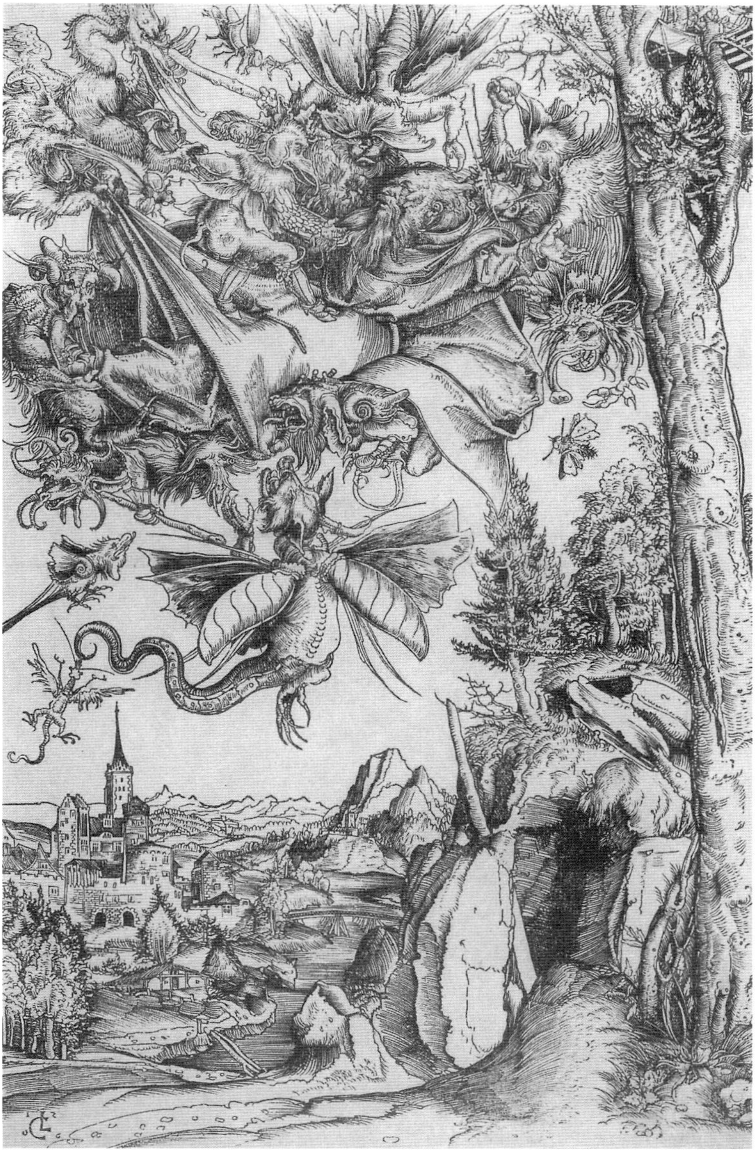

The Temptation of St Anthony, 1506.
Woodcut, 40.6 x 27.8 cm.
Basel, Kunstmuseum.

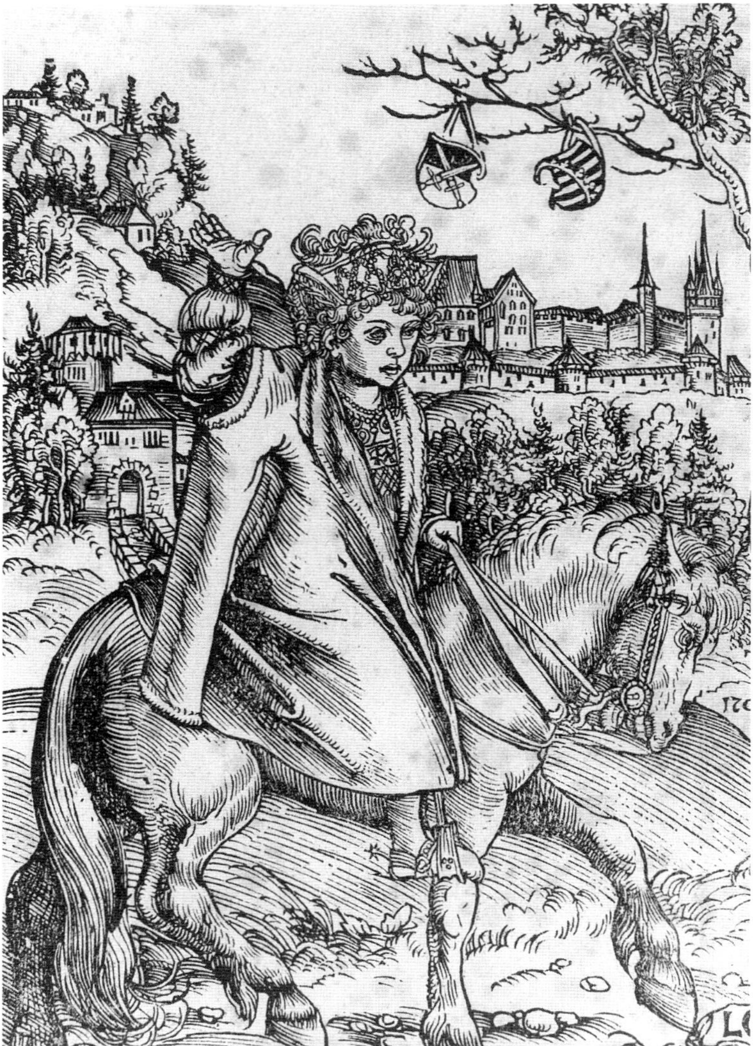

Saxon Prince on Horseback Before the North Side of the Veste in Coburg (Duke John Frederick on Horseback), 1506.
Woodcut, 27.7 x 12.5 cm.
Gotha, Stiftung Schloss Friedenstein.

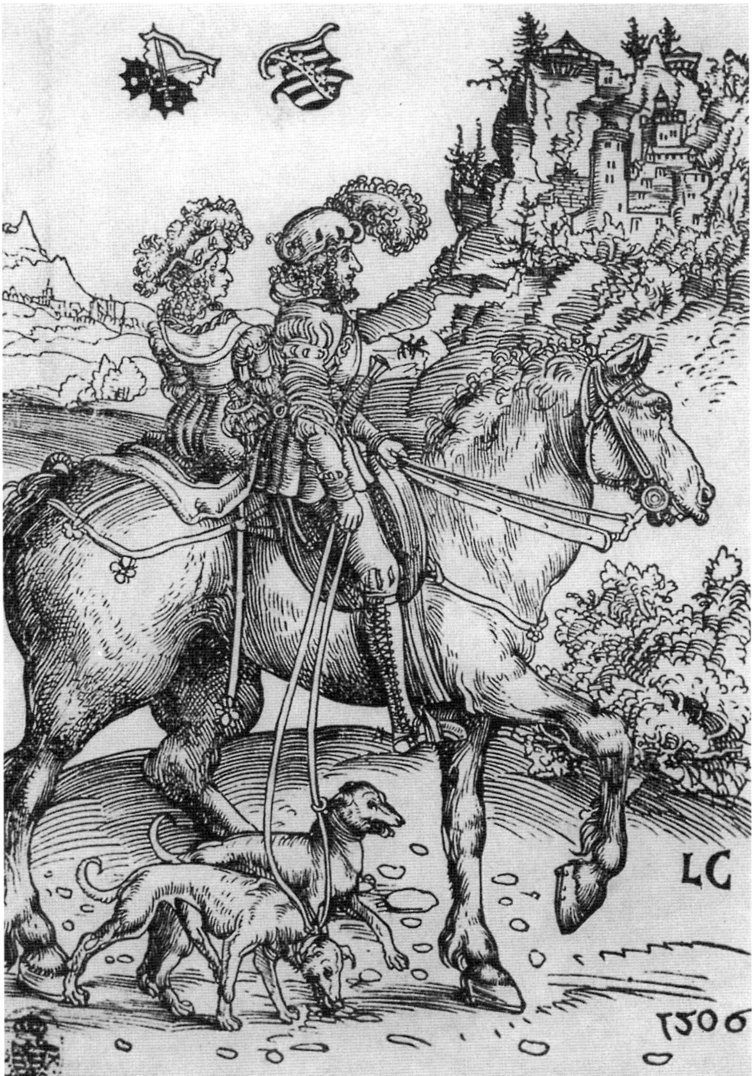

Noble Couple on Horseback, 1506.
Woodcut, 17.8 x 12.4 cm.
Dresden, Staatliche
Kunstsammlungen.

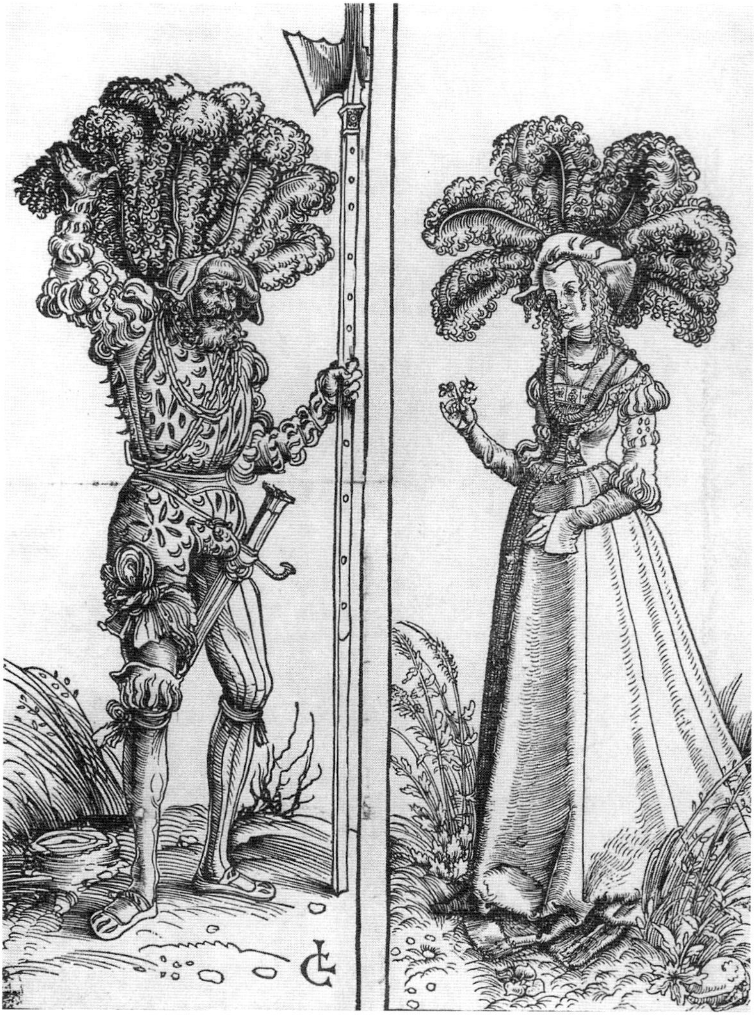

Landsknecht and Lady, around 1506.
Woodcut, each 24.3 x 9.2 cm.
Dresden, Staatliche Kunstsammlungen.

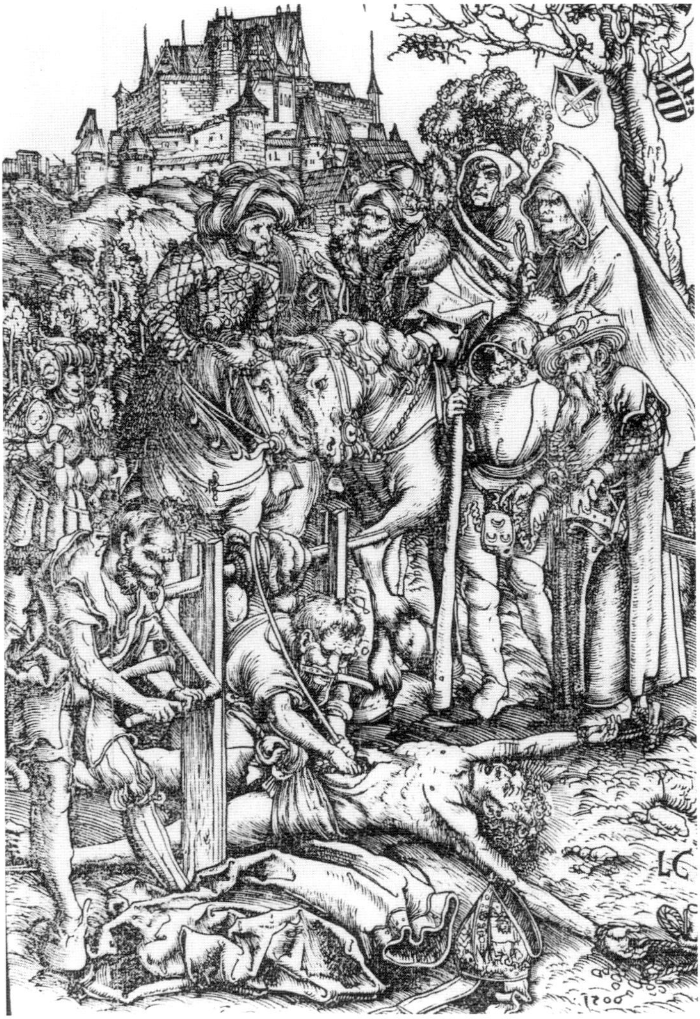

The Martyrdom of St Erasmus, 1506.
Woodcut, 22.6 x 15.3 cm.
Gotha, Stiftung Schloss Friedenstein.

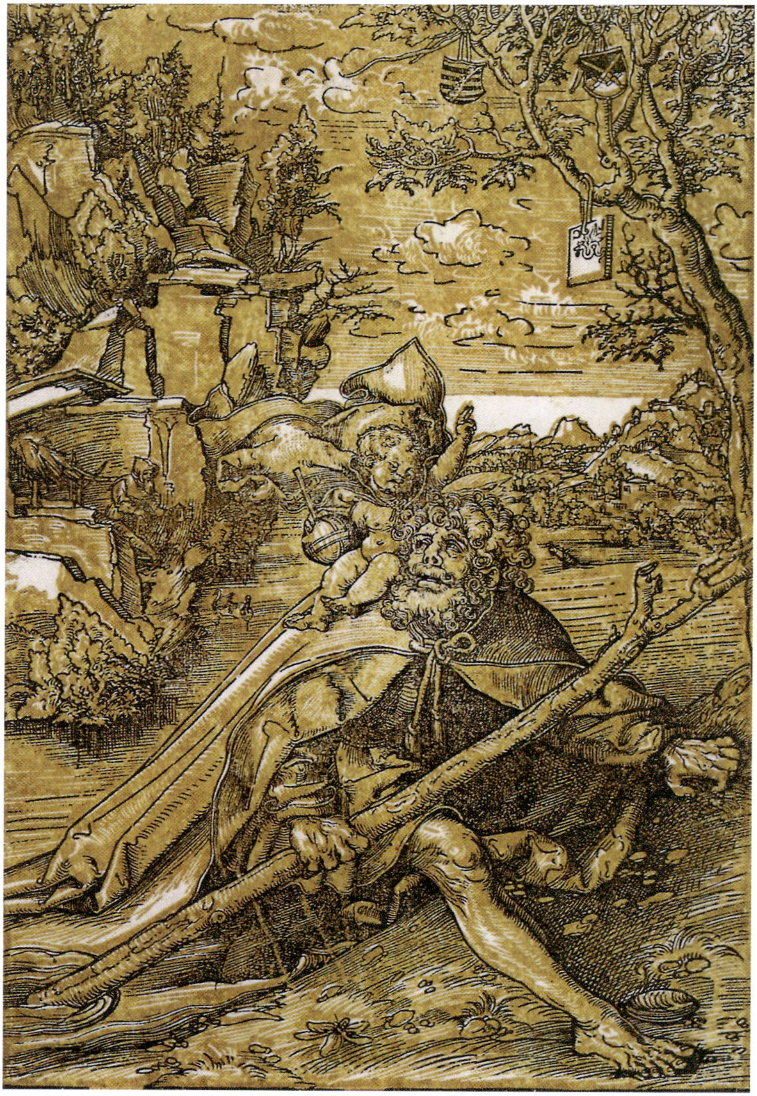

St Christopher, 1506.
Woodcut, 28 x 19.7 cm.
Gotha, Stiftung Schloss Friedenstein.

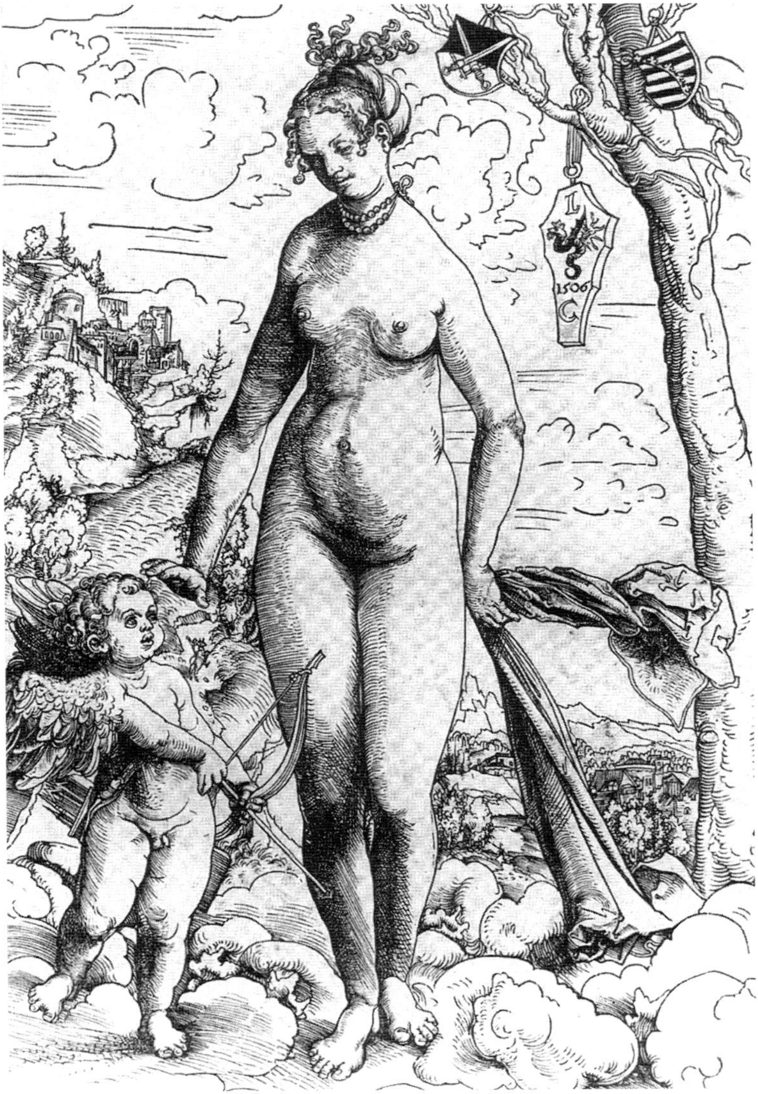

Venus and Cupid, 1506.
Woodcut, 27.9 x 19.3 cm.
Gotha, Stiftung Schloss Friedenstein.

1507

☐ In the bills from Coburg, there is first mention of a boy, a helper in Cranach's workshop. In 1509, there were two apprentices, in 1512, two apprentices and a journeyman; later there were numerous helpers in the workshop. Konrad Meit, the sculptor, used Cranach's workshop.

☐ Frederick the Wise was given the title of a General Governor of the Empire at the Diet (assembly) of Constance by King Maximilian (who, in 1508, became Emperor).

☐ After completing his studies of law in Bologna in 1507, the Humanist, Christoph Scheurl, who was born in Nuremberg, was appointed Rector of the University of Wittenberg at the age of 26.

☐ The 64-year-old Pope Julius II issued an indulgence (the commutation for money of part of the temporal penalty due for sin) in favour of a new St Peter's Basilica in Rome.

☐ On 03.04.1507, at the age of 23, Luther was ordained as a priest in Erfurt Cathedral.

1508

☐ On 06.01.1508 in Nuremberg, Frederick III the Wise granted the 36-year-old Lucas Cranach the right to bear a winged serpent as his coat of arms; in 1537, his coat of arms was modified.

☐ In June, Cranach undertook a trip from Wittenberg to Altenburg and back with the goldsmith Christian Döring.

☐ In summer (mid-July or the second half of July until 18.11.1508 at the latest), Cranach travelled to the Netherlands (amongst other places, to Antwerp and Mecheln). It is likely that this trip was in connection with a secretly planned political marriage of Frederick the Wise and with other political issues. The artist painted portraits of the 8-year-old Archduke and later Emperor, Charles V.

☐ In mid-December, Cranach and his apprentice received their winter apparel in Torgau.

☐ Albrecht Dürer delivered the painting *The Martyrdom of the Ten Thousand* (99 x 87 cm) to Frederick the Wise.

☐ The Humanist Conrad Celtis, who was born in Wipfeld by Schweinfurt, died on 04.02.1508 at the age of 49 in Vienna. In 1487 at Nuremberg Castle, he had been the first German to be created Poet Laureate by the Emperor Frederick III. In Vienna, he had been a Professor of Poetry and Rhetoric.

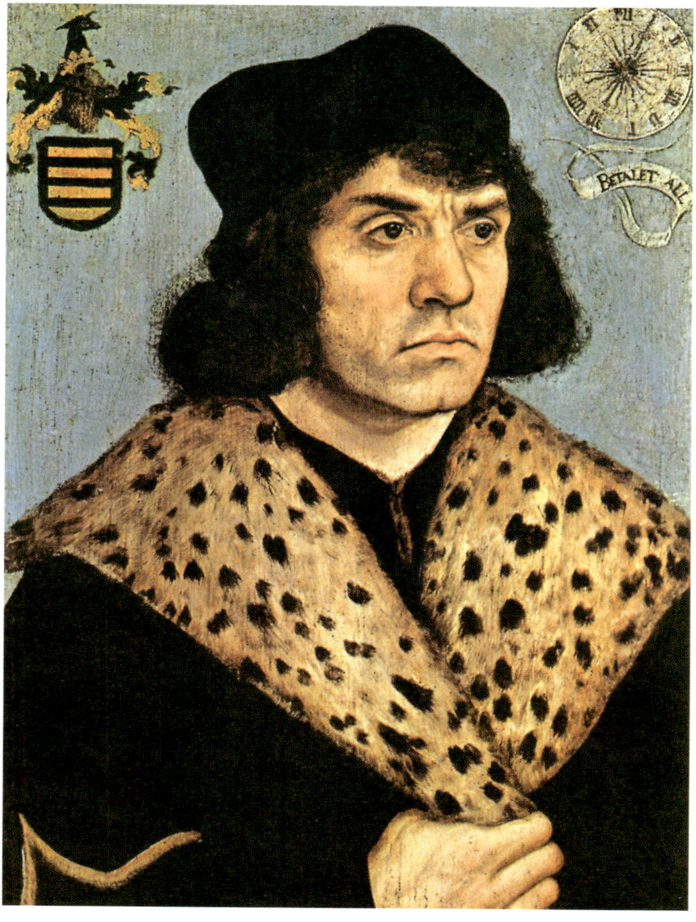

Clean-Shaven Man with a Spotted Fur Collar, approx. 1508–12. Oil on oak wood, 48.4 x 36.4 cm. Kreuzlingen, Heinz Kisters collection.

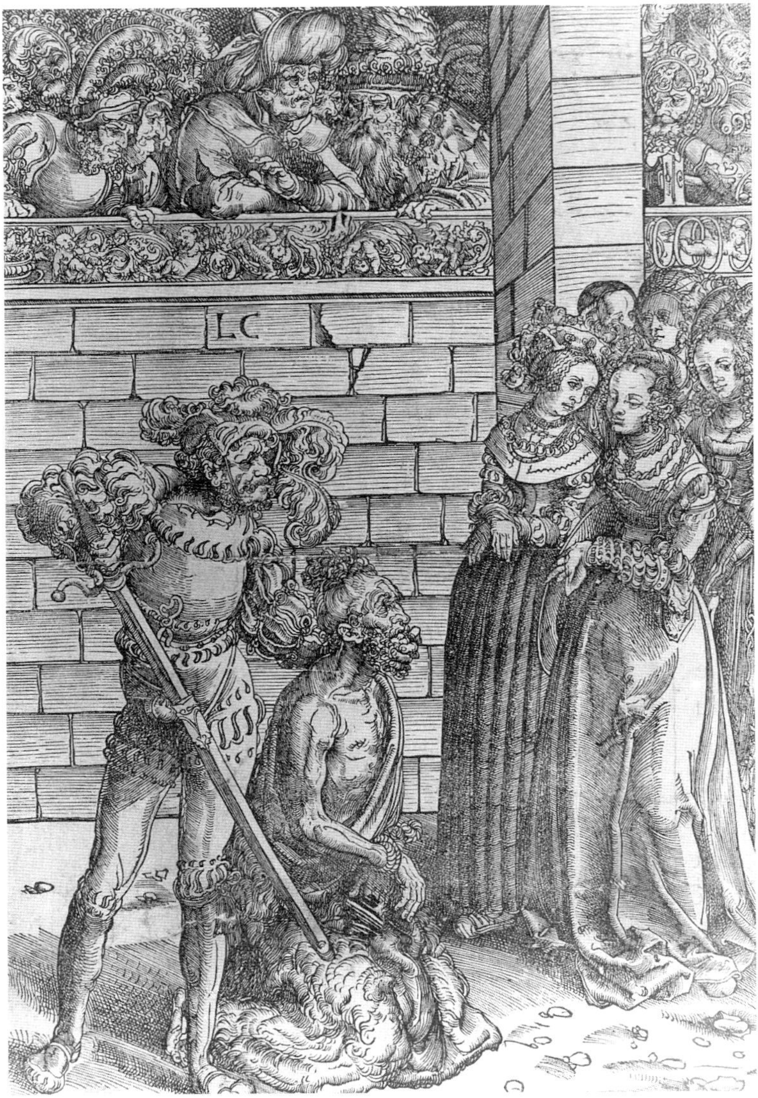

The Beheading of St John the Baptist, 1508.
Woodcut, 39 x 27.2 cm.
Gotha, Stiftung Schloss Friedenstein.

1509

□ In a letter of dedication by the Nuremberg Humanist and Wittenberg professor Dr Christoph Scheurl published on 01.10.1509 in Leipzig, Lucas Cranach was named as being the foremost of the living painters. Praise was also given to the speed with which he created his paintings and his *trompe l'oeil* works (optical illusions).

□ The theologian Andreas Karlstadt testified to Cranach's knowledge of Latin.

□ The artist and his journeymen worked in Wittenberg, Lochau and Torgau. Lucas Cranach lived in Wittenberg Castle: the lock on his door was repaired and, in the workshop, a tiled stove was newly installed.

□ Four of his eight copper engravings were created in this year: for example, *The Penance of St Chrysostom*; it was only around 1520 that the remainder were created.

□ The series of woodcuts entitled *The Passion of Christ* with 14 individual plates is the only large and significant graphic series dealing with the theme of the passion of Christ to be created by Cranach. In 1540, the series appeared for the first time in German.

□ In this year, Cranach also illustrated the Wittenberg *Book of Saints*, a catalogue of the 5,005 reliquaries stored in Wittenberg's Castle Church. The reliquaries almost exclusively came from the collection of Frederick the Wise, who displayed them publicly once a year with an indulgence linked to this event. Cranach produced 117 woodcuts for this book.

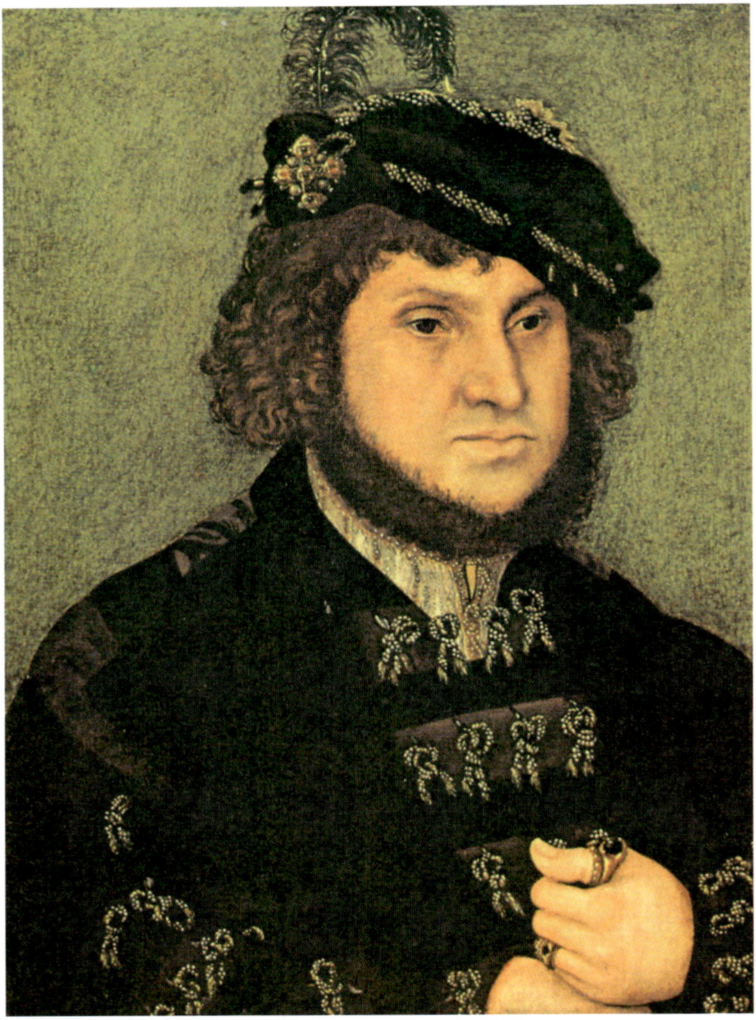

*Duke John of Saxony (later John the Steadfast)
and his Six-Year-Old Son John Frederick (later John Frederick
the Magnanimous), 1509.
Oil on lime wood, each 42.8 x 32.3 cm.
Private collection.*

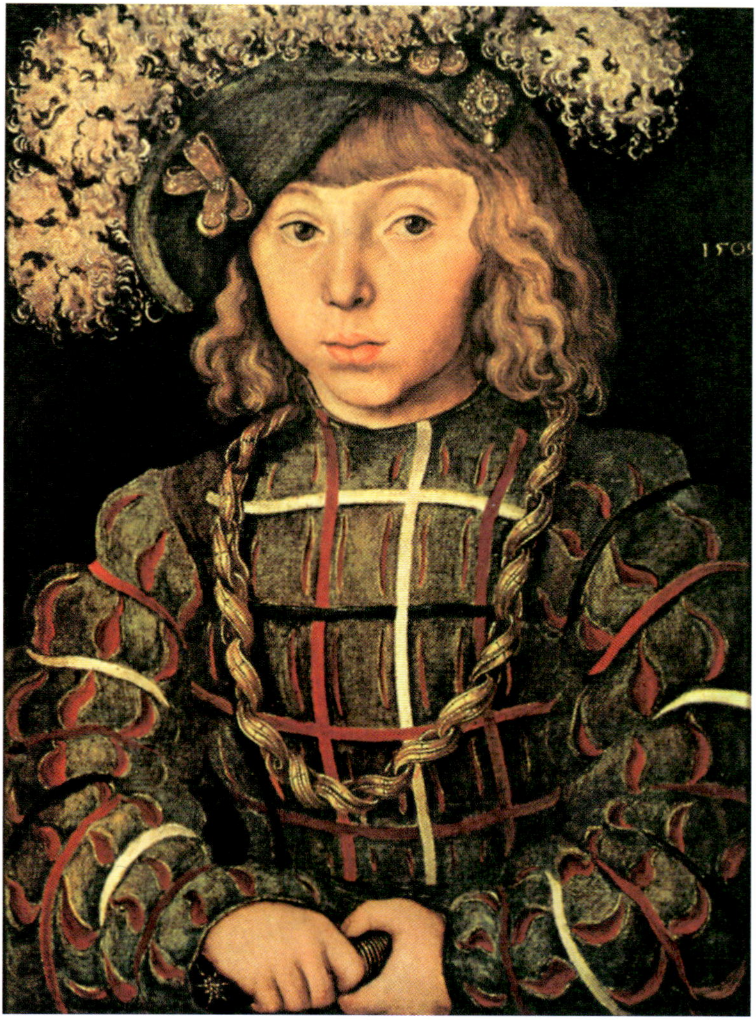

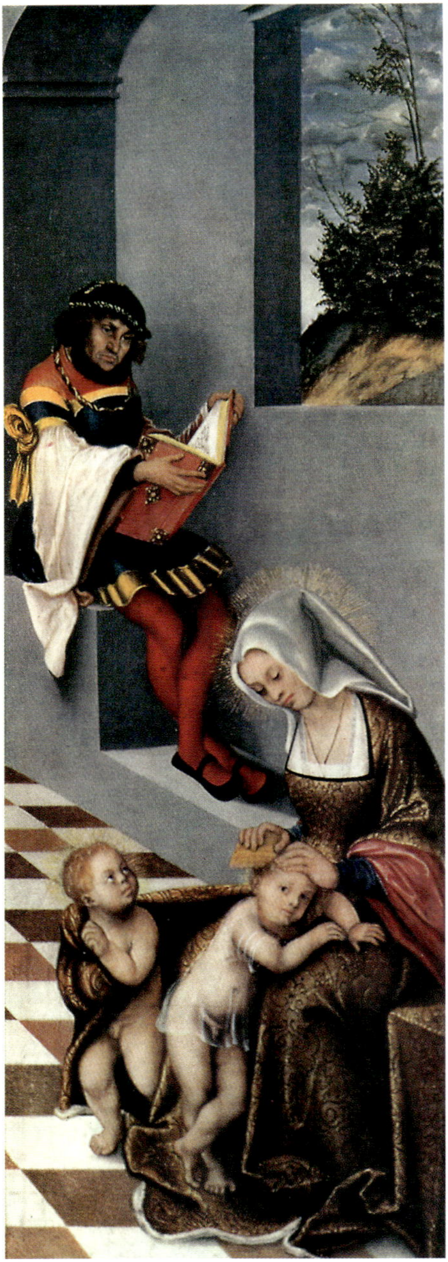

St Anne (right wing of altar-piece): The Holy Kinship, 1509. Oil on panel, 120 x 44 cm. Frankfurt am Main, Städelsches Kunstinstitut.

Venus and Cupid, 1509. Oil on panel transferred to canvas, 170 x 84 cm. St Petersburg, Hermitage.

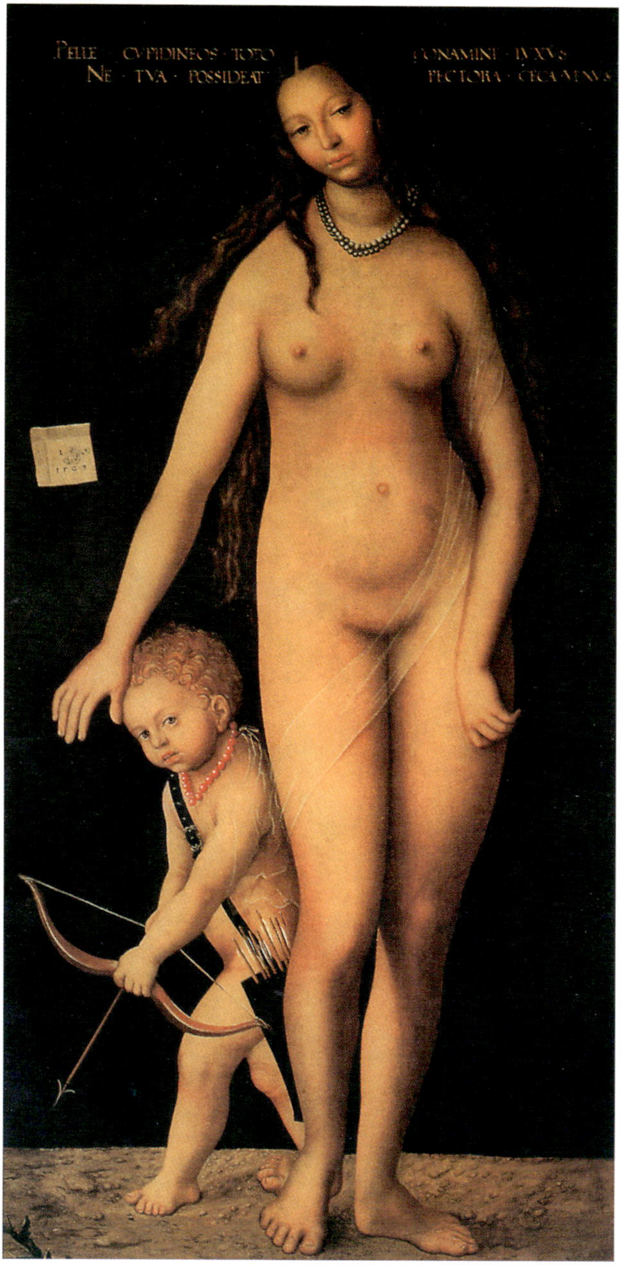
PELLE · CVPIDINEOS · TOTO CONAMINE · LVXVS
NE · TVA · POSSIDEAT PECTORA · CECA · VENVS

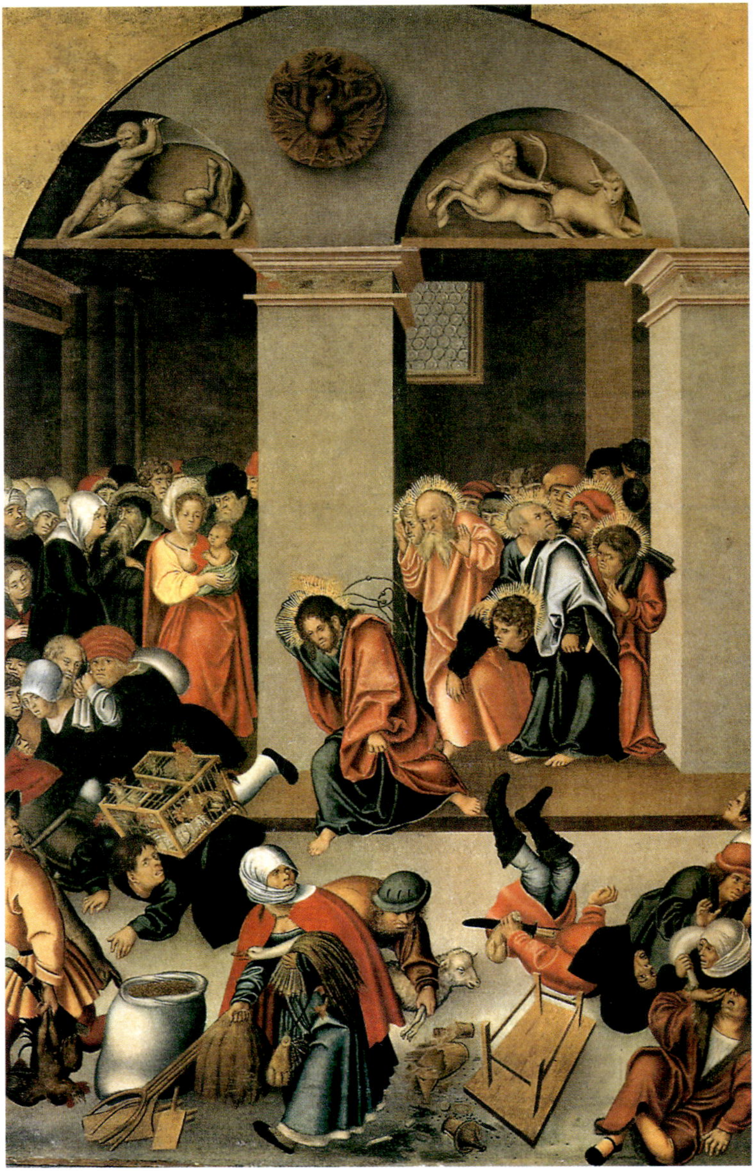

Christ Driving the Money-Changers from the Temple, around 1509.
Oil on lime wood, 144 x 98 cm.
Dresden, Staatliche Kunstsammlungen.

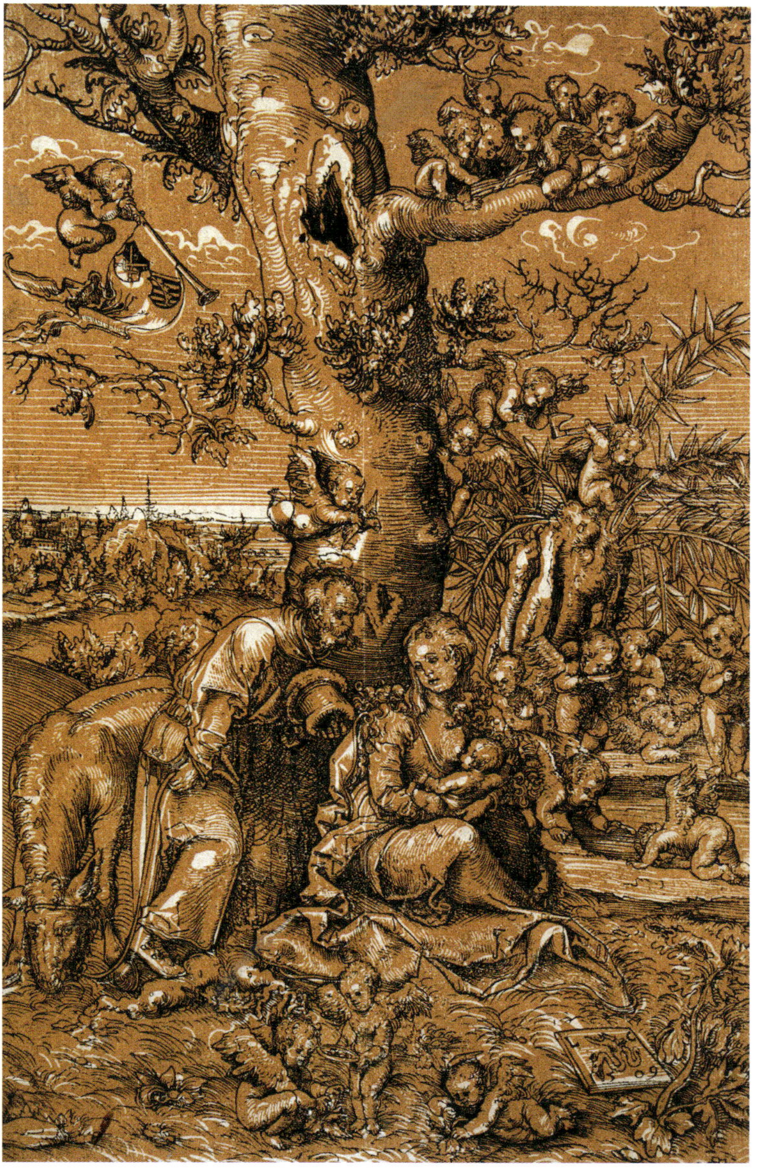

The Rest on the Flight into Egypt, 1509.
Woodcut, 28.5 x 18.5 cm.
Gotha, Stiftung Schloss Friedenstein.

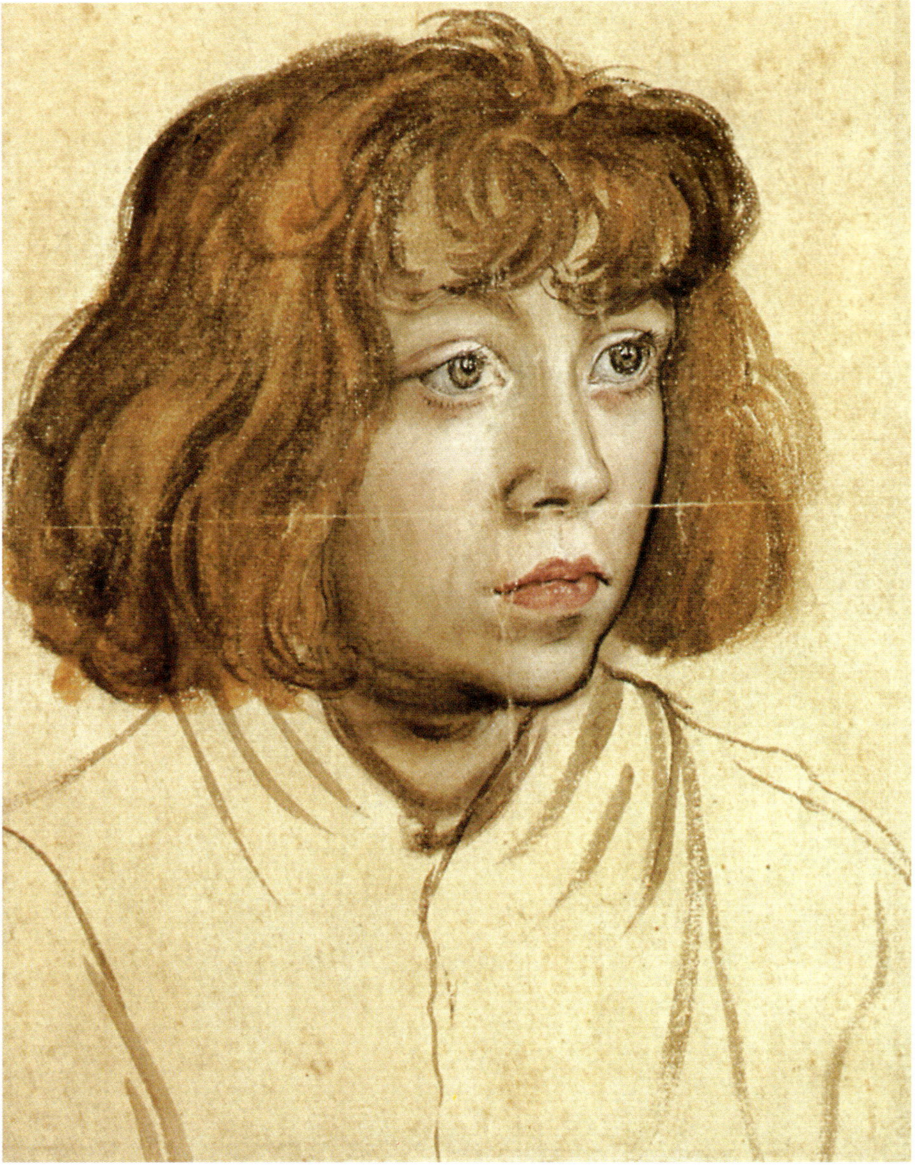

Portrait of a Boy, around 1509.
Chalk, watercolour and opaque watercolour, 21.8 x 17 cm.
Paris, Louvre.

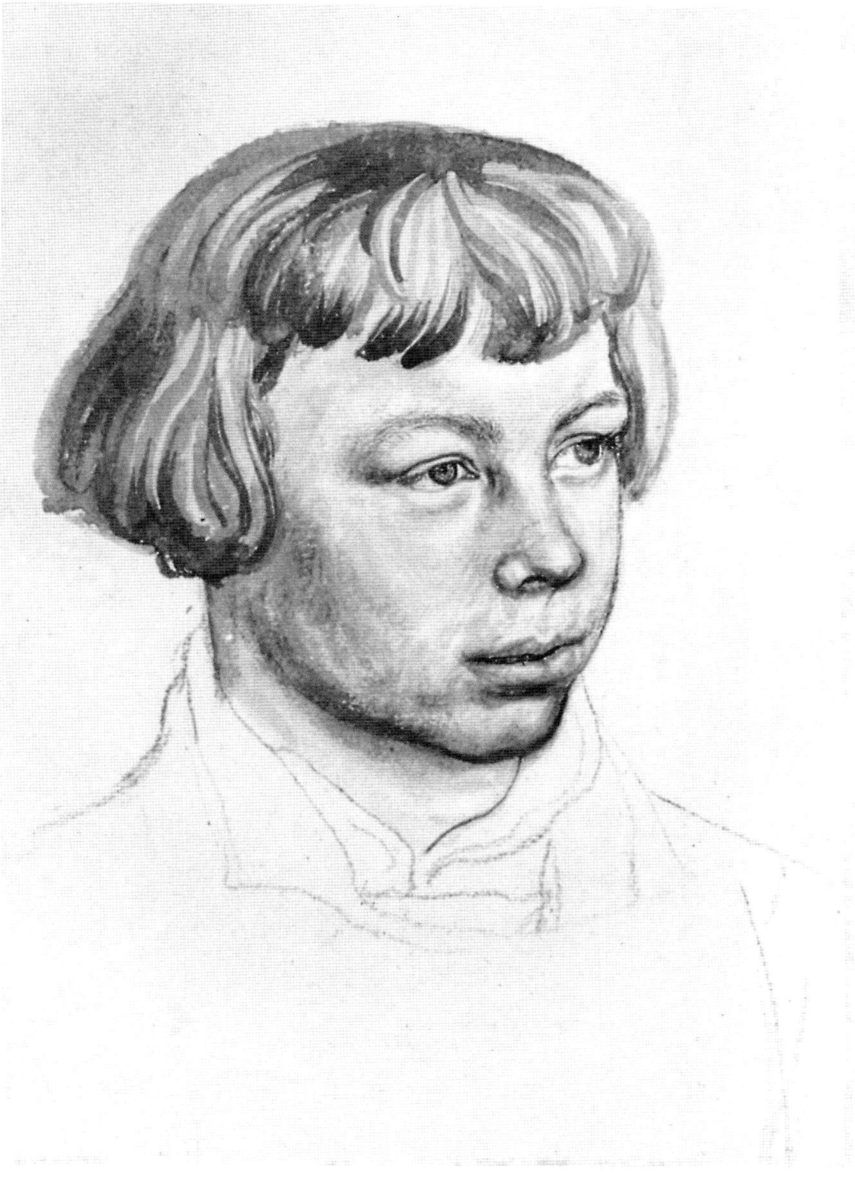

Portrait of a Boy, around 1509.
Chalk, watercolour and opaque watercolour, 24.5 x 17.8 cm.
Paris, Louvre.

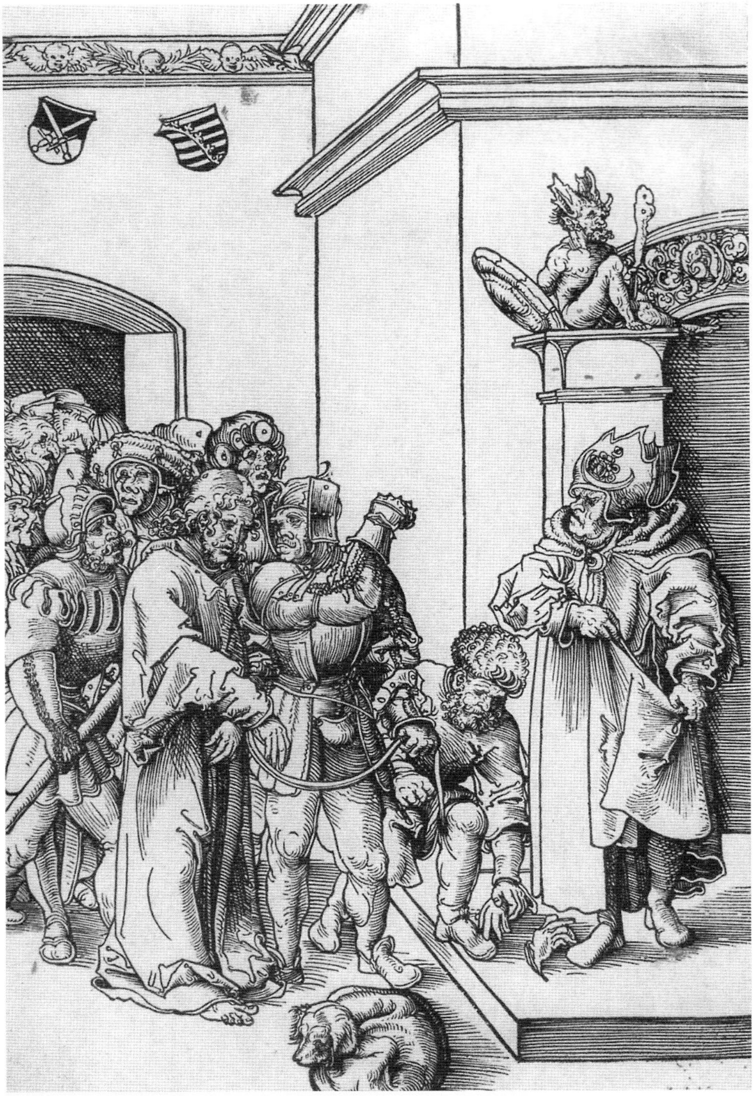

Christ Crowned with Thorns (Christ before Annas), from the series: 'The Passion of Christ', 1509.
Woodcut, 25 x 17.2 cm.
Gotha, Stiftung Schloss Friedenstein.

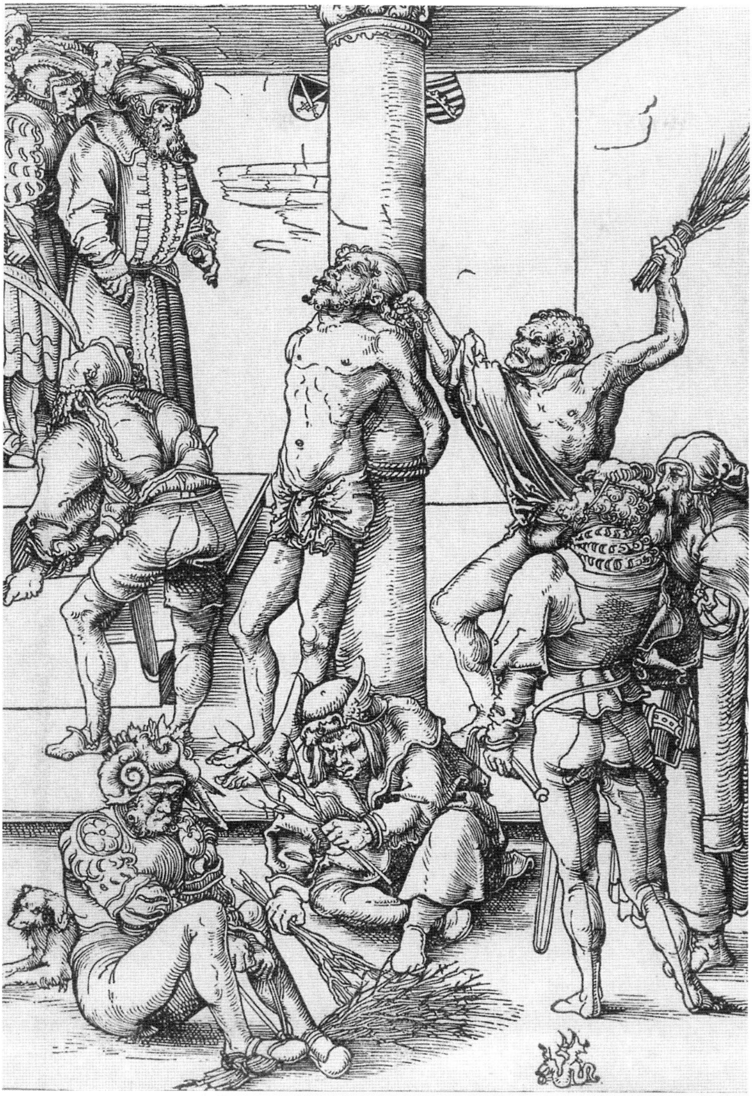

The Scourging of Christ, from the series:
'The Passion of Christ', 1509.
Woodcut, 25 x 17.2 cm.
Gotha, Stiftung Schloss Friedenstein.

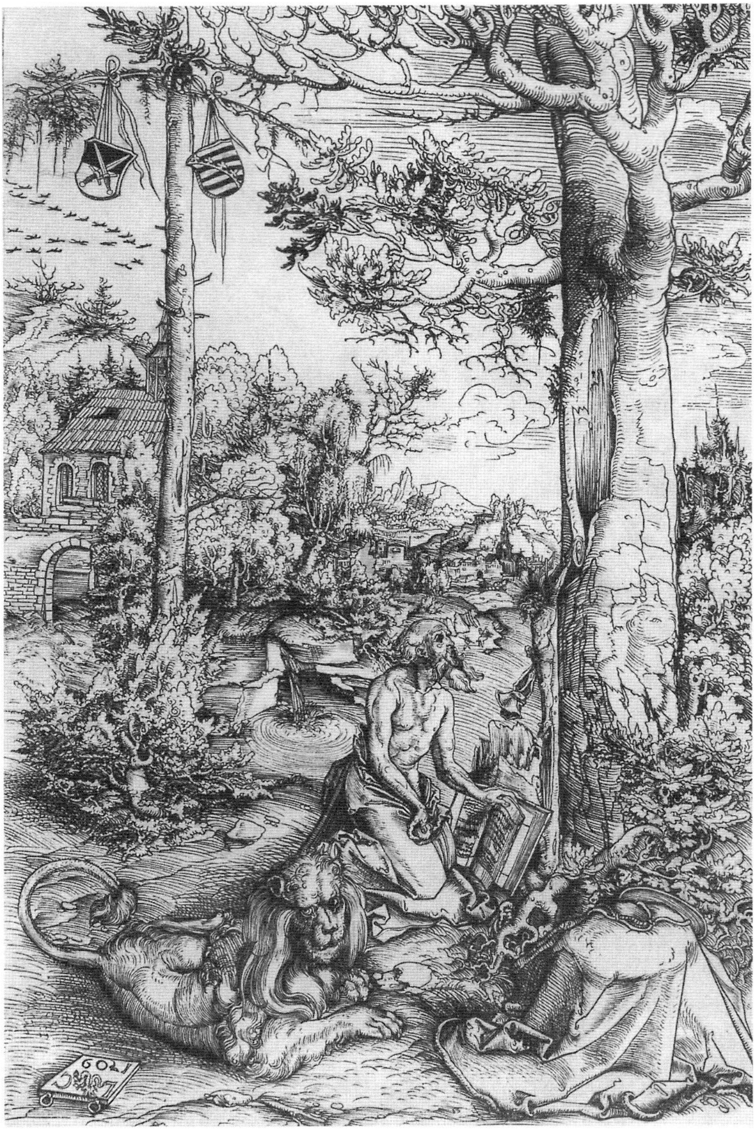

The Penitence of St Jerome, 1509.
Woodcut, 33.2 x 23.2 cm.
Gotha, Stiftung Schloss Friedenstein.

1510

□ Lucas Cranach bought 750 bricks from the town brickworks. From this time onwards, he established a large painter's workshop in the town in which he was able to carry out many commissions.

In the accounts of the Wittenberg treasury, *Lucas Moler* was registered as having had to pay a special tax for the building of the great bastion.

□ The series of woodcuts entitled *Christ, the Twelve Apostles and St Paul* appeared between 1510 and 1515 with 14 large-scale individual plates. By adding the instruments of torture employed in their martyrdom, the apostles are identifiable for the viewer.

□ At the beginning of November, Martin Luther set off with a fellow monk to Rome on monastery business. They travelled via Nuremberg, Ulm, western Switzerland, Milan, Florence and Siena to Rome. They left Rome again in February 1511, arriving back in Erfurt at the beginning of April and in Wittenberg in the late summer. Rome represented a highly ambiguous experience in Luther's life ('If there be a hell, then Rome is built on it').

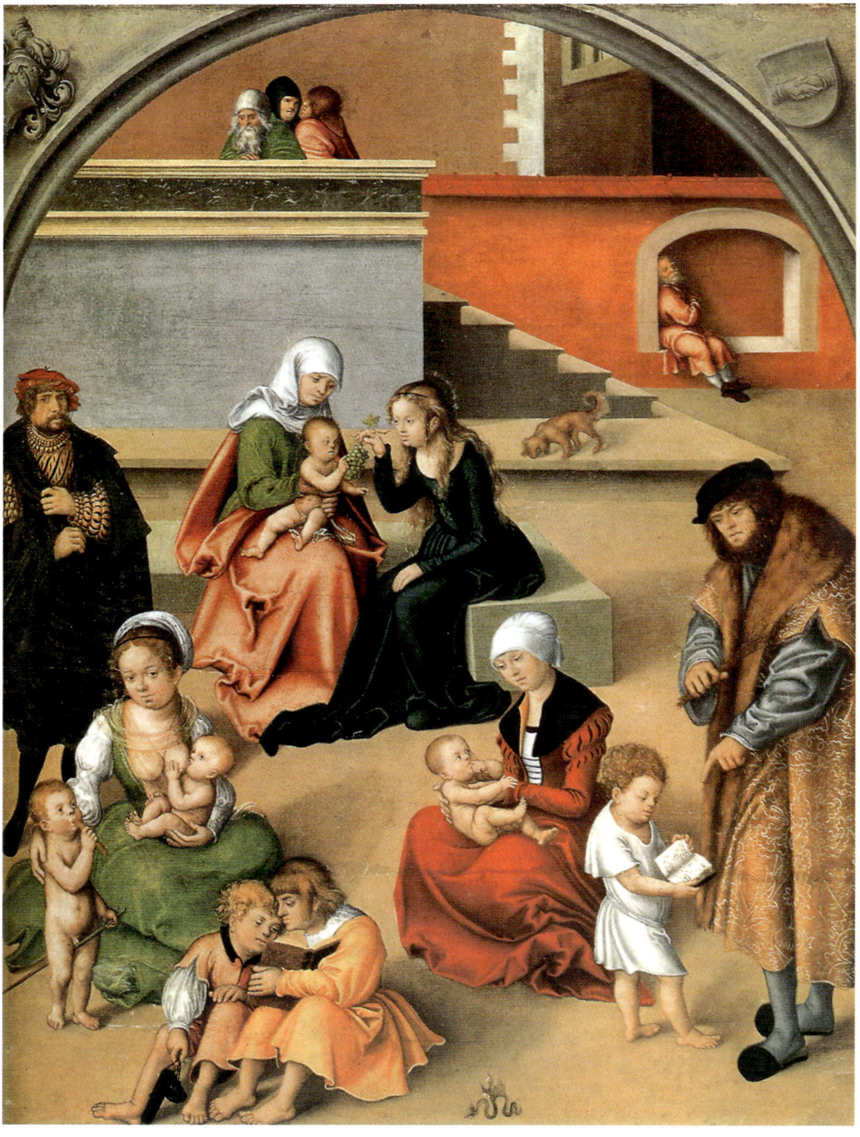

The Holy Kinship, around 1510.
Oil on lime wood, 88 x 71 cm.
Vienna, Akademie der bildenden Künste.

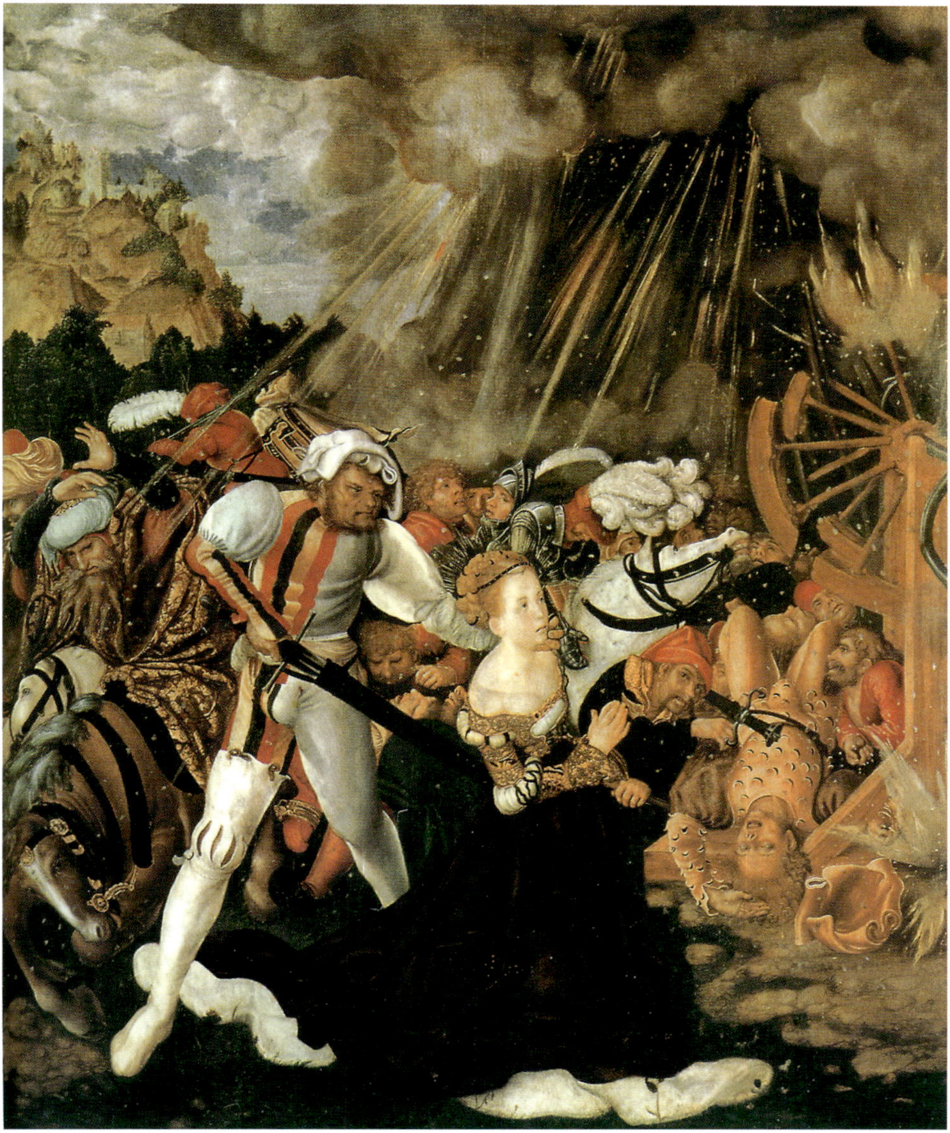

The Martyrdom of St Catherine, around 1510.
Oil on panel, 112 x 95 cm.
Budapest, Library of the Reformed Congregation.

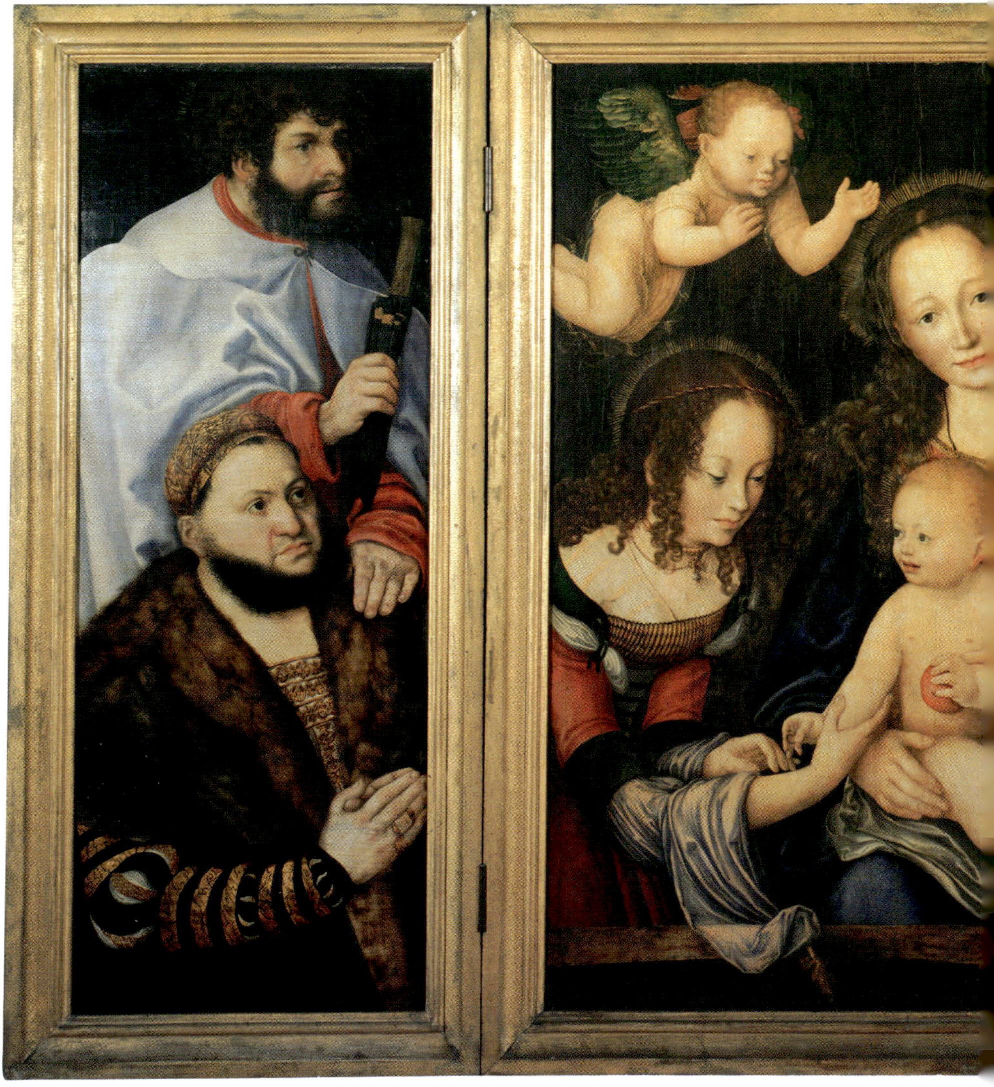

The Dessau Altarpiece of the Princes, approx. 1510–12.
Oil on lime wood, central panel 106 x 92.5 cm, side panel 106 x 42 cm.
Dessau, Anhaltische Gemäldegalerie.

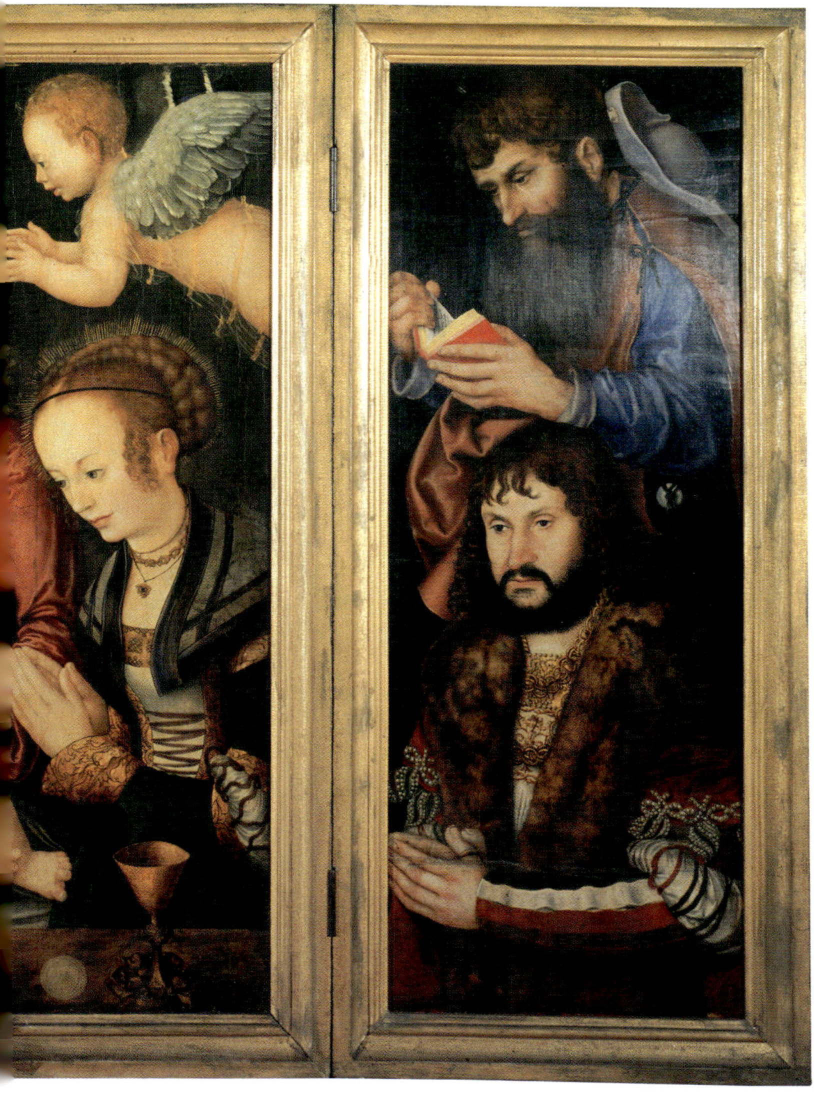

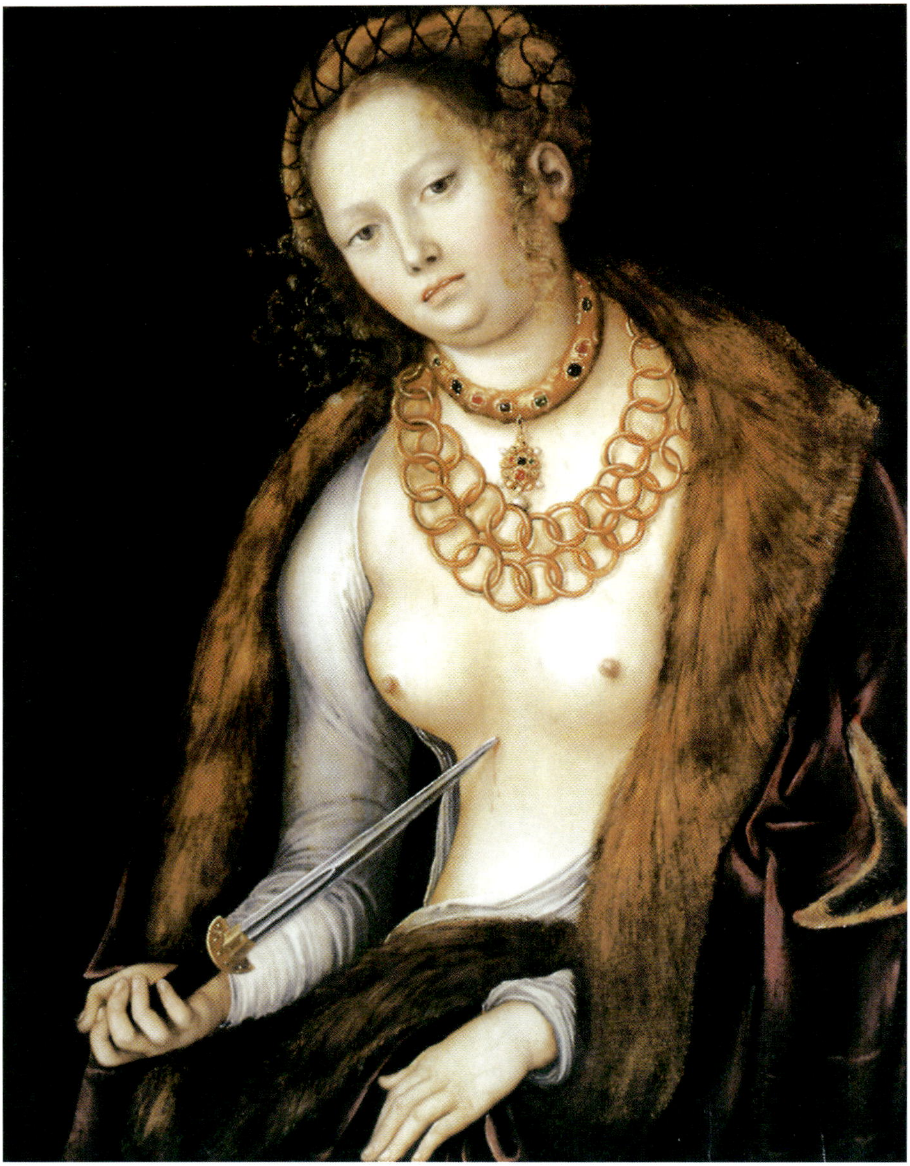

Lucretia, approx. 1510–13.
Oil on lime wood, 60 x 47 cm.
Private collection.

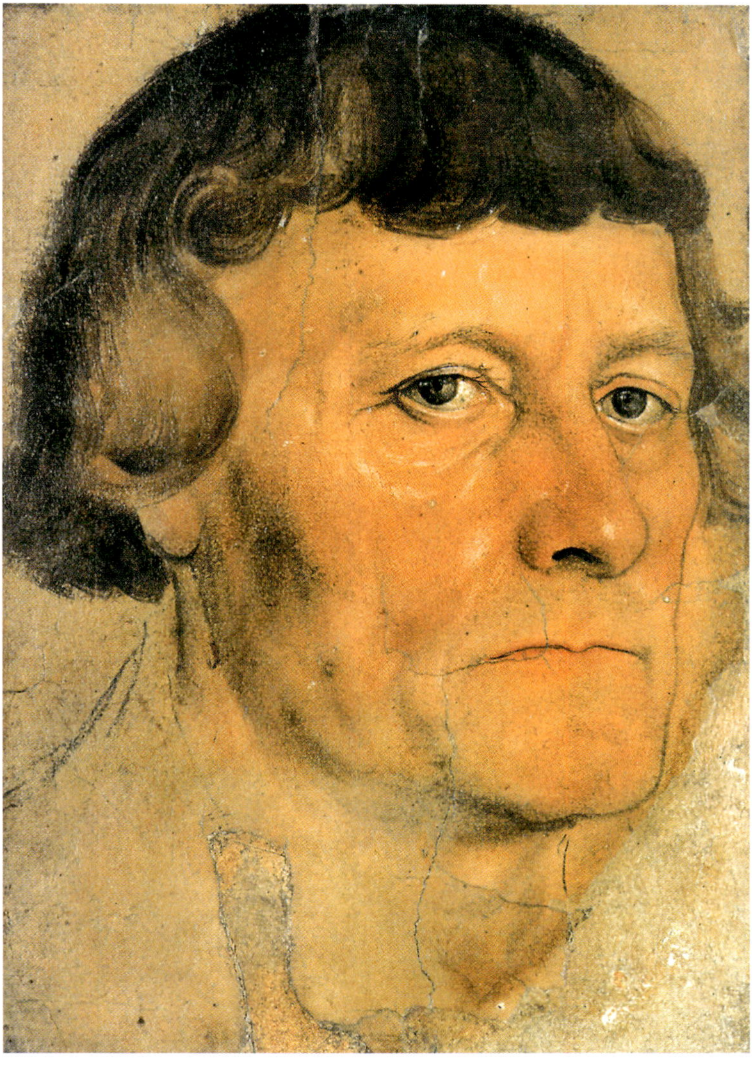

Clean-Shaven Man, approx.1510–15.
Oil on paper with a brownish undercoat, 22.3 x 16 cm.
Berlin, Staatliche Museen.

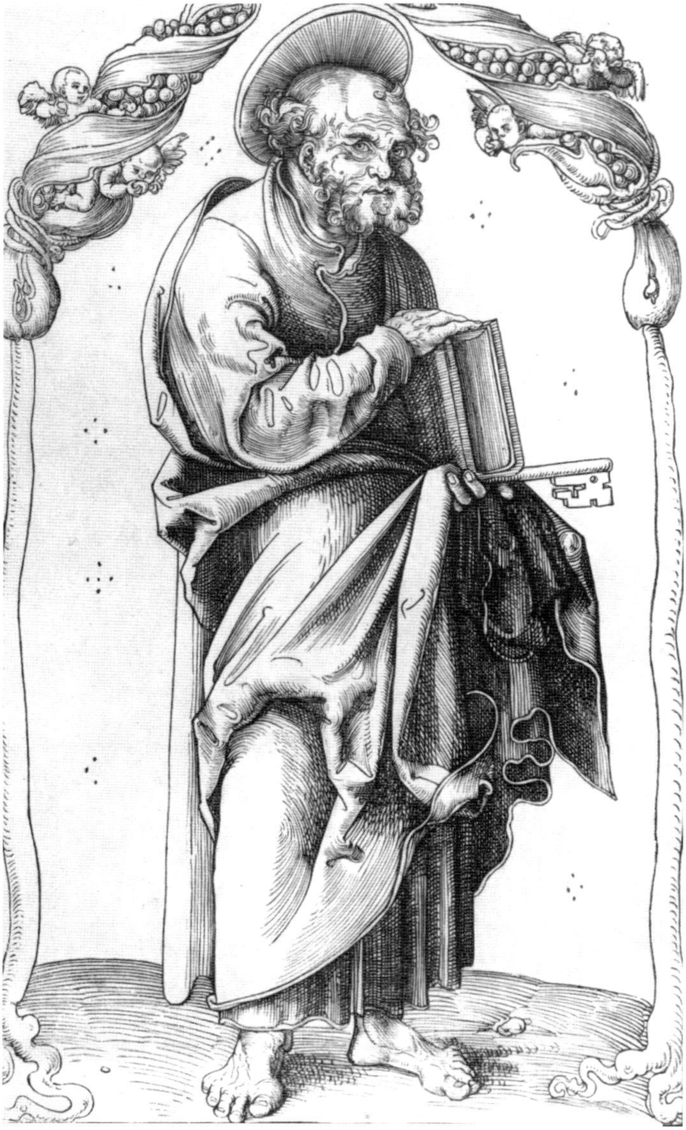

St Peter, from the series:
'Christ and the Apostles', approx. 1510–15.
Woodcut, 30.9 x 18.2 cm.
Gotha, Stiftung Schloss Friedenstein.

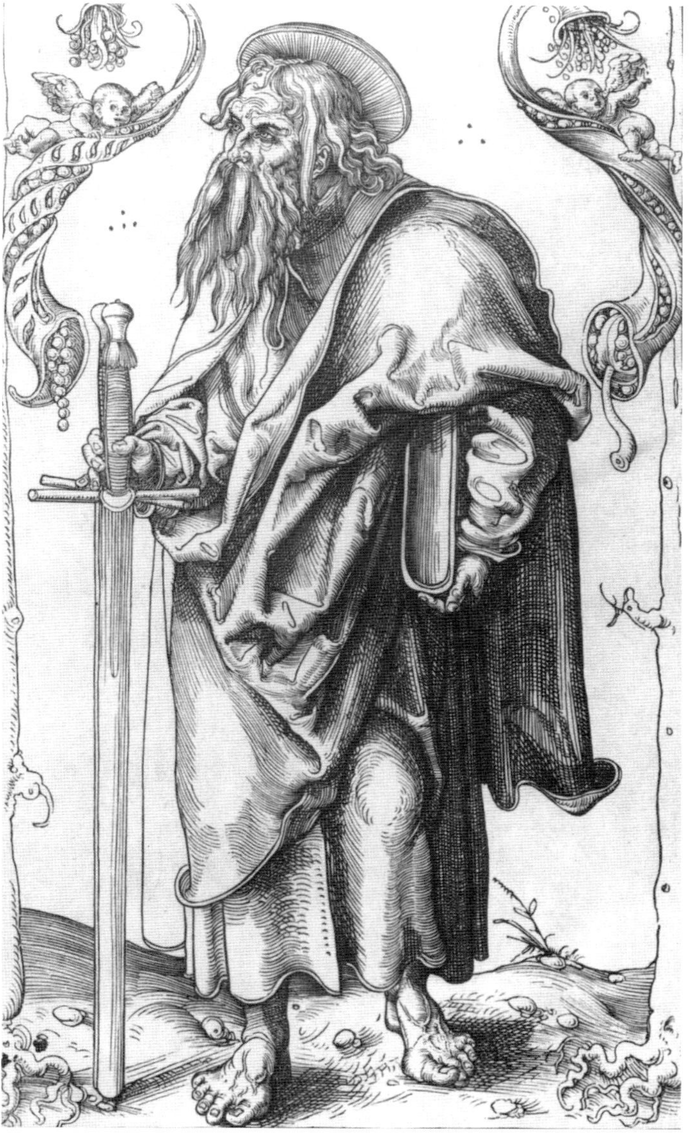

St Paul, from the series:
'Christ and the Apostles', approx. 1510–15.
Woodcut, 30.9 x 18.2 cm.
Gotha, Stiftung Schloss Friedenstein.

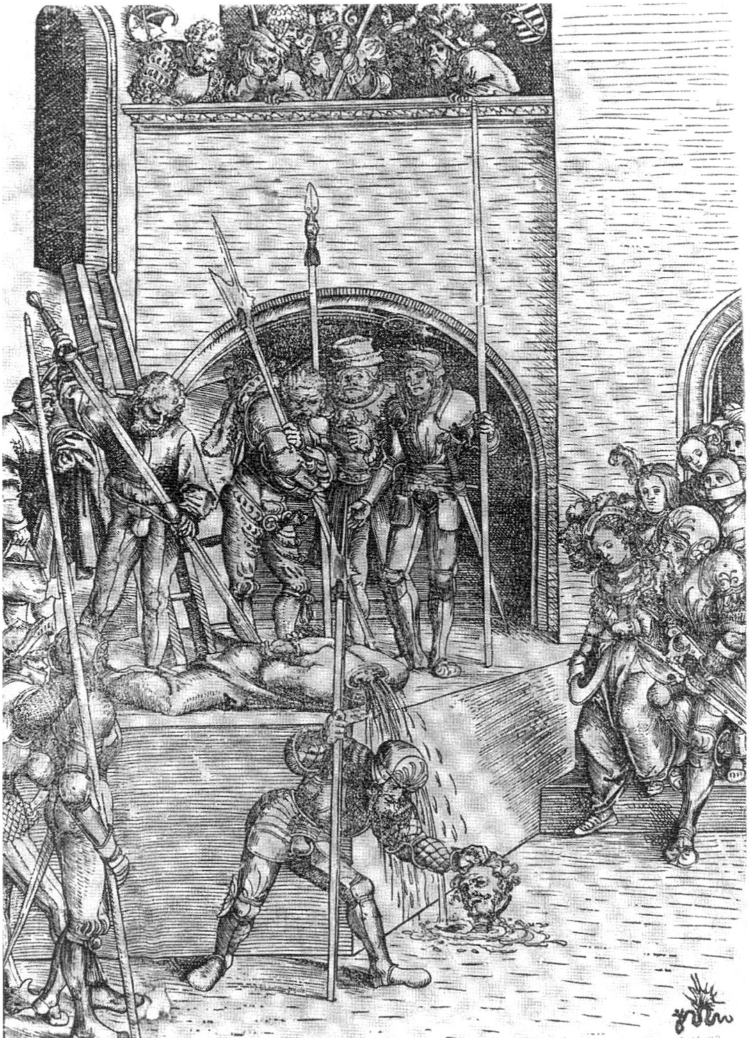

The Beheading of St John the Baptist, approx. 1510–14.
Woodcut, 33 x 23.3 cm.
Gotha, Stiftung Schloss Friedenstein.

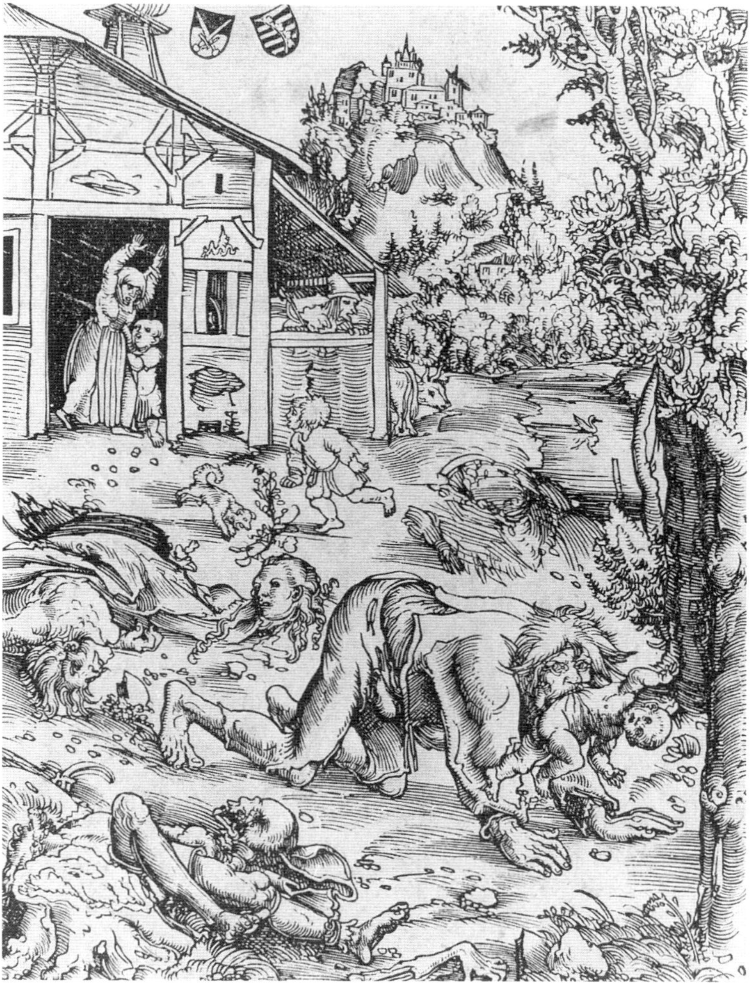

The Werewolf, approx. 1510–15.
Woodcut, size of plate: 16.1 x 12.5 cm.
Gotha, Stiftung Schloss Friedenstein.

1511

□ It cannot be determined whether Cranach was already married at this time. It can be assumed, however, that he married at some time between 1510 and 1511. His wife, Barbara Brengbier, came from Gotha and was the daughter of the Gotha alderman Jobst and his wife Katharina Brengbier, née Jahn. The marriage produced five children: two sons and three daughters. Both sons took up their father's profession: Hans (around 1513–37) and Lucas (1515–86) both became artists.

□ Cranach's brother, Mathias (*around 1490), started to study at the University of Wittenberg. He received summer clothing from the court and helped his brother until at least 1512.

□ The 21-year-old Albert II, Margrave of Brandenburg-Ansbach (1490–1568), was conferred with the title of a Grand Master of the Teutonic Order by Emperor Maximilian I. Albert II was the last Grand Master of the Teutonic Order (1511–25). He transformed the German state into a secular hereditary dukedom under Polish suzerainty and called himself thereafter Albert II of Prussia. Albert was the first German duke to introduce the Reformation and it was he who founded the University of Königsberg in 1544.

Margrave Albert of Brandenburg-Ansbach, approx. 1511–12.
Oil on panel, 38 x 26 cm.
Private collection.

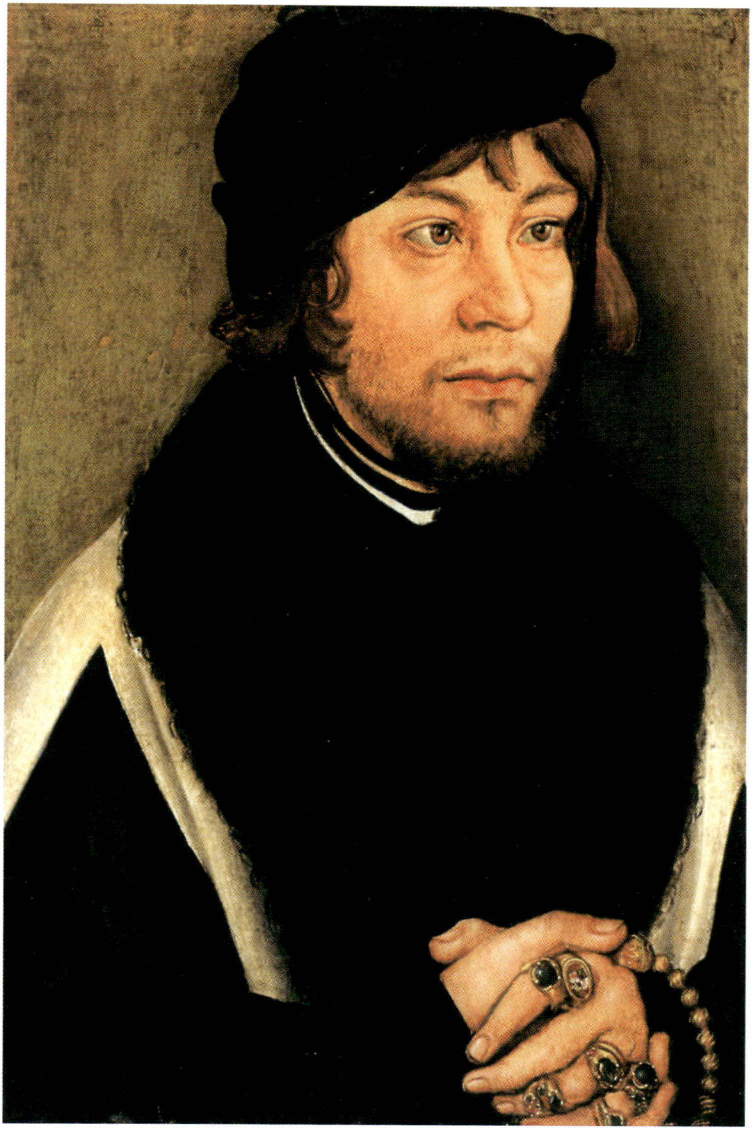

1512

☐ According to the accounts of the Wittenberg treasury, Lucas Cranach owned two houses in Wittenberg, for which he paid taxes. It is possible that he already had bought one of these houses in 1511, but the treasury accounts for this year have been lost. In any case, there must have been a great deal of building in progress in 1512 or large building projects were being planned. In this year, Cranach bought 11,500 building bricks, 6,000 roof slates as well as 40 wagon-loads of lime from the town brickworks.

☐ The 28-year-old Georg Spalatin, who had been ordained as a priest in 1508 in Erfurt and who had been the tutor to Prince John Frederick I of Saxony since December of this year, founded and administered the Wittenberg University library from autumn 1512 onwards at the behest of Frederick the Wise. The library was located within Wittenberg Castle. Spalatin was

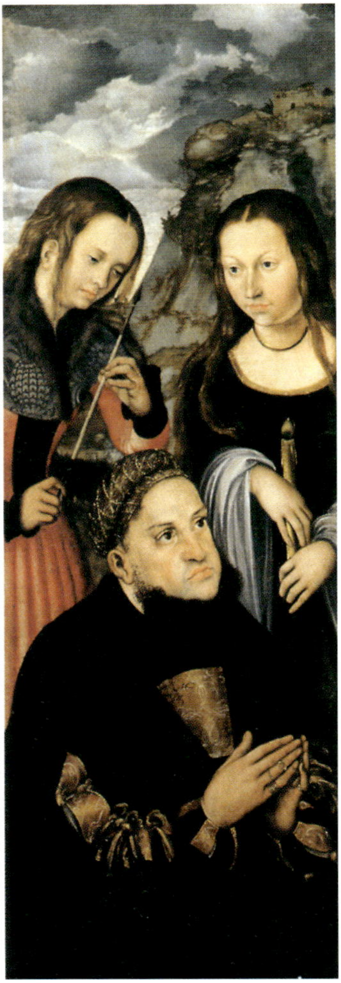

Frederick the Wise, Kneeling with Sts Ursula and Genevieve, around 1512.
Oil on panel, 100 x 35 cm.
Copenhagen, Statens Museum for Kunst.

to become the decisive defender and mediator at the Elector's court in the matter of Martin Luther.

☐ Martin Luther became a Doctor of Theology and took over the Chair of Biblical Theology from Johannes von Staupitz at the University of Wittenberg.

☐ The series of woodcuts entitled *The Martyrdom of the Twelve Apostles* with 12 plates appeared around 1512. Cranach depicted the martyrs' deaths of the Apostles – except for John, who died a natural death. The woodcuts were subsequently used in many publications.

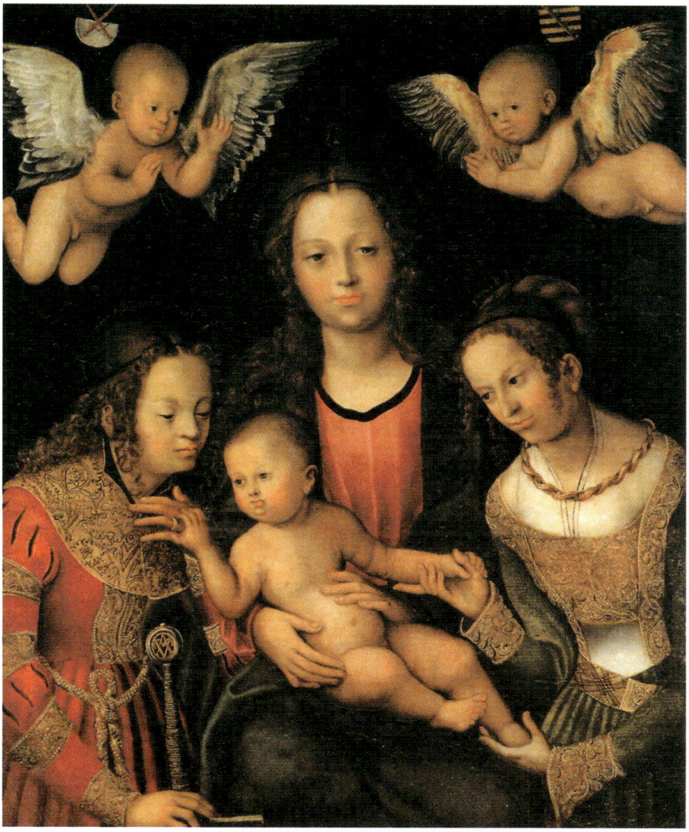

Virgin and Child with Sts Catherine and Barbara, around 1512. Oil, originally painted on wood and later transferred to canvas, 96.5 x 80.5 cm (centre altarpiece). Copenhagen, Statens Museum for Kunst.

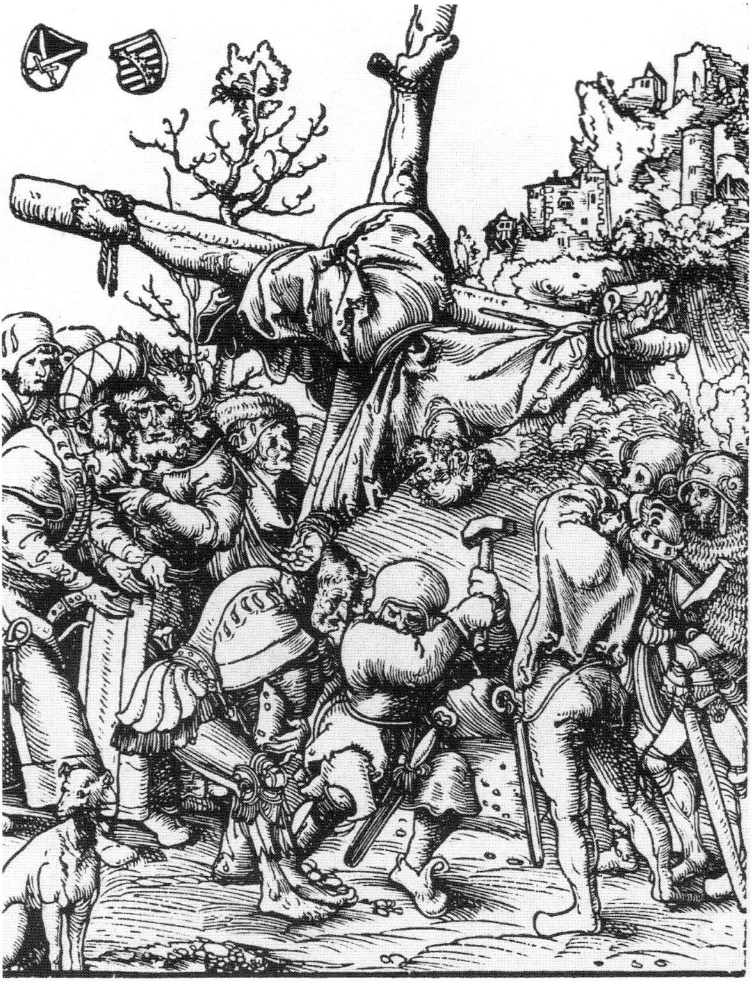

Martyrdom of St Peter, from the series:
'Martyrdom of the Twelve Apostles', 1512.
Woodcut, 16 x 12.3 cm.
Gotha, Stiftung Schloss Friedenstein.

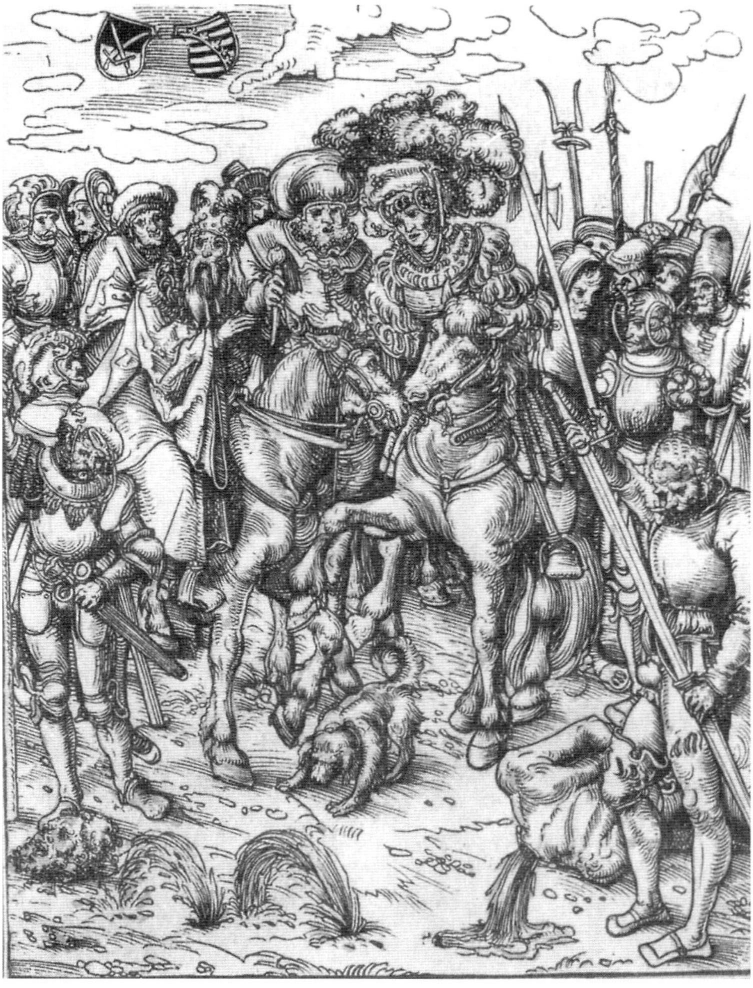

Martyrdom of St Paul, from the series:
'Martyrdom of the Twelve Apostles', 1512.
Woodcut, 15.8 x 12.2 cm.
Gotha, Stiftung Schloss Friedenstein.

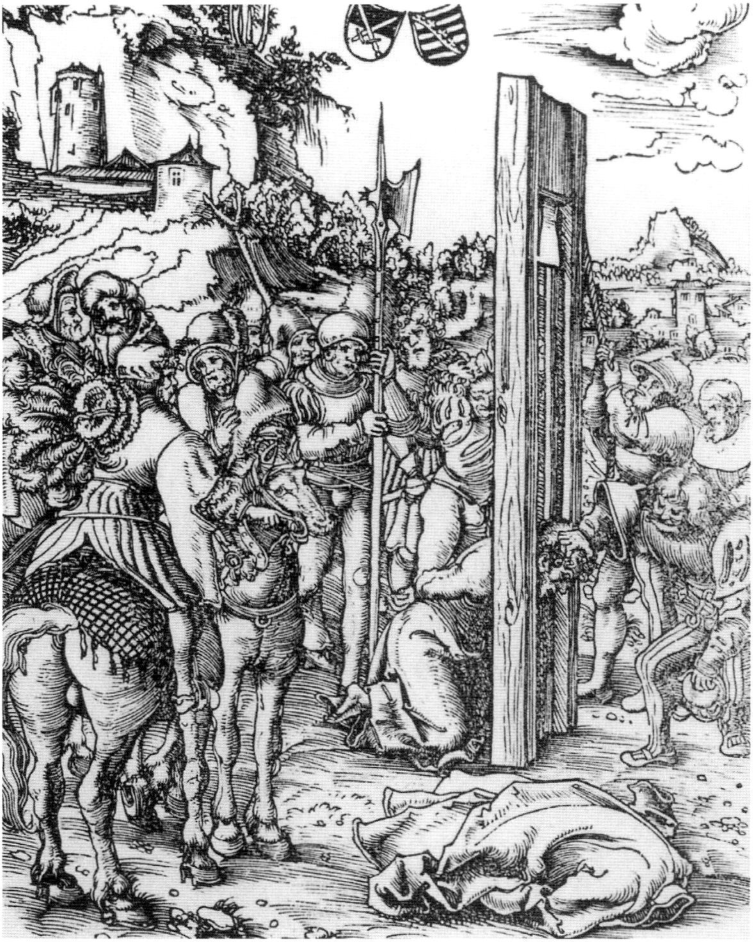

Martyrdom of St Matthew, from the series: 'Martyrdom of the Twelve Apostles', 1512. Woodcut, 16 x 12.3 cm. Gotha, Stiftung Schloss Friedenstein.

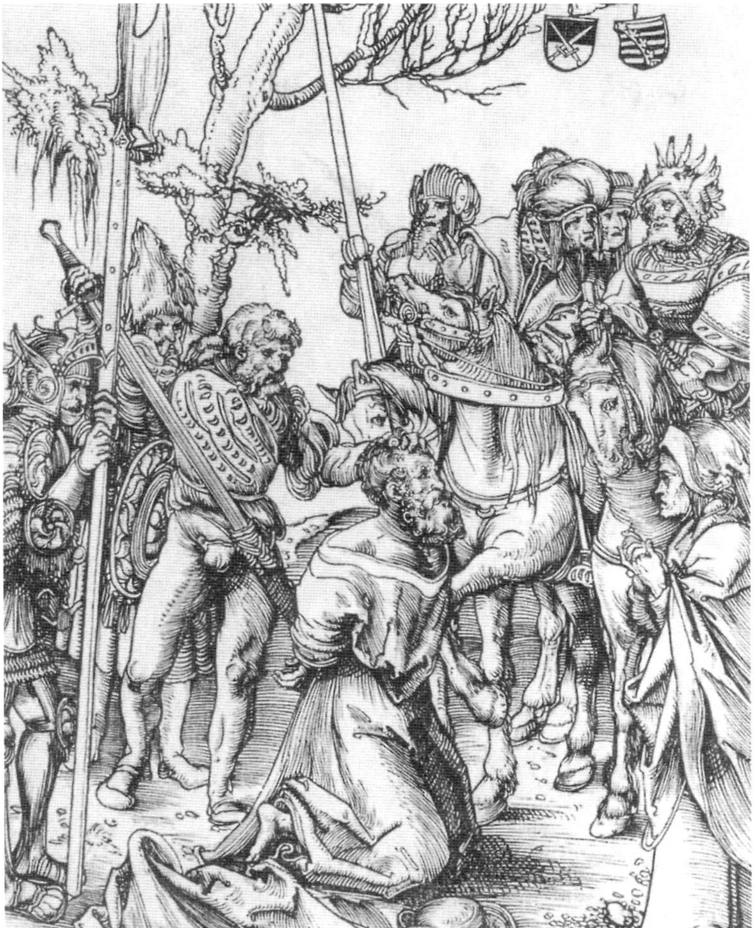

Martyrdom of St James the Greater, from the series:
'Martyrdom of the Twelve Apostles', 1512.
Woodcut, 16.1 x 12 cm.
Gotha, Stiftung Schloss Friedenstein.

1513

□ The accounts of the Wittenberg treasury for 1513 show, in addition to the two houses (for which Cranach paid the taxes mentioned in 1512 until 1517), tax relief, which was for the first time granted to him, for a house which had changed ownership from Caspar Teuschel to Cranach. Caspar Teuschel, a town alderman and judge in Wittenberg, had apparently started building work five years previously on the corner of the Schlossstraße/Elbgasse. However, he had not managed to complete the work within the five years of his tax relief with the consequence that Lucas Cranach obtained another period of five years from the council. For the aforementioned house, from 1518 onwards, he paid a yearly tax of 5 florins and 15 pennies, thus making the property the most highly taxed residential and commercial property in the whole town.

In this year, he also paid excise duties to the town for the first time for the running of a wine merchant's.

□ Around 1513, Cranach's first son, Hans, was born; Hans also later became a painter (+1537, Bologna).

□ Cranach received four florins for supplying pieces of tournament equipment (caparisons, painted printed coats of arms and various helmet plates) which Duke John the Steadfast took with him on his journey to Mecklenburg, Pomerania and Brandenburg (24.04.1513).

□ The 45-year-old co-regent Duke John the Steadfast married Margarethe, the daughter of Duke Waldemar VI of Anhalt-Zerbst in Torgau on 13.11.1513, a day after the bride's 19th birthday. His first wife, Sophie of Mecklenburg, had died in 1503, at the age of 22, after the birth of their son, John Frederick I, the later Elector.

The marriage to Margarethe of Anhalt-Zerbst produced four children: Marie (1516–83), Margarethe (+1535), John II (dates not known as he died shortly after his birth) and John Ernst I (1521–53), Duke of Saxe-Coburg.

□ Cranach, together with ten journeymen, decorated Hartenfels Castle above Torgau four weeks before the wedding, supplying the marital bed, tournament trappings, carpets, helmet decorations and coats of arms.

□ Ernst, Archbishop of Magdeburg and Bishop of Halberstadt, died on 03.08.1513 at the age of 49. Ernst was the brother of Frederick the Wise and his co-regent, John the Steadfast. His successor, from 30.08.1513 onwards, was the 23-year-old Albert II, Margrave of Brandenburg, who had been the Canon of Mainz since 1509.

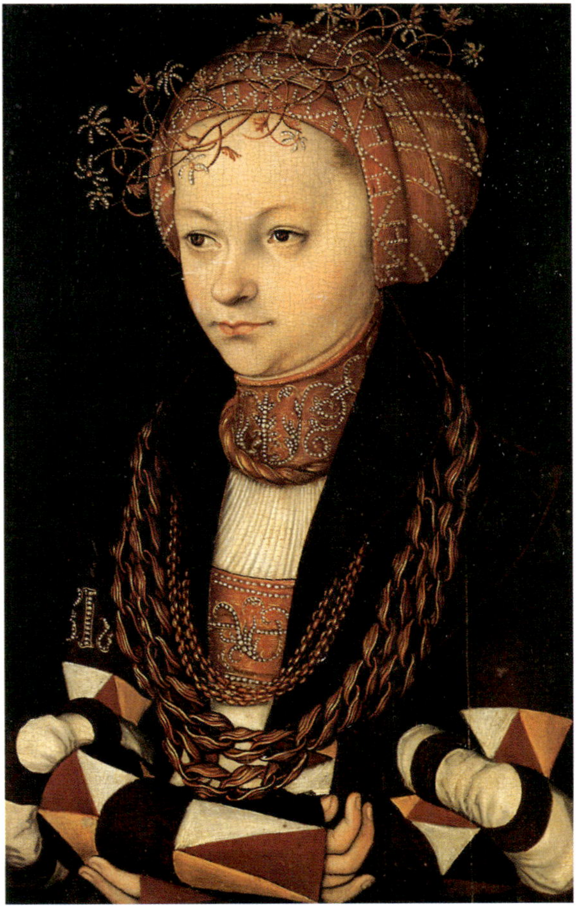

Female Portrait, around 1513.
Oil on panel, 47 x 35 cm.
Private collection.

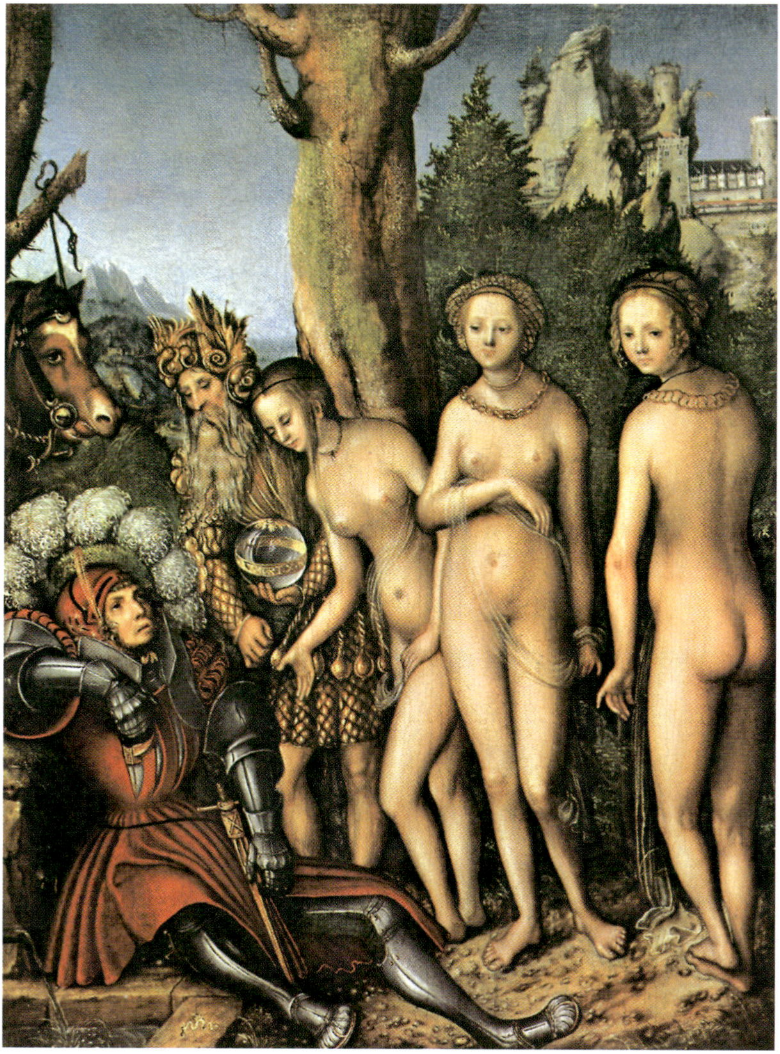

The Judgment of Paris, around 1513.
Oil on lime wood, 43 x 32.2 cm.
Cologne, Wallraf-Richartz-Museum.

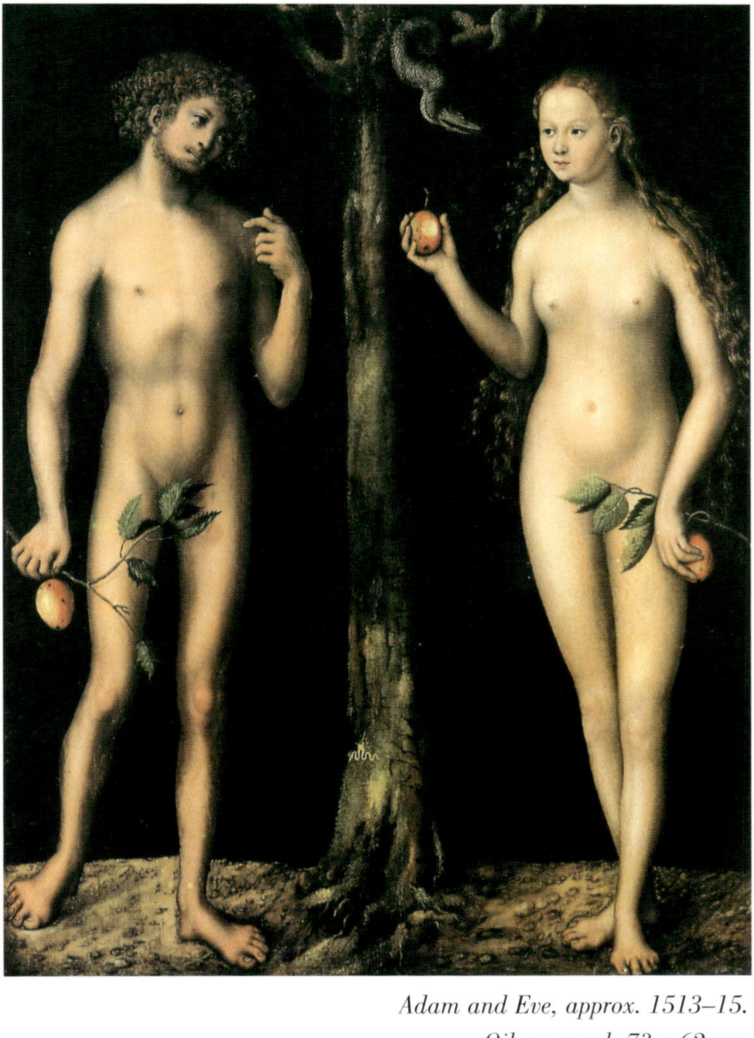

Adam and Eve, approx. 1513–15.
Oil on panel, 73 x 62 cm.
Würzburg, Mainfränkisches Museum.

1514

□ The 24-year-old Albert II (1490–1545), Margrave of Brandenburg, Canon of Mainz since 1509, from 1513 onwards Archbishop of Magdeburg and administrator of the bishopric of Halberstadt, also became Archbishop and Elector of Mainz; in 1518, he was appointed cardinal by the Pope. Albert II was the second son of Elector Johann Cicero of Brandenburg (1455–99) and the brother of the Elector Joachim I of Brandenburg.

To pay the high pallium-money (the tax on the papal confirmation of ecclesiastical promotion) and monies accrued from dispensations (due to his holding more than one diocese) to the Vatican, Albert was forced to take out a loan of 29,000 florins from the banking family Fugger. To repay these funds, Albert was granted half the proceeds of the sale of indulgences (the commutation for money of part of the temporal penalty due for sin) in his church provinces and within the secular realm of the House of Hohenzollern, which then constituted a contribution towards the rebuilding of St Peter's Basilica in Rome. In 1517, these widespread excesses of selling indulgences were the basis of Luther's condemnation of this practice in his Ninety-Five Theses.

Luther was not protesting against indulgences as such, but against the fact that indulgences were not granted, but sold. The indulgence is based on a complex theological construct: although the repentant Christian was forgiven for his sins through confession, the confession rescued him from Hell, but there remained penalties imposed by God in purgatory which the penitent had to endure before he could enter Heaven. These penalties could be remitted totally or in part while the believer was still alive through good deeds, such as by going on a pilgrimage or carrying out an act of compassion. However, the indulgence could also be offered on behalf of a person who was already dead. The latter's release from purgatory was thus hastened and he reached paradise more quickly. The church had the right to issue such letters of indulgence for this purpose.

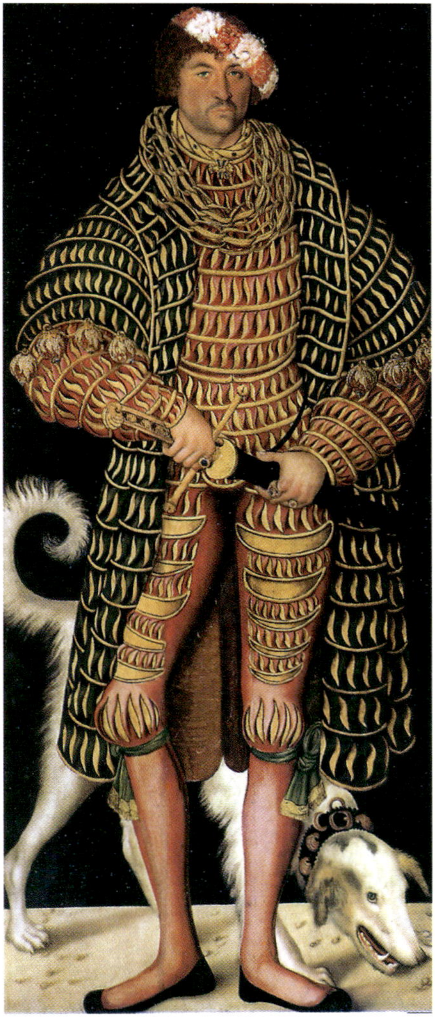

Duke Henry the Pious of Saxony, 1514.
From lime wood to canvas, divided,
original format 185 x 165 cm.
Dresden, Staatliche Kunstsammlungen.

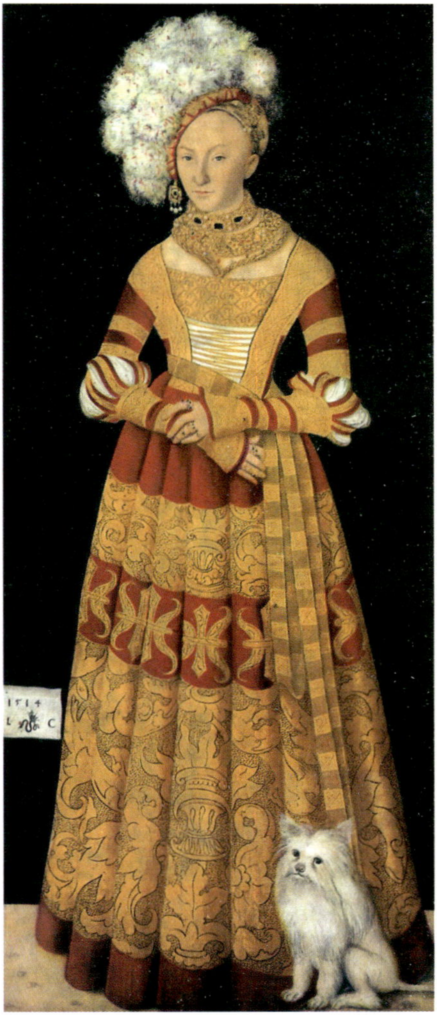

Duchess Catherine of Saxony, 1514.
From lime wood to canvas, divided,
original format 185 x 165 cm.
Dresden, Staatliche Kunstsammlungen.

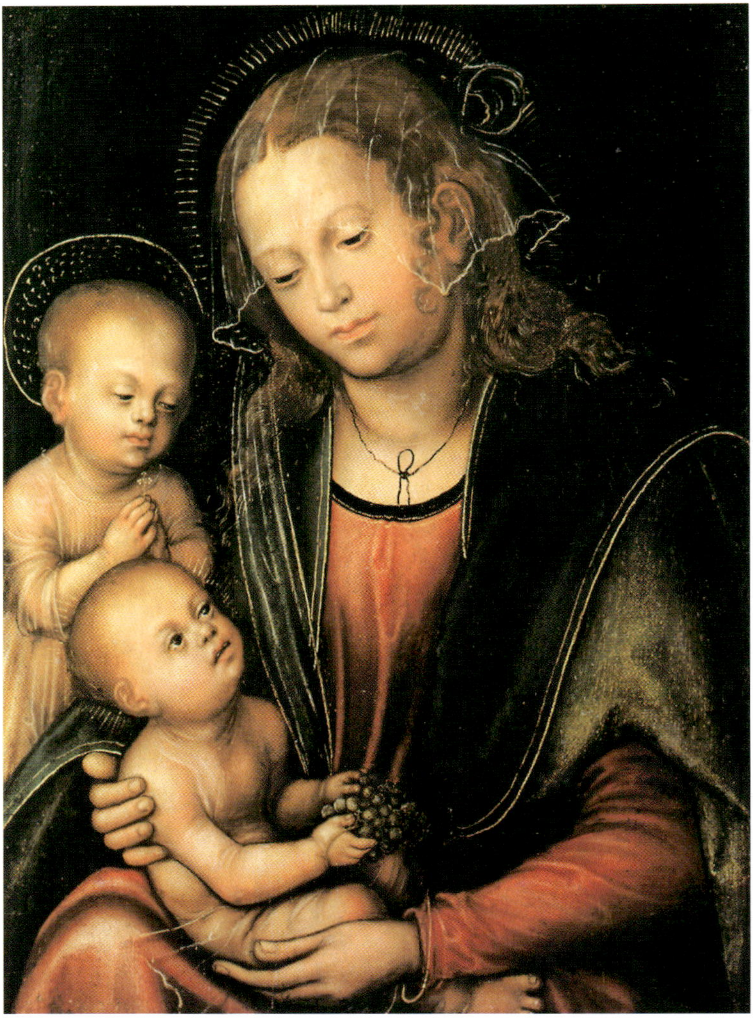

Virgin and Child, 1514.
Oil on panel, 71.3 x 44.3 cm.
Florence, Uffizi.

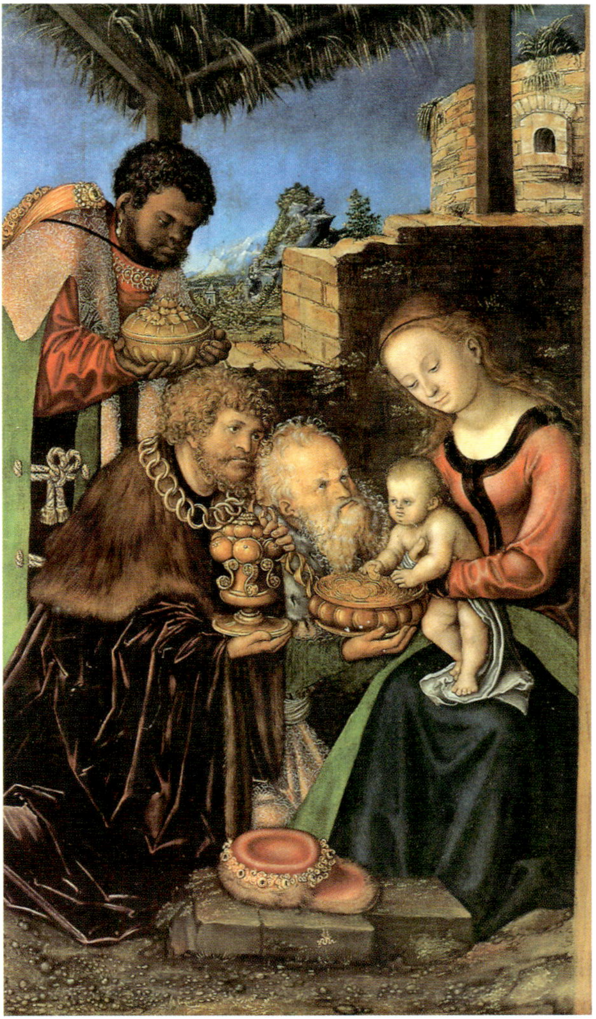

The Adoration of the Magi, around 1514.
Oil on pine wood, 122 x 73 cm.
Gotha, Stiftung Schloss Friedenstein.

1515

□ Cranach's second son, Lucas the Younger, was born on 04.10.1515; he was later to become a painter, too (+1586, Weimar). In addition to two sons, the marriage also produced three daughters: Ursula (dates unknown), Barbara (1520–1601) and Anna (1520/7–1577).

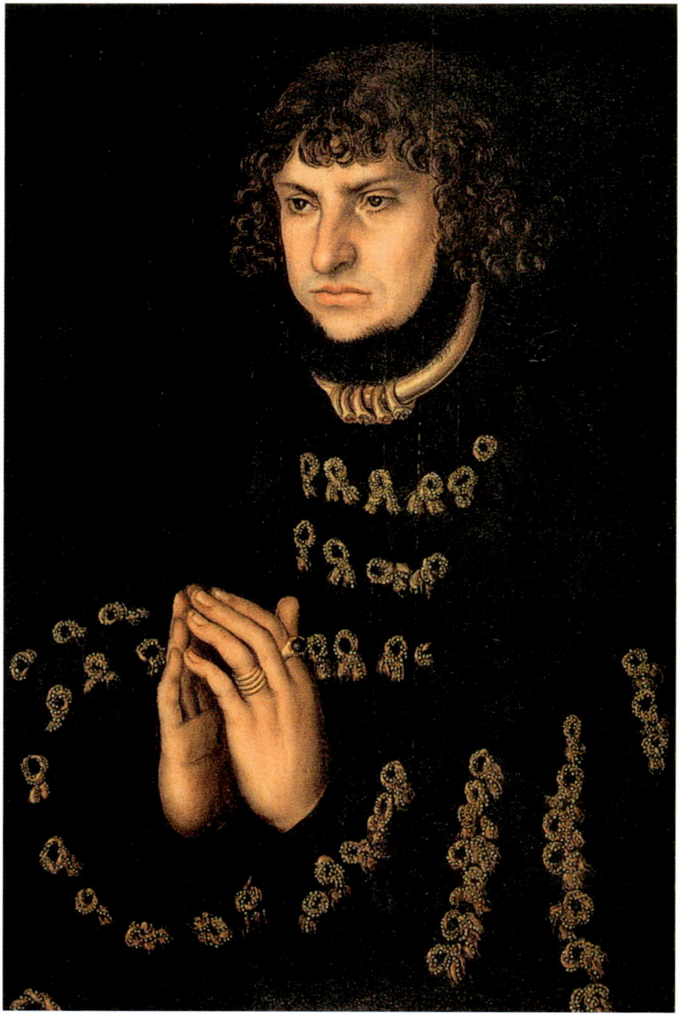

Duke John the Steadfast, around 1515. Oil on conifer wood, 64.7 x 49.3 cm. Coburg, Kunstsammlungen der Veste.

☐ Lucas Cranach, alongside Albrecht Dürer, Albrecht Altdorfer, Hans Baldung (who was known as Grien), Hans Burgkmair and others, worked on the artistic decoration of Emperor Maximilian I's prayer book.

☐ For work on the towers of the castles in Wittenberg and Torgau, Cranach received a payment of 60 florins.

☐ The 40-year-old Pope Leo X (from 1513 onwards) authorised plenary indulgences for the dioceses of Albert II, Margrave of Brandenburg, Archbishop of Magdeburg, Bishop of Halberstadt and the Brandenburg territories in order to build St Peter's Basilica in Rome.

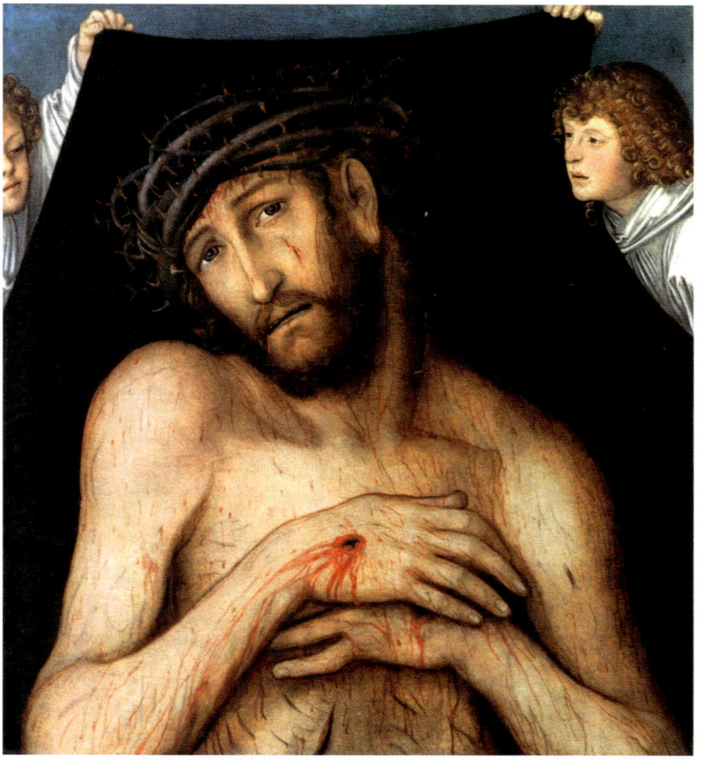

Christ as the Man of Sorrows, around 1515.
Oil on lime wood, 56.2 x 52.2 cm.
Weimar, Stiftung Weimarer Klassik und Kunstsammlungen.

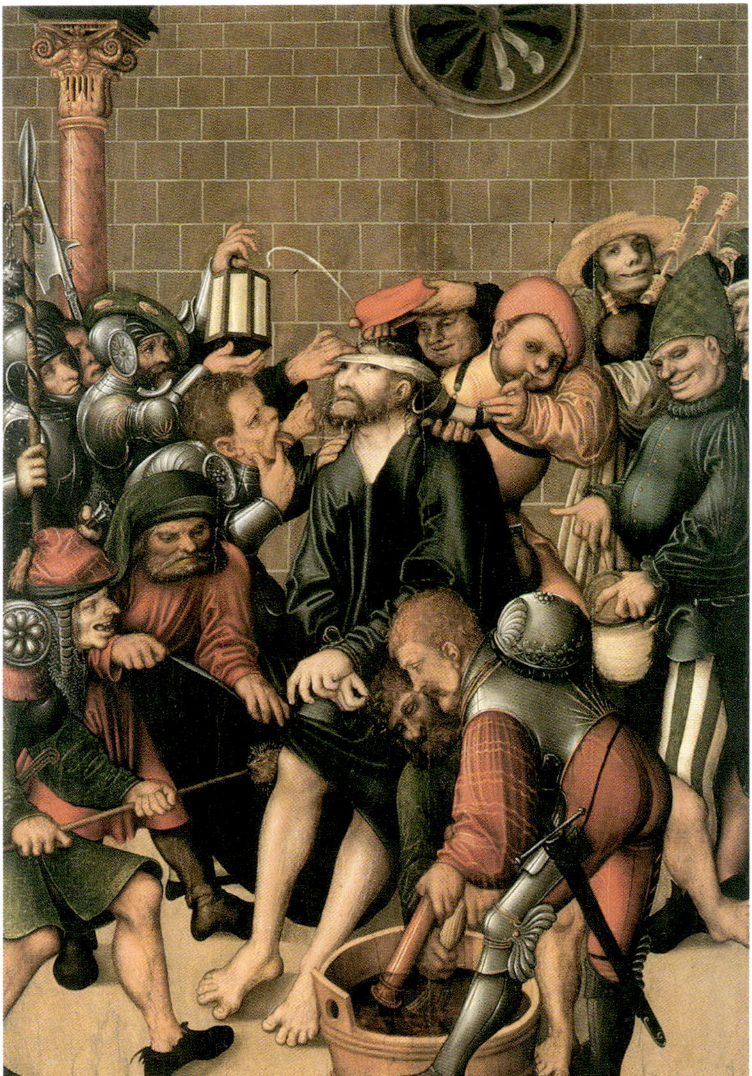

The Scourging of Christ, approx. 1515–20.
Oil on lime wood, 86.5 x 59.4 cm.
Weimar, Stiftung Weimarer Klassik und Kunstsammlungen.

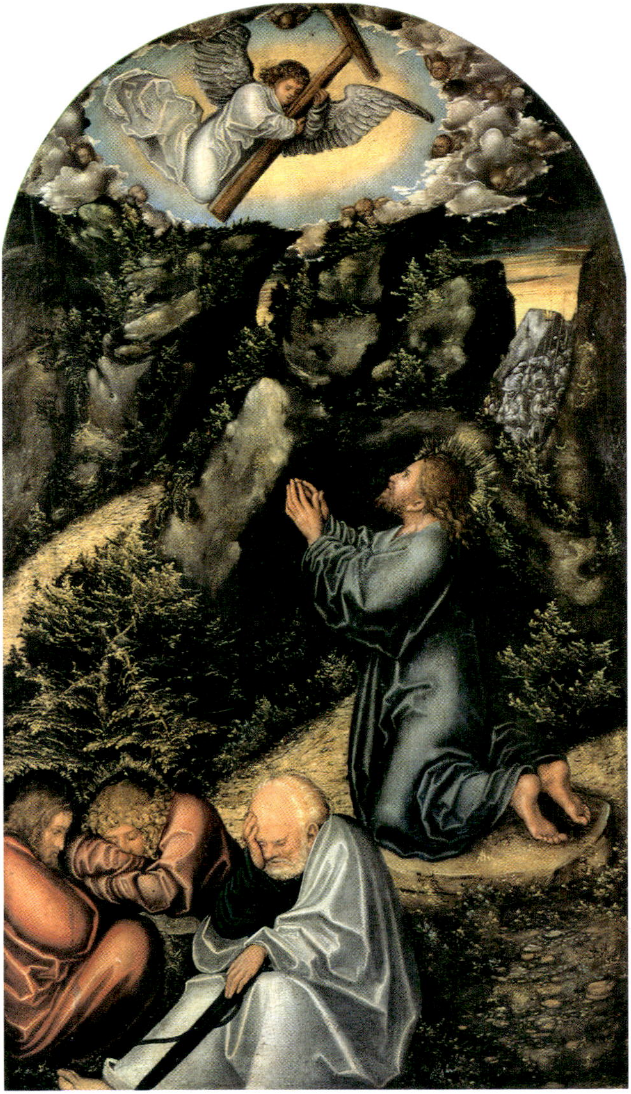

The Agony in the Garden, approx. 1515–20.
Oil on lime wood, 58 x 41 cm.
Dresden, Staatliche Kunstsammlungen.

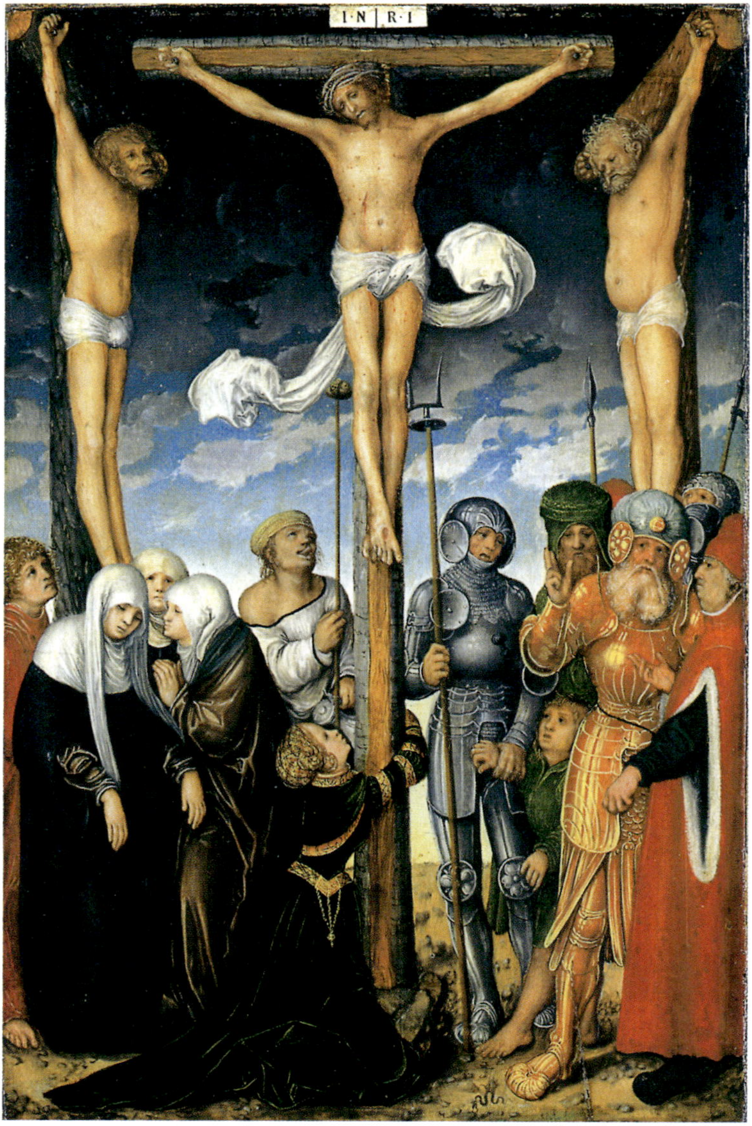

The Crucifixion, around 1515.
Oil on panel, 42 x 28 cm.
Frankfurt, Städelsches Kunstinstitut.

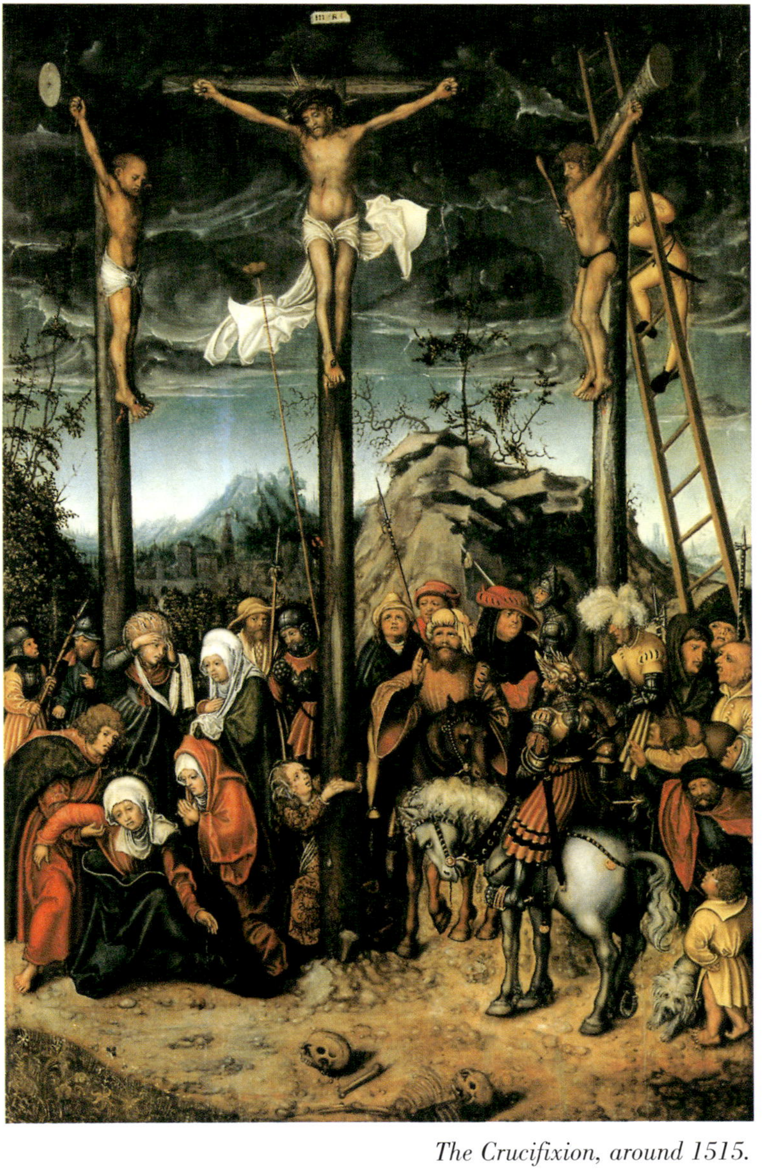

The Crucifixion, around 1515.
Oil on panel, 67 x 46.5 cm.
Copenhagen. Statens Museum for Kunst.

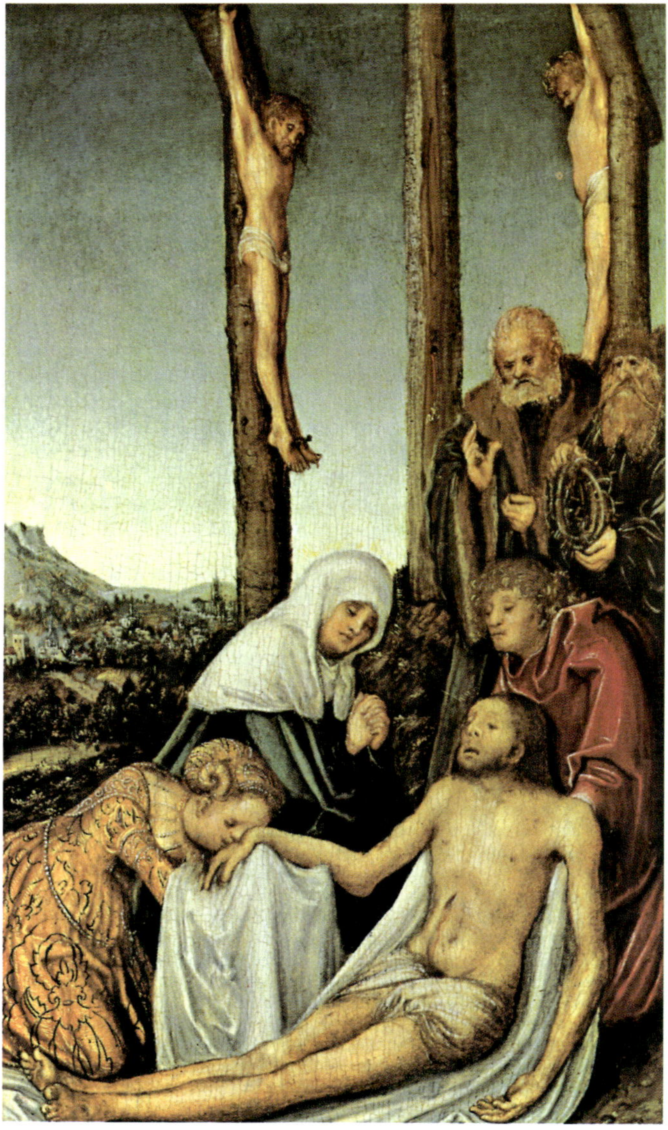

The Lamentation, around 1515.
Oil on panel, 29 x 17.5 cm.
Boston, Museum of Fine Arts.

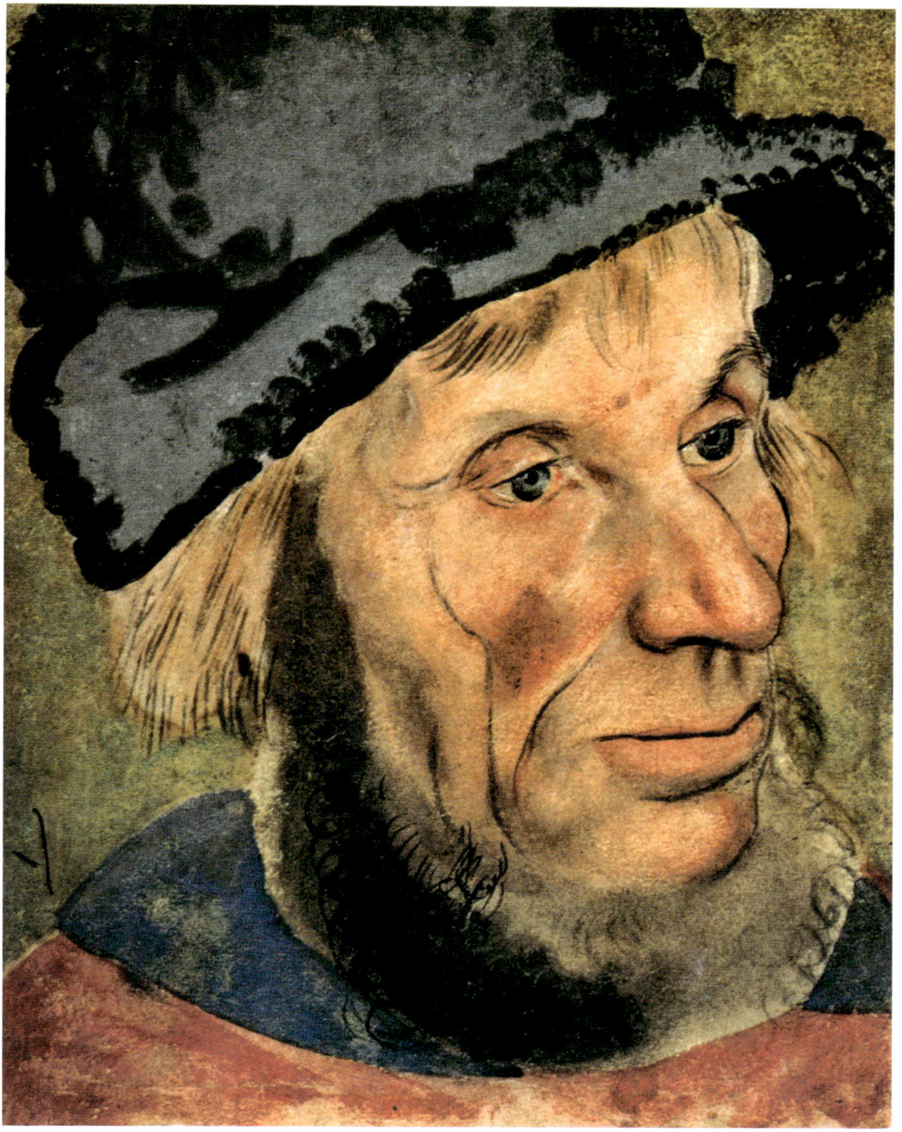

Portrait of a Farmer, around 1515.
Watercolour, 19.3 x 15.7 cm.
Basel, Kunstmuseum.

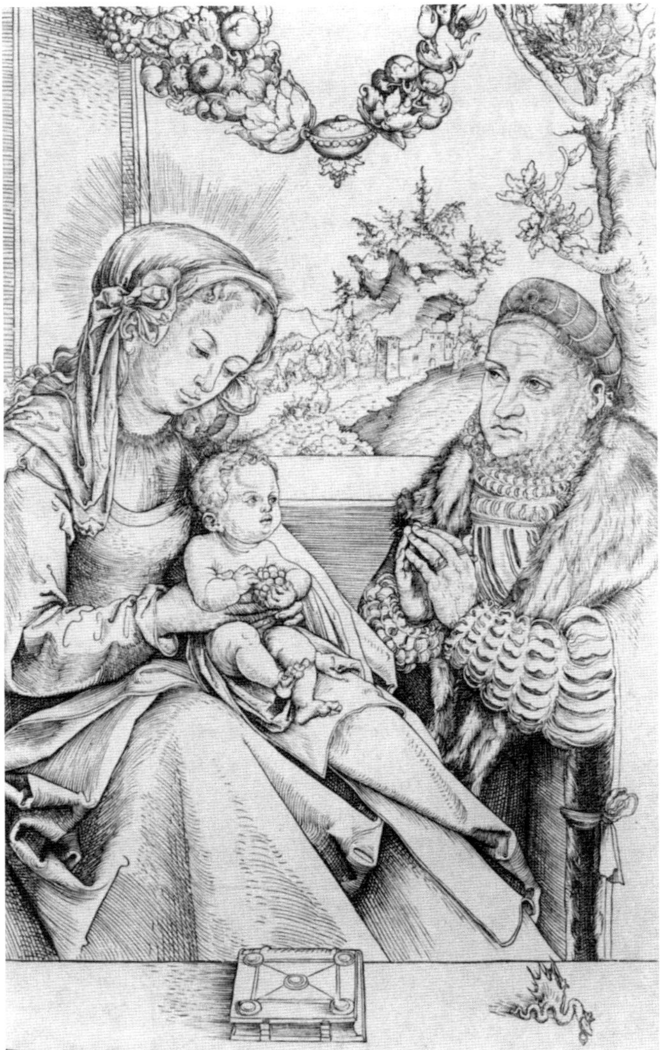

Madonna and Child with Frederick the Wise of Saxony, around 1515.
Woodcut, 36.9 x 23 cm.
Dresden, Staatliche Kunstsammlungen.

1516

□ At the end of March, Lucas Cranach was driven from Torgau to Leipzig to visit the Easter market.

□ One of his pupils worked for Archbishop Albert II, Margrave of Brandenburg.

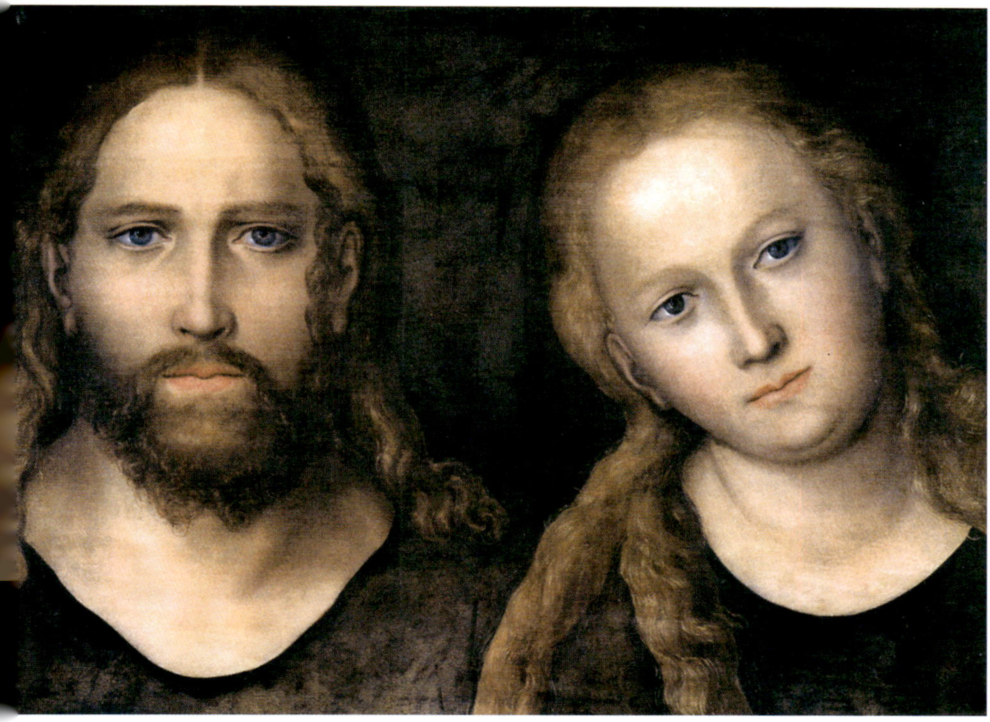

Christ and Mary, approx. 1516–20.
Oil, vellum on wood, 34.2 x 52.7 cm.
Gotha, Stiftung Schloss Friedenstein.

1517

☐ Lucas Cranach had been ill since January and was only able to go to work at the court of Duke George of Saxony in Dresden at the beginning of March. There he painted the *Holy Trinity* and decorated two sleighs.

☐ On 31.10.1517, Martin Luther posted his Ninety-Five Theses on the door of the Castle Church in Wittenberg – at least that is what history records. In reality, the Theses were the publication of a call, originally penned in Latin, for an academic disputation on the value of indulgences. Luther's Theses were translated into German and printed by the Leipzig printer Melchior Lotter the Elder. The Theses were rapidly circulated and provoked an unexpected response. In the Theses, Archbishop Albert II of Mainz was called upon to put an end to the misuse of indulgences. He responded by reporting Luther to the Pope. The Curia saw the Theses as an attack on papal authority.

1518

☐ The new residential and commercial property on the corner of the Schlossstraße/Elbgasse was completed in this year; the two smaller houses Cranach had purchased in 1512 were sold. Until 1520, Cranach only paid taxes for the large, new property. The artist was also mentioned as the owner of a house in Gotha (24.03.1518).

☐ In autumn, the 49-year-old papal legate Cardinal Thomas de Vio, who was known as Cajetan, summoned Luther to the Diet (imperial assembly) in Augsburg. The Elector's court chaplain and secretary Spalatin tried to obtain imperial safe conduct for Luther on his journey to Augsburg, but Emperor Maximilian refused. Eventually, the Cardinal agreed not to send Luther to Rome. However, the interview with Luther strengthened Cajetan's belief that he was dealing with a full-blown heretic. Luther refused to recant the Theses which had been condemned as heresy by Rome (12.–14.10.1518).

Frederick the Wise refused Cajetan's request to extradite Luther to Rome into the hands of Pope Leo X or to banish him from the country (08.12.1518). Supporters in Augsburg aided Luther's flight from the city and he rode to Wittenberg via Leipzig.

☐ The 21-year-old Philipp Melanchthon was appointed Professor of Greek at the University of Wittenberg and, from 1521 onwards, he worked at the Faculty of Theology, too.

☐ Cranach's *Reclining Water Nymph* lies in the style of a Classical sculpture in the landscape. The inscription reads in translation: 'I am the nymph of the holy spring. Do not disturb me in my sleep, I am resting here.' The inscription is not of Classical origin, but is often regarded as such. In fact, it stems from late 15th century Italy and was already known to the German Humanist Conrad Celtis before 1500.

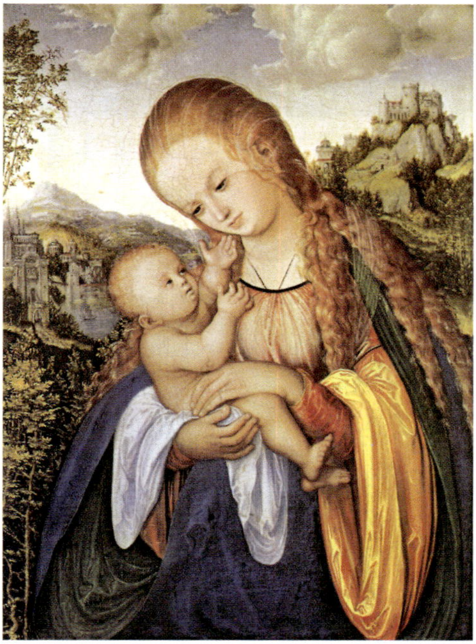

Virgin and Child in a Luxuriant Landscape, around 1518.
Oil on lime wood, 40.7 x 31.2 cm.
Karlsruhe, Staatliche Kunsthalle.

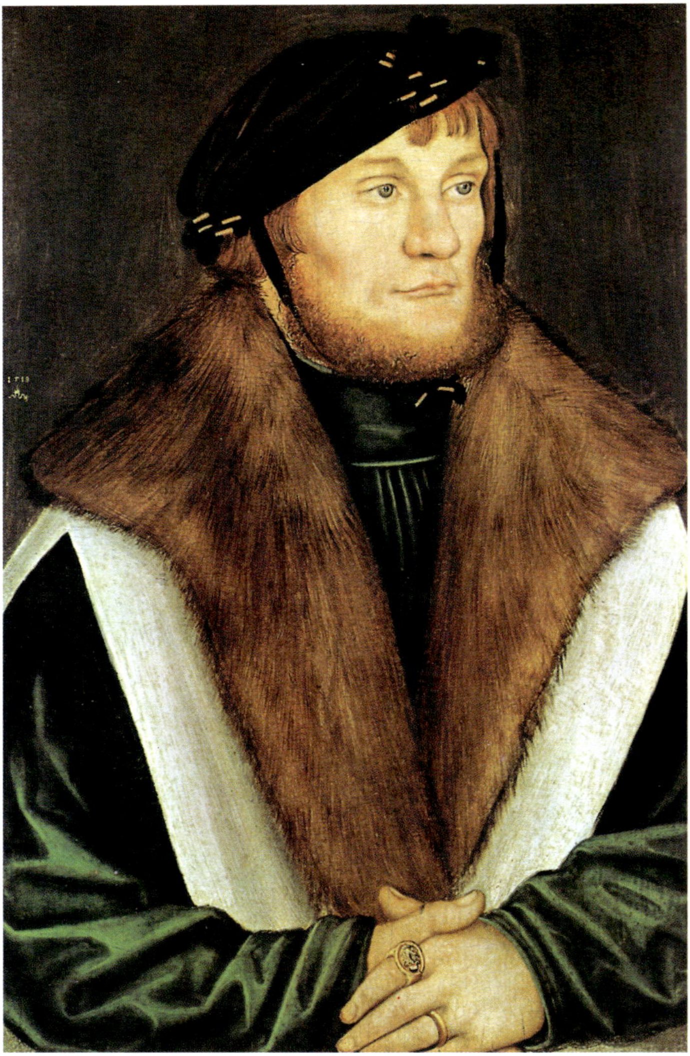

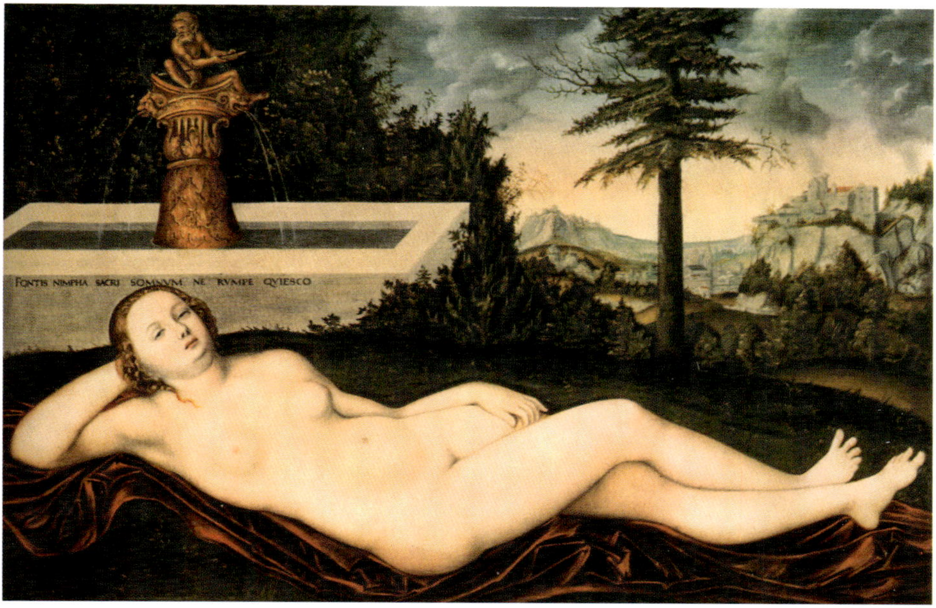

Reclining Water Nymph, 1518.
Oil on panel, 59 x 92 cm.
Leipzig, Museum der bildenden Künste.

Bearded Young Man, 1518.
Oil on lime wood, 42 x 28 cm.
Private collection.

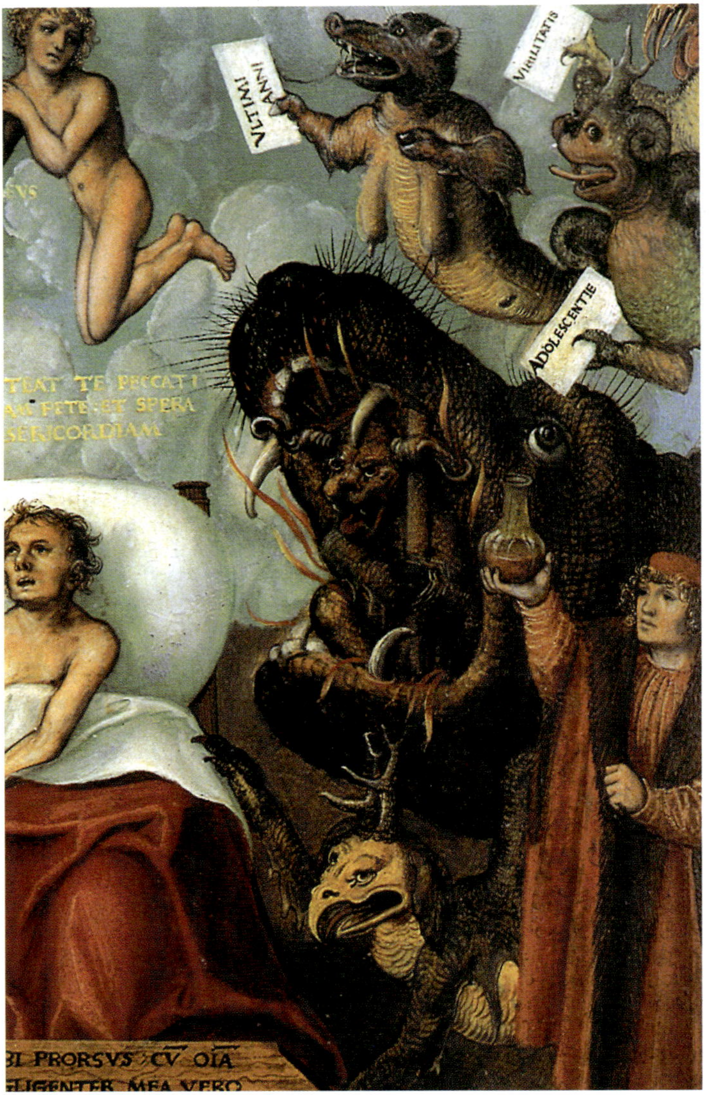

At Death's Door (detail), 1518.
Oil on lime wood, 93 x 36.2 cm.
Leipzig, Museum der bildenden Künste.

1519

☐ Lucas Cranach, at the age of 47, was elected to Wittenberg council for the first time. He was a member of the town council for 26 years until 1544/45. He was appointed mayor of Wittenberg for the first time in 1537 and also served in this office in 1540 and 1543.

☐ The first pamphlet of the Reformation, the *Carriage* (*Fuhrwagen*), as it is known, written by Andreas Karlstadt, was depicted graphically in a woodcut by Cranach. An allegorical image was the result which was to intended to make people realise that a person cannot reach a state of bliss by his own wealth or endeavours, but solely through God's grace. The *carriage* with a layperson as a passenger thus reached its destination, namely the Redeemer, whilst the second wagon filled with clerics and oiled with money landed in the jaws of Hell. The woodcut was also sent to Albrecht Dürer and Christoph Scheurl.

☐ In June/July, the Leipzig disputation took place between Johannes Eck and Martin Luther/Andreas Karlstadt. Duke George of Saxony also took part in the disputation and henceforth became an opponent of Luther. Johannes Eck assisted in the condemnation of Luther and, in 1520, was commissioned with publishing the papal bull (a decree issued under the papal seal), *Exsurge Domine* (Lord, cast out). This document is the first written statement by the church against Luther's teachings.

☐ Frederick the Wise traded paintings by Cranach with the mother of the French King Francis I in order to obtain reliquaries for the Castle Church in Wittenberg (correspondence 1517/1519). Francis was a candidate for the imperial election and sought to win Frederick the Wise over so that the latter would support him.

☐ Maximilian I, who had been the Emperor since 1518, died on 12.01.1519 at the age of 60 in Wels. After Maximilian I's death, the Pope was interested in Frederick the Wise as an ally against Spain. Frederick could have become Emperor himself, but refused the candidacy at the last minute.

□ The 19-year-old Charles V (*24.02.1500, Ghent) was chosen as the German Emperor on 28.06.1519 in Frankfurt; the 25-year-old French king, Francis I (*12.09.1494, Cognac), who had been supported by the Pope, lost the election.

Charles received the news of his election whilst at the Spanish north coast. It was only in summer 1520 that he was once again to stand on German soil.

1520

□ On 08.12.1520, the 48-year-old Lucas Cranach was given the privilege to be an apothecary in Lochau (dispensing medicines, selling paint, spices, sealing wax, oil, ink, sugar and, above all, wine). He had sought this privilege in March of the same year from the Elector's court.

With the apothecary's privilege, Cranach gained a unique monopoly in Wittenberg as no other apothecary was allowed to work in the town. The apothecary's privilege also comprised the right to serve fortified wines, though only on condition that the town council be paid excise duties. Since 1513, Cranach had been running one of the most important private wine merchant's in the town, the turnover from which was only exceeded by that of the wine cellars in the town hall. In addition to wine, he also served imported beer. From 1526, the businessman Cranach started to pay brewery taxes to the town so as to be able to sell his own brew.

□ Barbara, the daughter of Lucas and Barbara Cranach, was born as their fourth child, after Hans (around 1513), Lucas (1515) and Ursula (dates unknown). The date of birth of their fifth and last child, Anna, is also unknown, but it is supposed that she was born between 1520 and 1527. Her godfather was Martin Luther.

□ When the monk and the painter had first met is not known. In any case, the two were bound both by a close private relationship (as godfather, best man and through correspondence) and by a close business connection (printing, pamphlets).

□ Up until 1522, Cranach's workshop produced numerous depictions of the Virgin. Numerous sources report about pictures of the Madonna by Cranach which were given as presents by the Electors of Saxony to other befriended rulers. In 1512, for example, two paintings at once were sent to Duke George of Saxony and his wife.

The recipients and commissioners of Cranach's depictions of the Virgin were not only to be found in the ranks of the believers in the old faith, but also found in the circle around Luther who himself had a picture of the Madonna with child, probably painted by Cranach, hanging in his room and who greatly enjoyed looking at it, as can be testified by one of his after-dinner speeches from 1532.

□ The three main Reformation texts by Martin Luther were printed in this year in Wittenberg: *An den christlichen Adel deutscher Nation* (Address to the Christian Nobility of the German Nation), *De Captivitate Babylonica Ecclesiae Praeludium* (A Prelude Concerning the Babylonian Captivity of the Church) and *Von der Freiheit eines Christenmenschen* (Of the Freedom of a Christian Man).

□ Copper engravings with depictions of Martin Luther and his opponent Cardinal Albert II of Brandenburg, Archbishop of Mainz, were produced by Lucas Cranach's workshop.

□ Dürer wrote to Spalatin that he would like to portray Luther in a copper engraving and sent him an engraving of Cardinal Albert II from the year 1519. Cranach used this as a model for later works.

□ There were conflicts in Wittenberg between aristocratic students, who were forbidden to carry weapons, and citizens of the town, especially Cranach's journeymen who carried arms as a form of 'provocation'.

□ Charles V set sail from La Coruna, Spain, via the Netherlands to Aachen (26.05.1520). On 23.10.1520, he was crowned the Roman Emperor-elect.

□ Rome threatened Luther and all who followed his teachings with excommunication in the papal bull (a decree issued under the papal seal), *Exsurge Domine* (Lord, cast out). His writings were to be seized and burnt. The accused was given 60 days in which to recant or he would be denounced as a heretic. In the latter case, Luther's ruler, Frederick the Wise, would be called upon to hand his clerical subject over without delay to the holy inquisition in Rome. As was to be expected, Luther did not recant. Instead, on 10.12.1520, he publicly set fire to the papal bull *Exsurge Domine* in front of the Elster Gate in Wittenberg.

□ 579 new students were registered at the University of Wittenberg in this year.

□ The painting of *Count Palatinate Philipp of Solms* was created around 1520. Philipp, the councillor to the Elector, ruled over Coburg from 1506–14 and served Frederick the Wise at the time of the imperial election. In 1543, Cranach was paid from the Elector of Saxony's funds for a painting of '*Lucretia,* sent to Count Palatinate Philipp of Solms'.

□ John of Brandenburg-Ansbach-Bayreuth had been born on 09.01.1493 at the Plassenburg in Kulmbach. His father was Margrave Frederick of Brandenburg-Ansbach. His brother Albert II became the last Grand Master of the Teutonic Order in 1511. John had lived from 1516 in Spain at the court of the later Emperor Charles V.

Before April 1519, he had married Germaine de Foix (*1490), the widow of King Ferdinand II the Catholic (+1516). Within the Hohenzollern dynasty he was one of the few members of the Habsburg Order of the Golden Fleece. In 1520, the 27-year-old came to Germany for the imperial coronation and it was probably at this time that his portrait was painted.

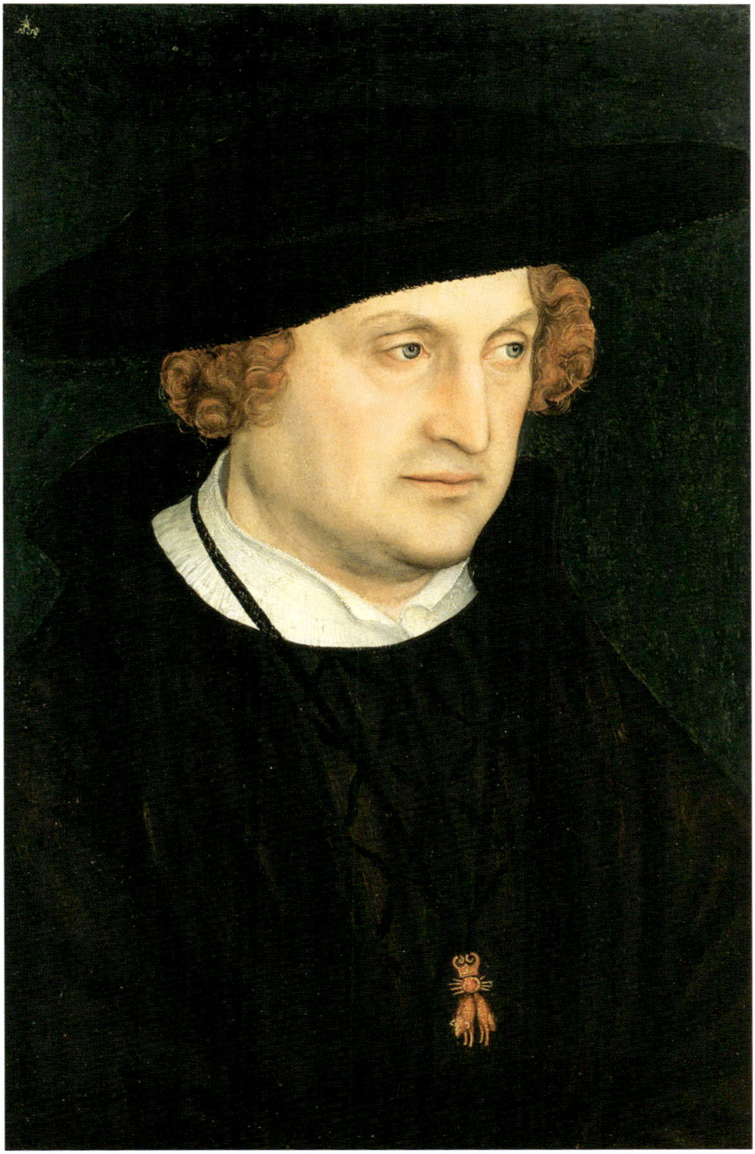

Margrave John of Brandenburg-Ansbach, around 1520.
Oil on panel, 42.3 x 29.5 cm.
Eisenach, Wartburg-Stiftung.

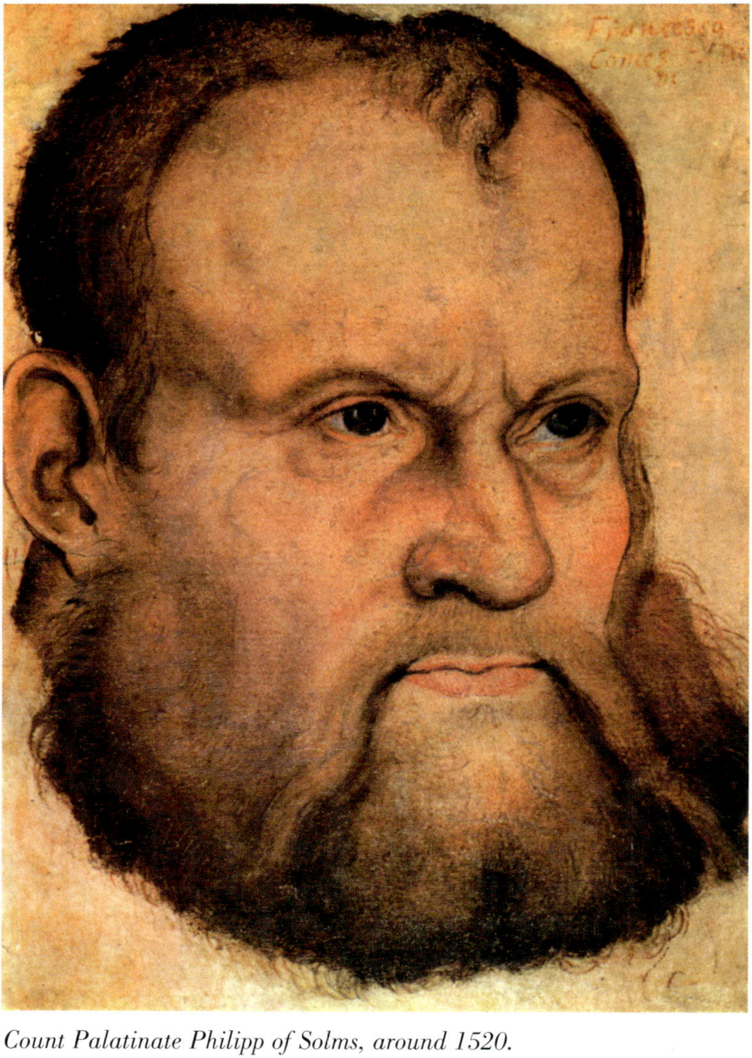

Count Palatinate Philipp of Solms, around 1520.
Oil on paper, 17.9 x 13.2 cm.
Bautzen, Stadtmuseum.

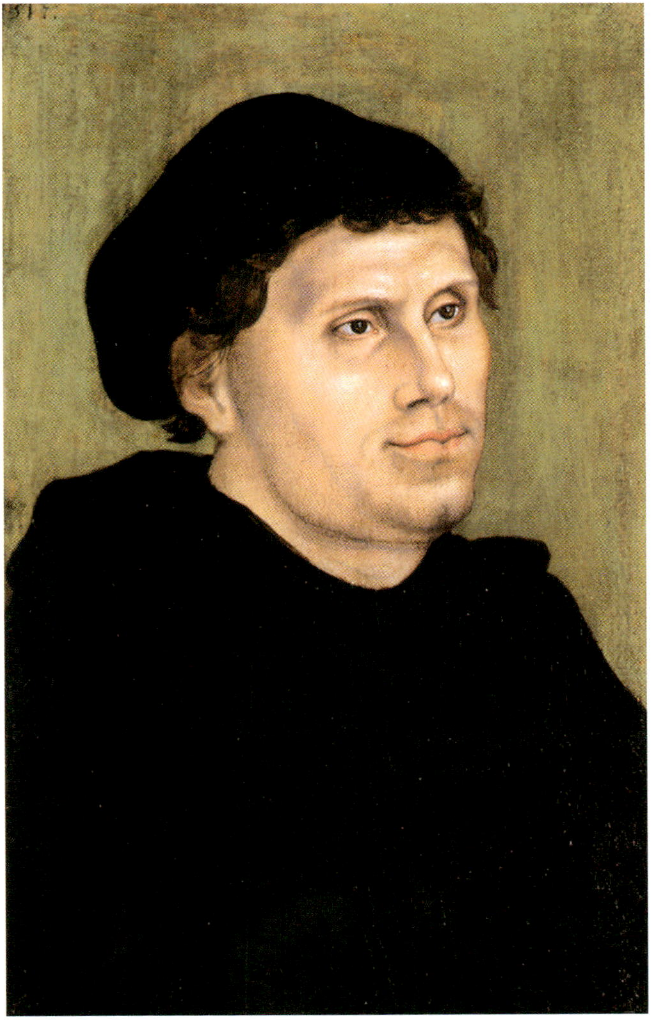

Martin Luther, around 1520.
Oil on panel, 40.3 x 26.5 cm.
Private collection.

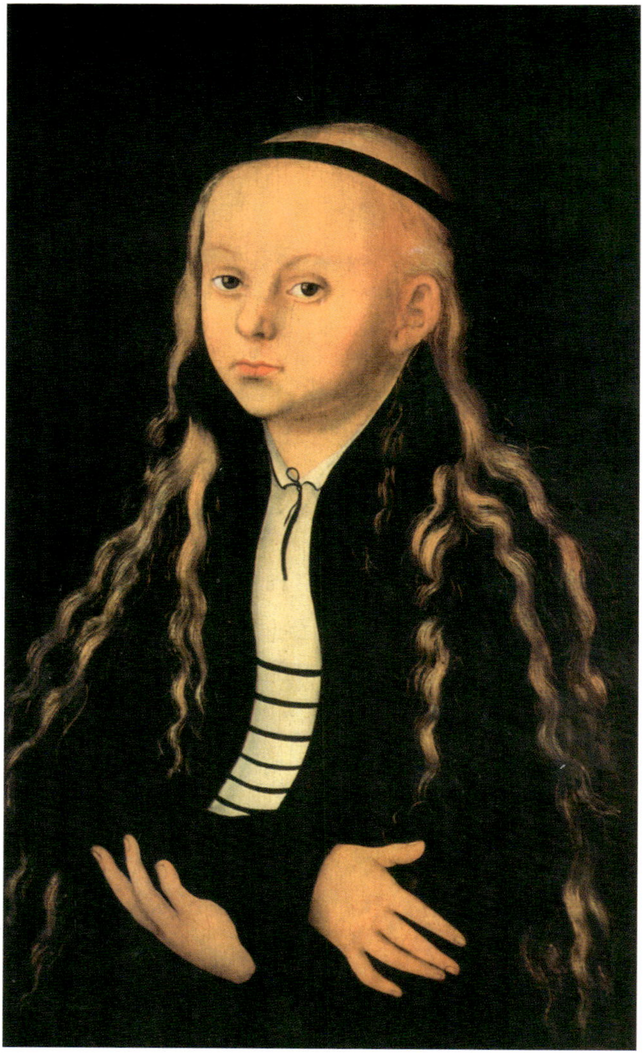

Portrait of a Young Girl (Magdalena Luther?), around 1520.
Oil on panel, 41 x 26 cm.
Paris, Louvre.

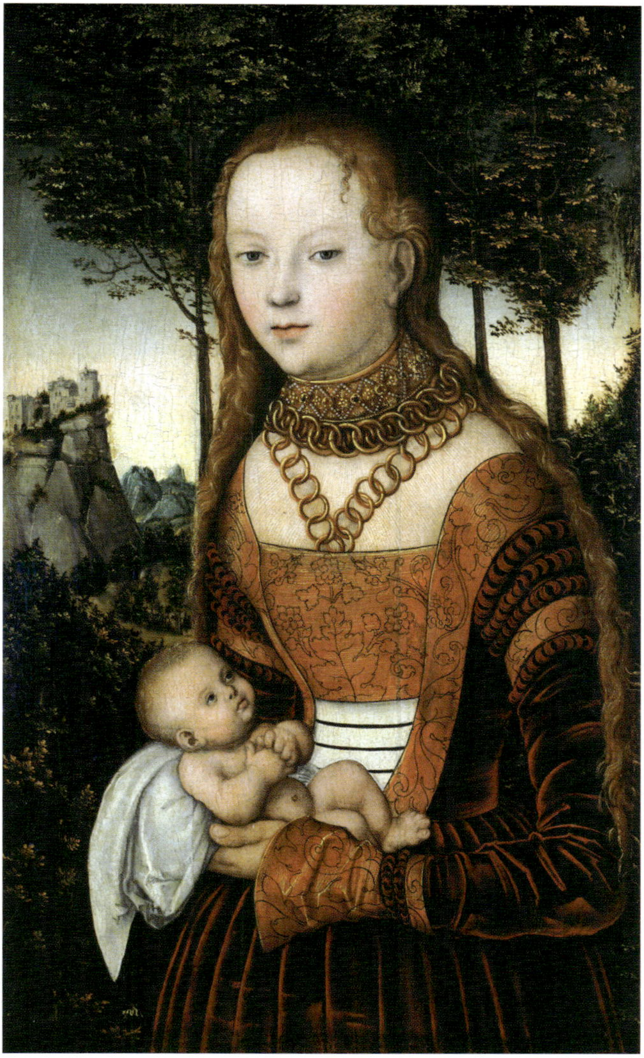

Woman Holding a Baby on a Napkin, around 1520.
Oil on panel, 37.5 x 60.5 cm.
Eisenach, Wartburg-Stiftung.

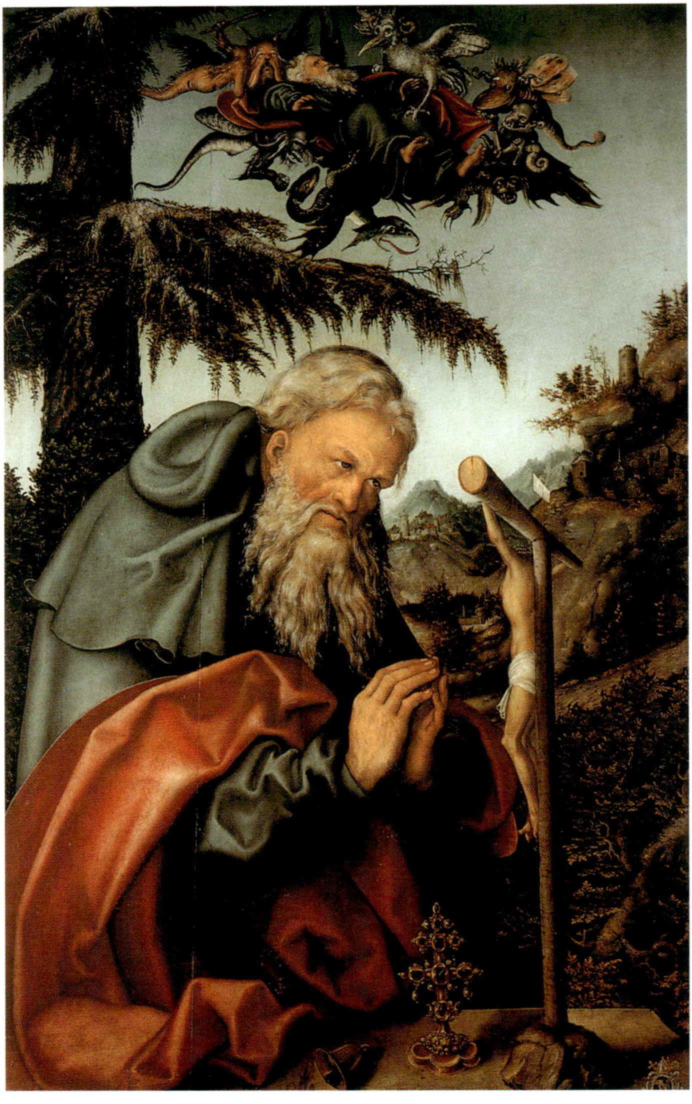

St Anthony as a Hermit, approx. 1520–25.
Oil on panel, 147 x 94.5 cm.
Biskupstvi Litomericke/Leitmeritz, Czech Republic.

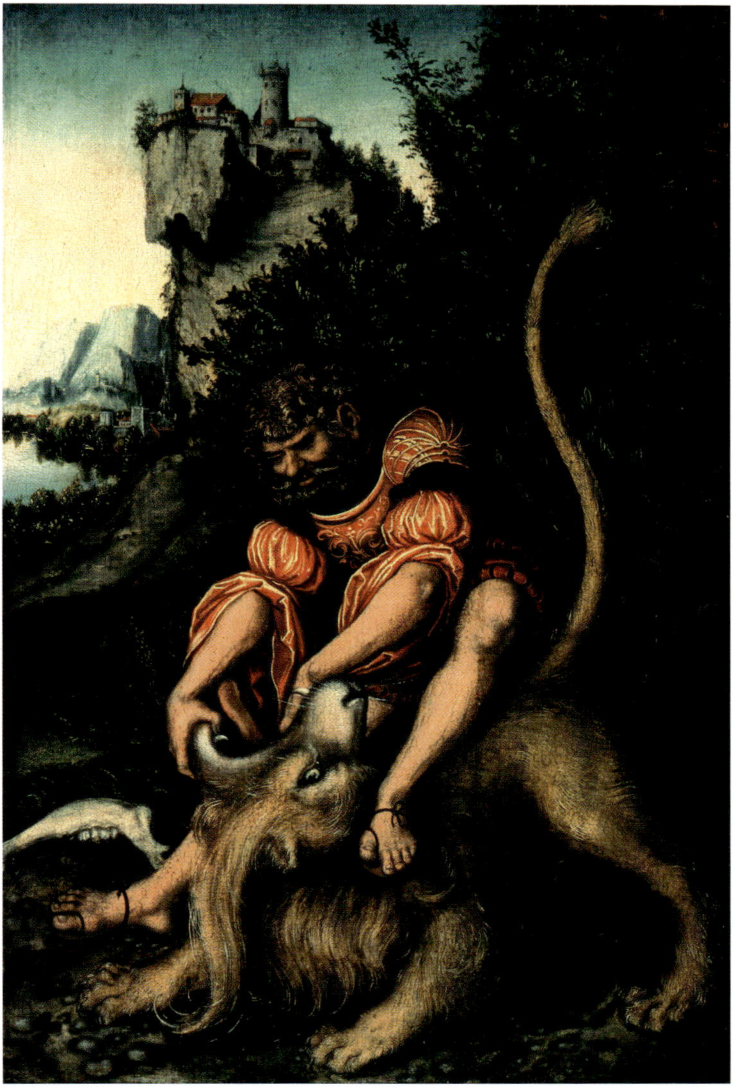

Samson Vanquishing the Lion, approx. 1520–25.
Oil on beech wood, 56.7 x 38 cm.
Weimar, Stiftung Weimarer Klassik und Kunstsammlungen.

1521

☐ Lucas Cranach received a payment of 66 florins for decorating the organ in the Castle Church in Weimar. His journeymen worked for four weeks and four days; they were provided with food and received travelling monies for the return journey to Wittenberg.

☐ Cranach delivered woodcuts for Reformation pamphlets such as the *Passional of Christ and Antichrist*, in which, in two series of 13 pictures, the honourable life of Christ was represented in opposition to the extravagant existence of the Pope (the *Antichrist*). The commentaries from the Bible and from papal decrees came from Philipp Melanchthon. The pamphlet was published anonymously at the printer's Grunenberg in Wittenberg.

☐ At the age of 36, Johannes Bugenhagen started his studies of theology at the University of Wittenberg. He became the priest of the Town Church in Wittenberg in 1523. In 1533, he was appointed professor. Bugenhagen worked closely with Martin Luther and was also his father confessor.

☐ On 03.01.1521, Pope Leo X issued the final papal bull excommunicating Luther from the church. Frederick the Wise did not comply with the imperial request to hand Luther over, which would probably have meant certain death for Luther on the pyre.

On 06.03.1521, Luther was summoned to the Diet (assembly) of Worms. His mentor, Frederick the Wise, whom Luther had never actually met in his lifetime, demanded Luther be granted safe conduct and the Emperor promised to ensure this would be the case.

On Cranach's initiative, the municipal authorities of Wittenberg placed a 'small dray cart' at the monk Martin Luther's disposal for the journey to Worms (02.–16.04.1521).

At the Diet of Worms, Martin Luther was heard before the Emperor and the Empire. Luther did not recant his Theses

(17.–18.04.1521). After the Diet, on 28.04.1521, Luther wrote from Frankfurt to Cranach. Amongst other matters, he informed Cranach that he would follow the advice of good people and would 'go into hiding' and remain hidden for some time ('There has to be a short time of silence and suffering'). This letter is evidence for the exchange of ideas and the close, trusting relationship between the two.

Close to Eisenach, Luther was taken into protective custody at the behest of his ruler, Frederick the Wise (04.05.1521), and he lived incognito, under the pseudonym of Junker Jörg or Knight George, in the Wartburg Castle until 01.03.1522. There he translated the New Testament from Greek into German in just eleven weeks and so became the founder of a standard German orthography which established itself from that point onwards.

☐ Rumour has it the Martin Luther interrupted his stay at the Wartburg at the beginning of December to pay a secret visit to Wittenberg, which is 210 kilometres away. The occasion for his visit was Andreas Karlstadt's radical church sermons. During this visit, it is reputed that his portrait was painted by Cranach, depicting Luther in the guise of Junker Jörg.

☐ The Diet passed the Edict of Worms (08.05.1521), signed by the Emperor on 26.05.1521, declaring Luther and his followers to be outlaws: 'And furthermore we forbid you all to offer shelter in your homes to the aforementioned Martin Luther, nor offer him food or drink, nor conceal him, nor offer help, alliance, support or protection in word or deed either publicly or in secret, but urge that, wherever you may encounter him, you should seize him, overpower him, take him into your custody and safely hand him over to us.'

☐ John Ernst I, the son of the Elector John the Steadfast, was born on 10.05.1521 in Coburg. Margarethe of Anhalt-Zerbst, the second wife of Elector John the Steadfast, died on 07.10.1521 at the age of 27 in Weimar. The marriage had produced four children.

□ Leo X, who had been Pope since 1513, died on 01.12.1521 at the age of 46 in Rome. His successors were Hadrian VI (1459–1523) and Clemens VII (1478–1534).

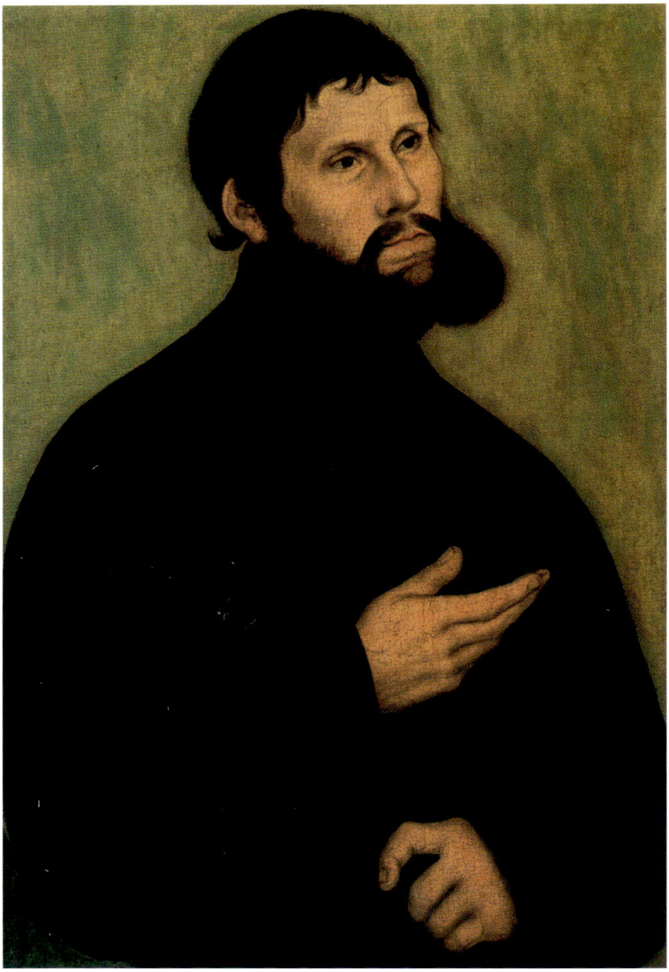

Martin Luther as Junker Jörg, approx. 1521–22.
Oil on beech wood, 52.8 x 37.3 cm.
Weimar, Stiftung Weimarer Klassik und Kunstsammlungen.

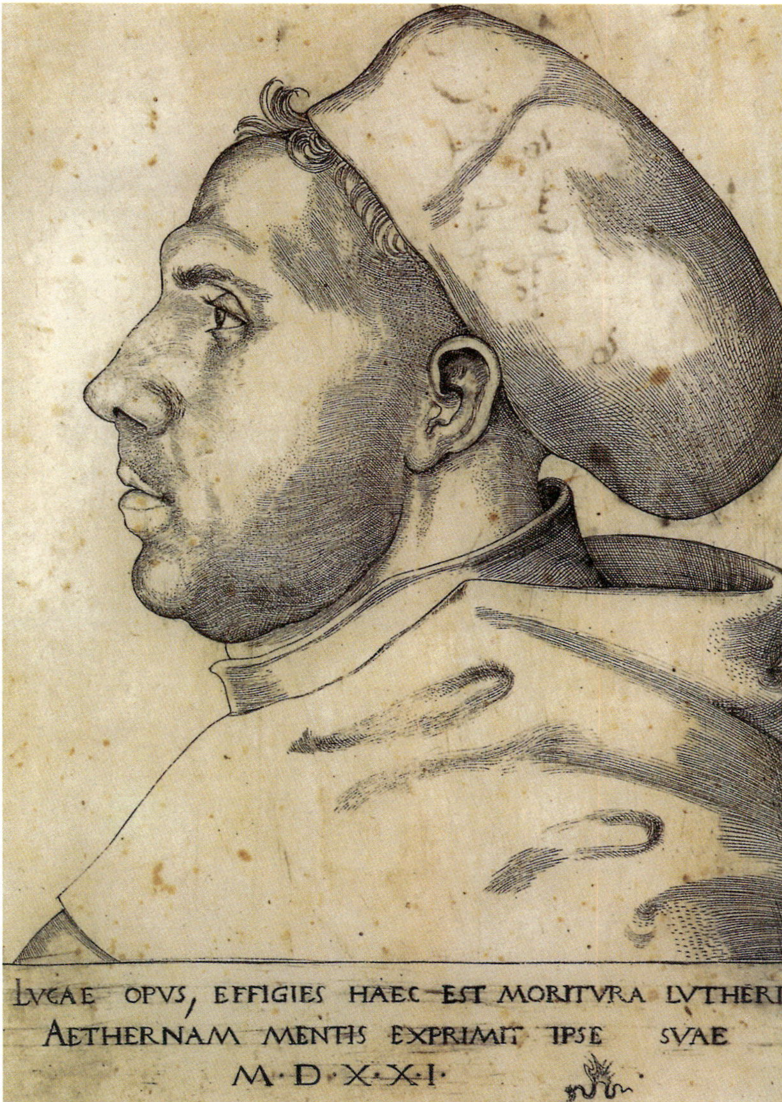

Martin Luther, 1521.
Copperplate engraving, 20.4 x 15 cm.
Gotha, Stiftung Schloss Friedenstein.

1522

□ Complete anarchy reigned in Wittenberg. The monasteries emptied, with Luther's own Order of the Augustinian Hermits taking the lead. The marriage of priests and monks began and the mass was changed. The priest and Professor of Theology Andreas Karlstadt placed the Host in the believers' hands during communion so that they could place it in their mouths themselves, which up until then had been considered a mortal sin. Karlstadt, in his iconoclastic tract *Von abtuhung der Bylder* (On the Rejection of Images), on 28.01.1521 called for the destruction of pictures. The town responded with rioting.

Shocked by reports of an impending revolt by the common people, who had been stirred up by Karlstadt, Martin Luther came out of hiding in the Wartburg on 06.03.1522 and, against the will of the Elector, hurried to Wittenberg. For a whole week, the preacher delivered daily sermons urging the citizens to show restraint. He was successful in restoring religious and civil order. Karlstadt left the town and went to join the Swiss reformer Ulrich Zwingli.

When Luther reappeared in Wittenberg, the Emperor did nothing to enforce his Edict of Worms and Luther was then able to move freely throughout the territories of the regent, who tended towards the Reformation.

□ Since Leipzig, the city of printers, was under the rule of Duke George of Saxony, who strictly adhered to the regulations of the Edict of Worms, it was no longer available for the publishing activities of the Reformers. The latter naturally returned to their origins in Wittenberg.

The Leipzig printer Melchior Lotter the Younger, whose father had printed Luther's Ninety-Five Theses in 1517, moved to Wittenberg. Lotter set up a printer's workshop in Cranach's house at Schlossstrasse 1.

For the major project of printing the New Testament, the house owner and his partner, the goldsmith Christian Döring, advanced the necessary sum of money. Cranach also supplied 21 full-page woodcuts. The bookshop, which Cranach had founded at the same time, was run from his house at Markplatz 3 until 1533. It also incorporated the trade in paper.

☐ Luther's New Testament was sold for 1½ florins. As a comparison: a whole pig, ready for slaughter, cost one florin and a cow, three florins. The first 5,000 copies were immediately sold out after their appearance in September (the 'September Testament'). In December, the second edition followed (the 'December Testament'). Up to the death of the Reformer 24 years later, more than 200,000 copies of his New Testament are reported to have been sold. Luther never took any payment for his work on this project.

☐ The court painter asked the Elector to look into the alleged poor state of affairs in his apothecary. He asked for a visitation and, at the same time, he stressed the fact that he had always bought fresh produce. The reason for this claim was a complaint from the University which alleged that 'the materials were not all fresh, good and sufficient and that they were offered at a much too high price…thus [we demand] that the apothecary be visited by Doctor Pistoris.'

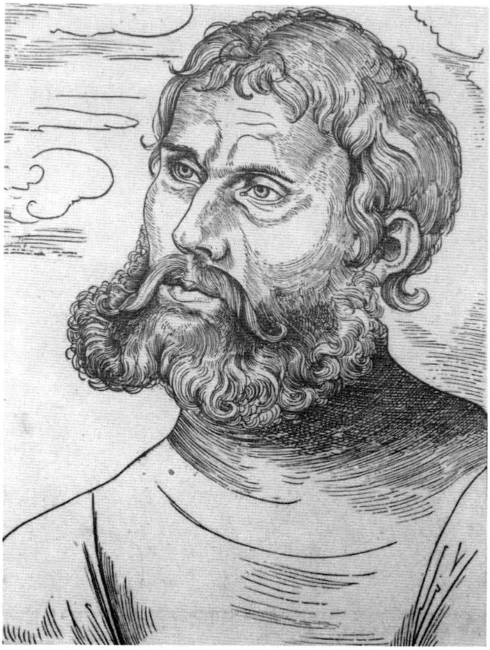

Luther as Junker Jörg, 1522.
Woodcut, 28.3 x 20.4 cm.
Dresden, Staatliche Kunstsammlungen.

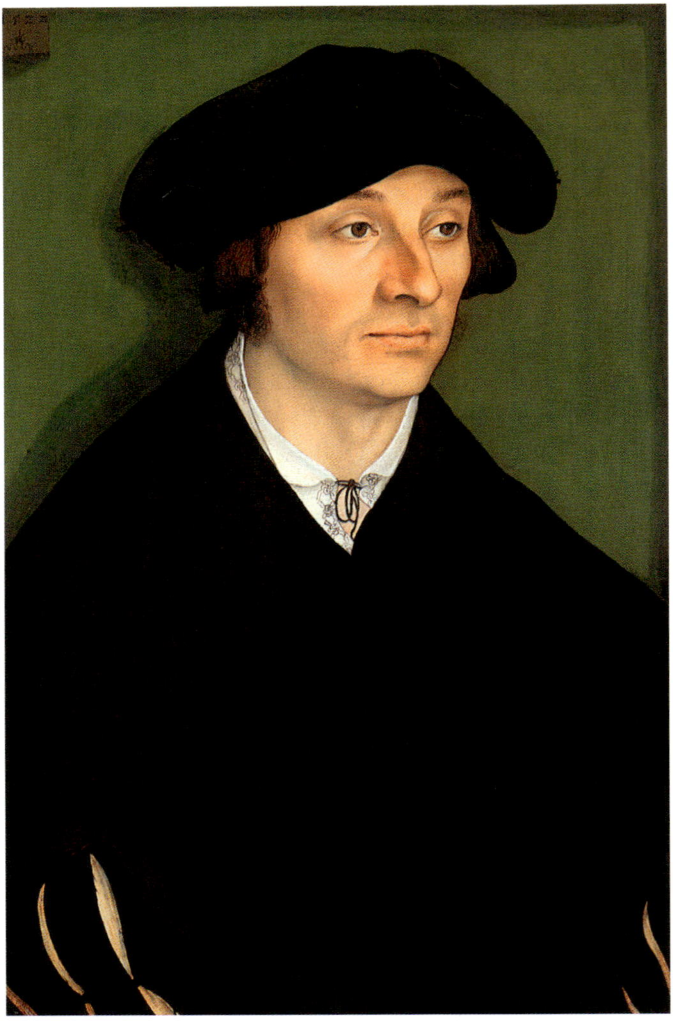

Portrait of a Man, 1522.
Oil on panel, 57.6 x 39.9 cm.
Washington, National Gallery of Art.

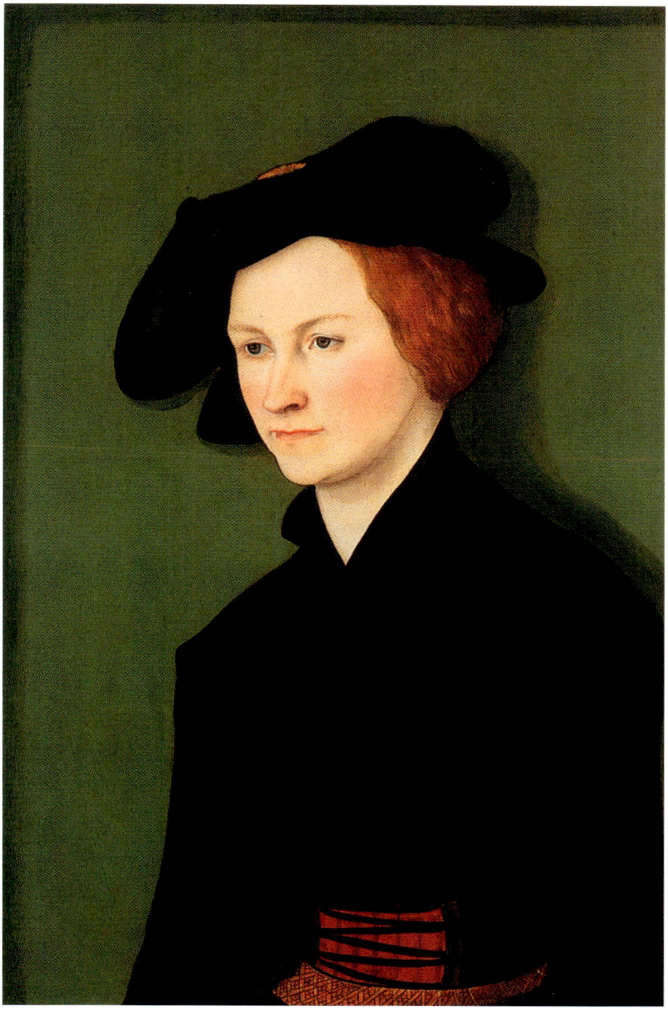

Portrait of a Woman, 1522.
Oil on panel, 58 x 39.8 cm.
Washington, National Gallery of Art.

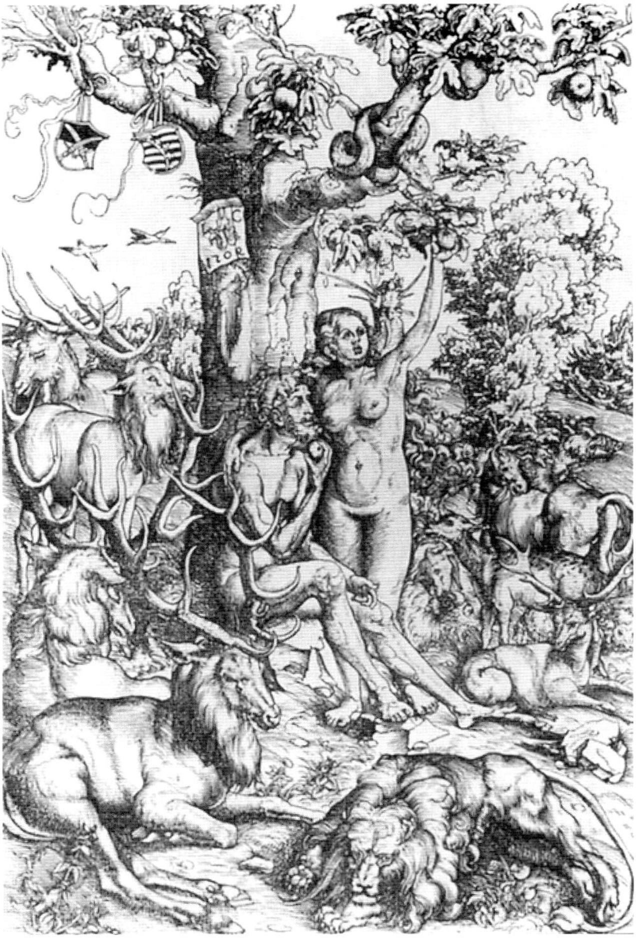

Adam and Eve, approx. 1522–30.
Woodcut, 21.8 x 17.4 cm.
Gotha, Stiftung Schloss Friedenstein.

1523

☐ Christian II, King of Denmark and Norway (1513–23), King of Sweden (1520–23), who had been driven from his country by Gustav Wasa, lived for some time from October onwards in Cranach's house in Wittenberg.

☐ Wittenberg: 'Numerous refugees arrived, expelled priests, former monks, even nuns. A small group of nine aristocratic nuns, who had fled from the convent in Nimbschen and, over Easter 1523, had been helped to escape by citizens from Torgau, were set down from the wagon in front of Luther's home and handed over to him. Luther stood somewhat perplexed in front of the distressed nuns, who still wore the habits of their order and were without any means. The quickest and most capable of them, the 24-year-old Katharina von Bora, was accommodated at his friend Lucas Cranach's house, who had a large and well-to-do household. She seemed somewhat arrogant, so Luther thought, and sought someone from amongst the students from good families. She started a relationship with the son of one of the great Patrician houses in Nuremberg, the Baumgärtners, who studied in Wittenberg; Luther eagerly sought to encourage this relationship.'

☐ On 11.12.1523, the 19-year-old Landgrave of Hesse, Philipp I, married the 18-year-old Christine of Saxony, the daughter of Duke George of Saxony, in Dresden. By 13.02.1539, the marriage had produced six children.

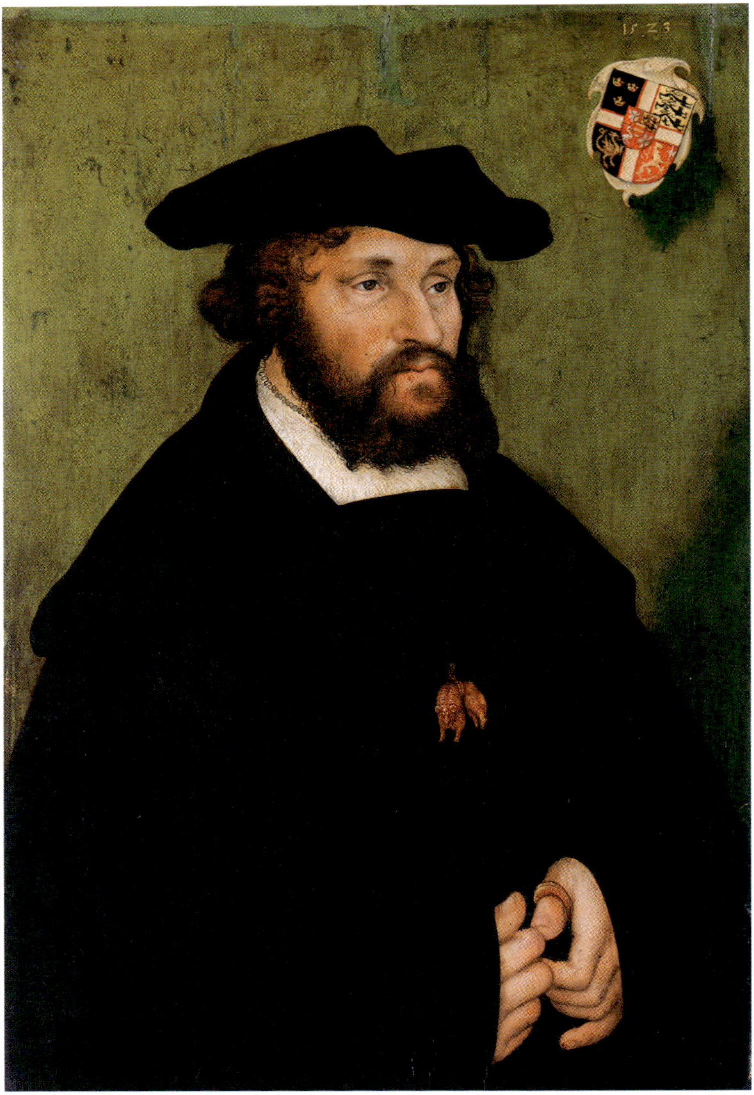

King Christian II of Denmark, 1523.
Oil on panel, 56 x 38 cm.
Nuremberg, Germanisches Nationalmuseum.

Der Bapstesel zu Rom

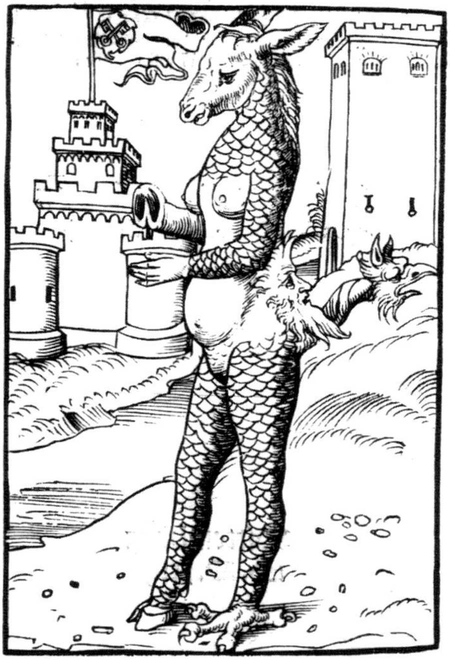

Das Munchkalb zu freyberg

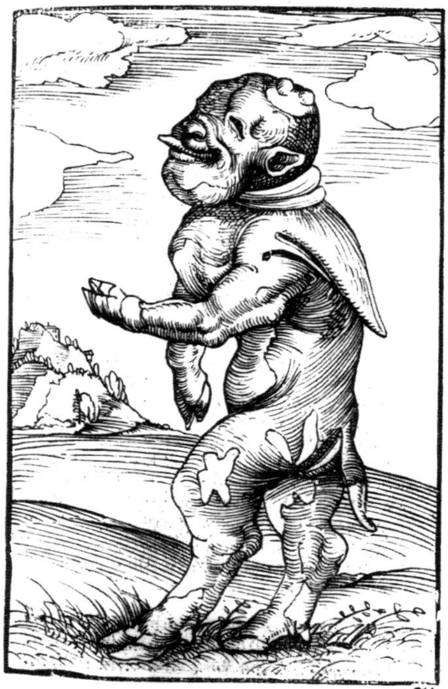

Pope-Donkey and Monk-Calf, 1523.
Woodcut, each 14.5 x 9.5 cm.
Gotha, Stiftung Schloss Friedenstein.

1524

□ In 1524, Lucas Cranach found himself amongst the entourage accompanying the Elector of Saxony to the Diet of Nuremberg. There, he met Albrecht Dürer, who made a silverpoint drawing of Frederick the Wise.

□ The printer and Cranach's business partner Melchior Lotter was forced to give up the joint business with Cranach and Döring (the printer's workshop and the publishing house). Luther still preferred to do business with the Cranach-Döring press. The printer Joseph Klug was employed as a technical manager. Even after this press was closed, Klug appeared as the representative of the two publishers at the Frankfurt book fairs in 1526/28. Klug was probably the son of Peter Klug, who was mentioned in 1478–81 by Anton Koberger (Nuremberg). The business partners Cranach and Döring apparently went their separate ways at the end of 1525.

□ The printer's run by the 30-year-old Hans Lufft in Wittenberg published several smaller texts by Luther. After the closure of Cranach's printer's workshop, Lufft became Luther's main publisher.

1525

□ The Elector of Saxony, Frederick III the Wise, died on 05.05.1525 at the age of 62 in his hunting castle in Lochau, which is today called Annaburg, 20 kilometres north of Torgau in the Annaburg Heath. He had no children. He was buried in the Castle Church in Wittenberg.

□ His 57-year-old brother, John the Steadfast, who had ruled with him since 1486 as co-regent, became his successor as the Elector of Saxony. Lucas Cranach was retained in his position as court painter. A relief gravestone cast in bronze by Peter Vischer in Nuremberg was completed in 1527 according to Cranach's design.

☐ The Peasants' War broke out in an area covering Southern Germany, Austria and Saxony. There were inflammatory sermons against the rich by Thomas Müntzer (*around 1490). His belief was 'they are the gentlemen who only guzzle, drink and gorge themselves and day and night strive to see how they can obtain food and put on many pounds'. He called on the farmers of Thuringia to join the Peasants' Revolt.

Luther was horrified by the 'murderous and thieving packs of farmers' (April–May 1525).

As the leader of the peasants' army, Müntzer was arrested in May 1525 and, after severe torture, was beheaded on 07.05.1525 close to Mühlhausen. The victors displayed his head on a pikestaff as a deterrent to others.

On 15.05.1525, the decisive battle took place at the Thuringian (Bad) Frankenhausen in the Kyffhauser Mountains. The peasants' army stood no chance against the Elector's mercenaries and 6,000 revolutionaries were allegedly slaughtered.

☐ On 13.06.1525, Martin Luther married the former nun Katharina von Bora. The witnesses to the marriage and guests in the five-person wedding party were Lucas Cranach, Johannes Bugenhagen and the lawyer Johann Apel. The marriage produced six children: three sons and three daughters.

☐ Katharina von Bora (*29.01.1499) came from an impoverished aristocratic family from Lippendorf, Borna, 20 kilometres south of Leipzig. After her mother's death (1504), she had been sent to be brought up in the Convent in Brehna (between Bitterfeld and Halle). At the age of nine, she went to the Convent Marienthron in Nimbschen, near Grimma, 28 kilometres southeast of Leipzig. She fled this Cistercian convent in the Easter night of 1523.

☐ As a wedding gift, Lucas Cranach, as the witness to the marriage, painted a diptych (altarpiece) depicting Luther and Katharina as well as the late Elector Frederick the Wise and the ruling Elector John the Steadfast.

□ The new Elector, John the Steadfast, initially paid Martin Luther an annual salary of 200 florins. In addition, he placed Wittenberg monastery at the couple's disposal as their home. Elector Frederick the Wise had paid a yearly sum of 100 florins to Luther from 1524 onwards.

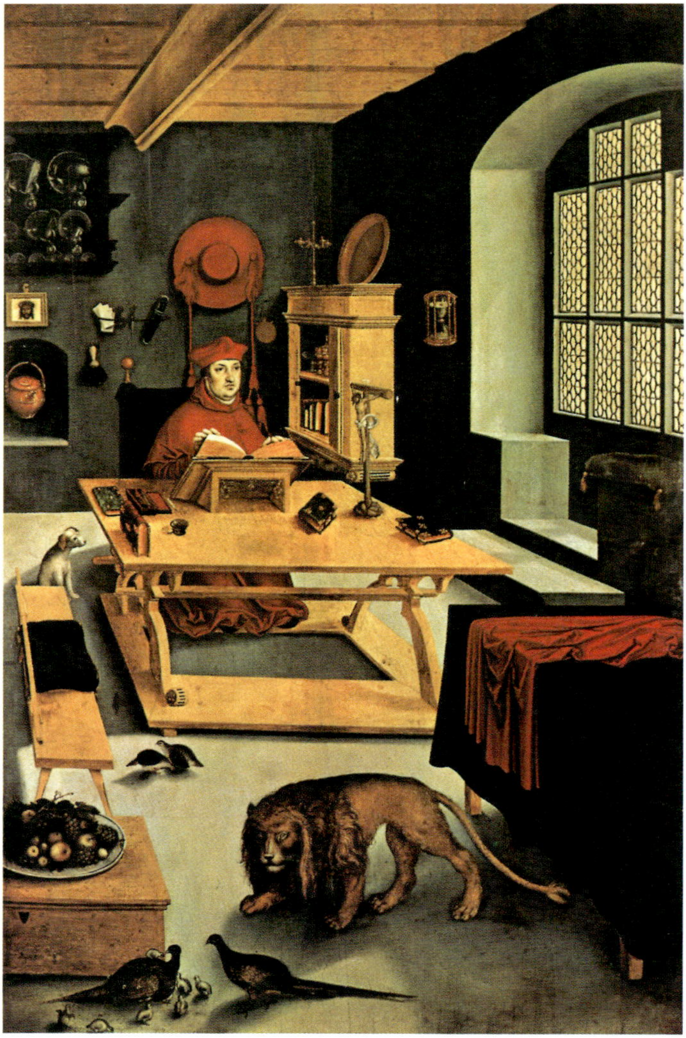

Cardinal Albrecht of Brandenburg, Elector of Mainz, 1525. Oil on panel, 116.5 x 77.5 cm. Darmstadt, Hessisches Landesmuseum.

Salome, approx. 1525–30. Oil on panel, 86 x 59 cm. Private collection.

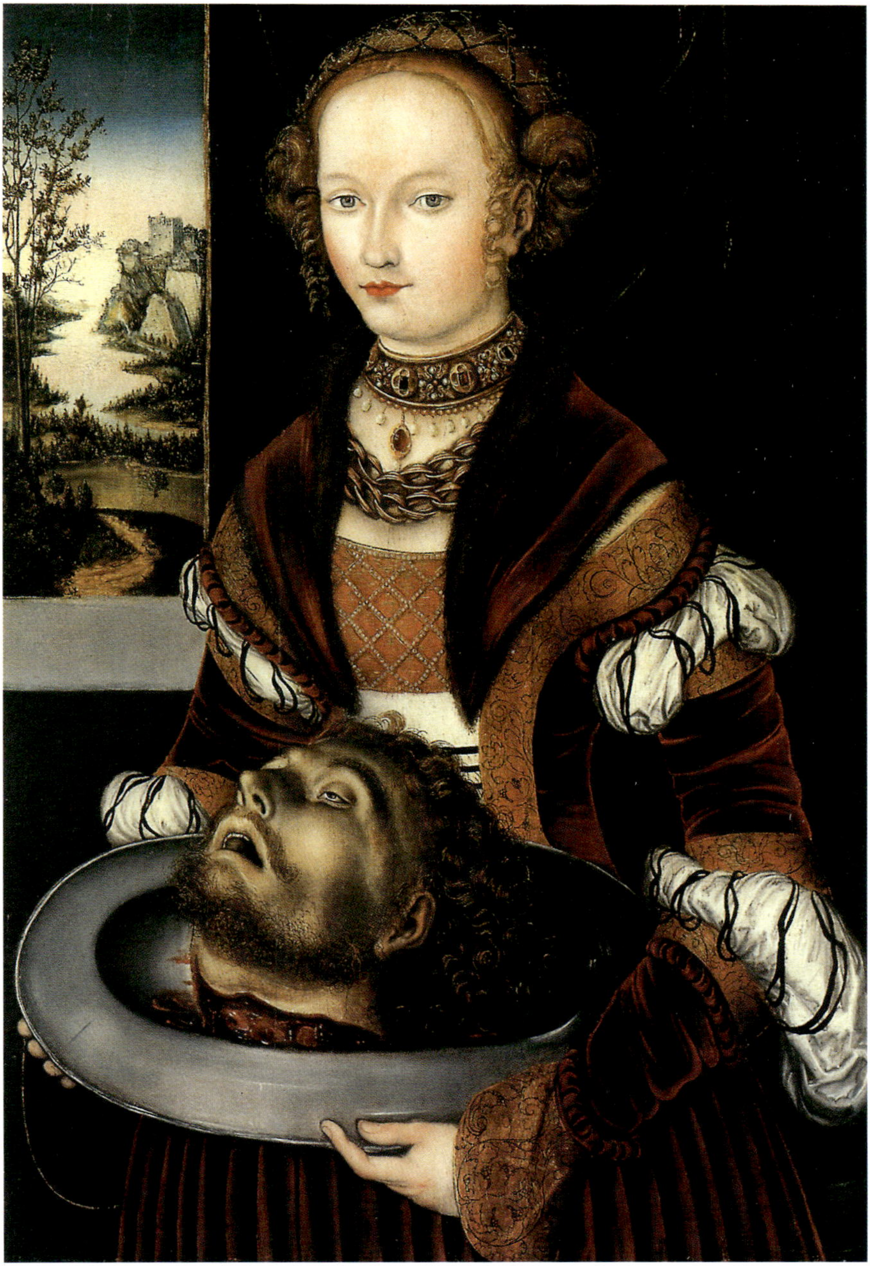

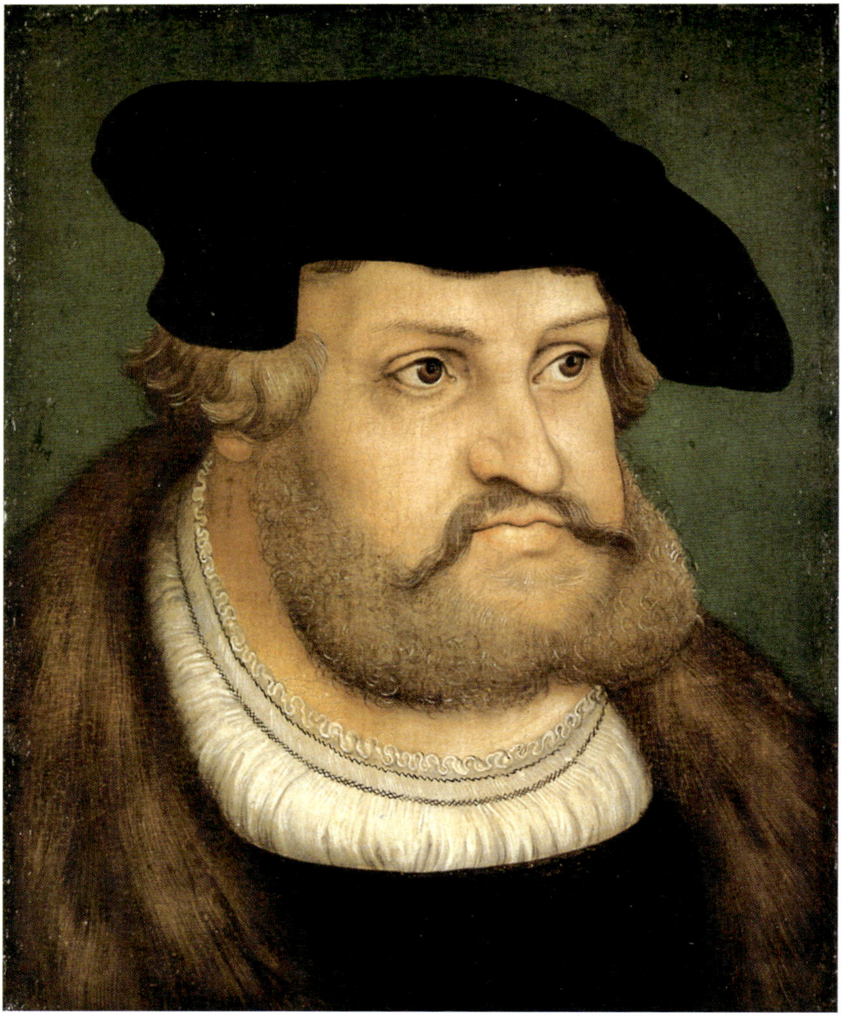

Elector Frederick the Wise, 1525.
Oil on panel, 28.5 x 23.5 cm.
Gottorf Castle, Schleswig-Holsteinische Landesmuseen.

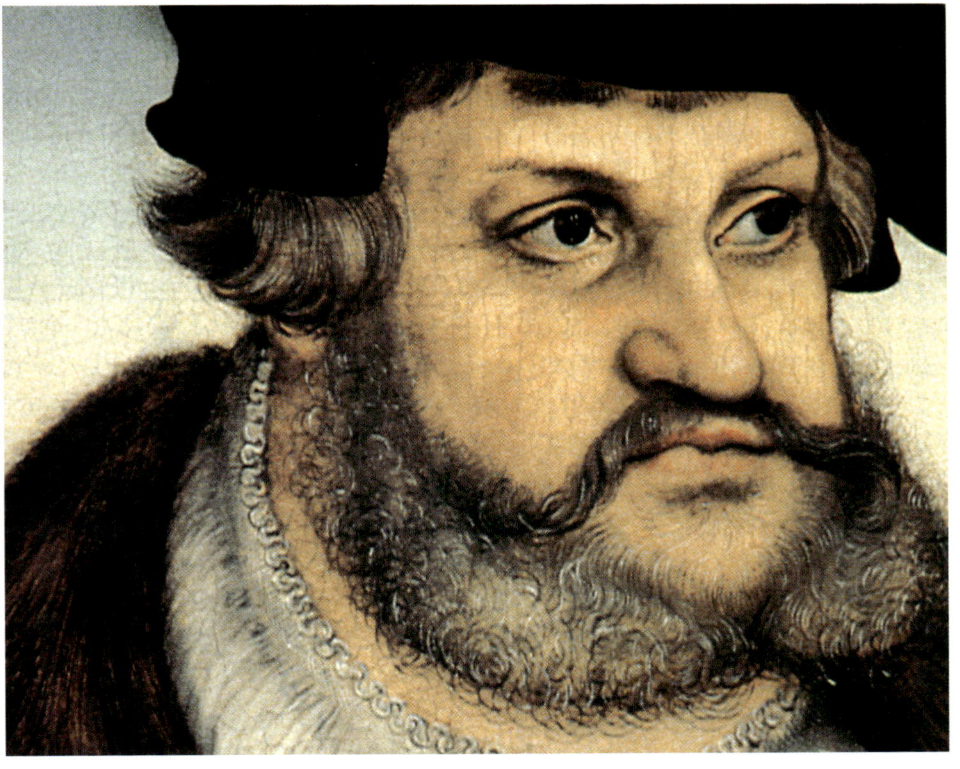

Elector Frederick the Wise, around 1525.
Oil on panel, 57.8 x 40.6 cm.
Private collection.

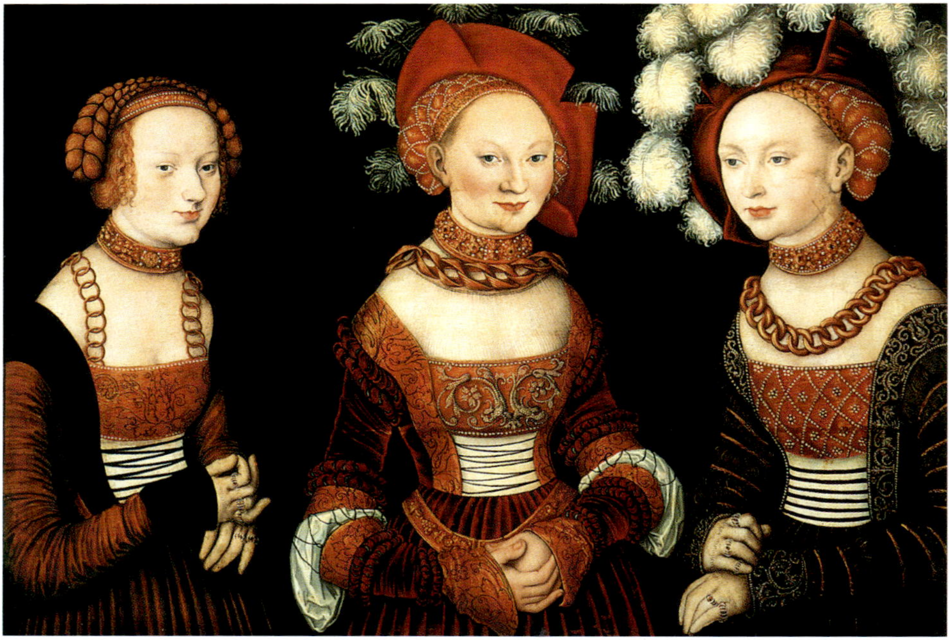

Study of Three Girls, approx. 1525–30.
Oil on panel, 62 x 89 cm.
Vienna, Kunsthistorisches Museum.

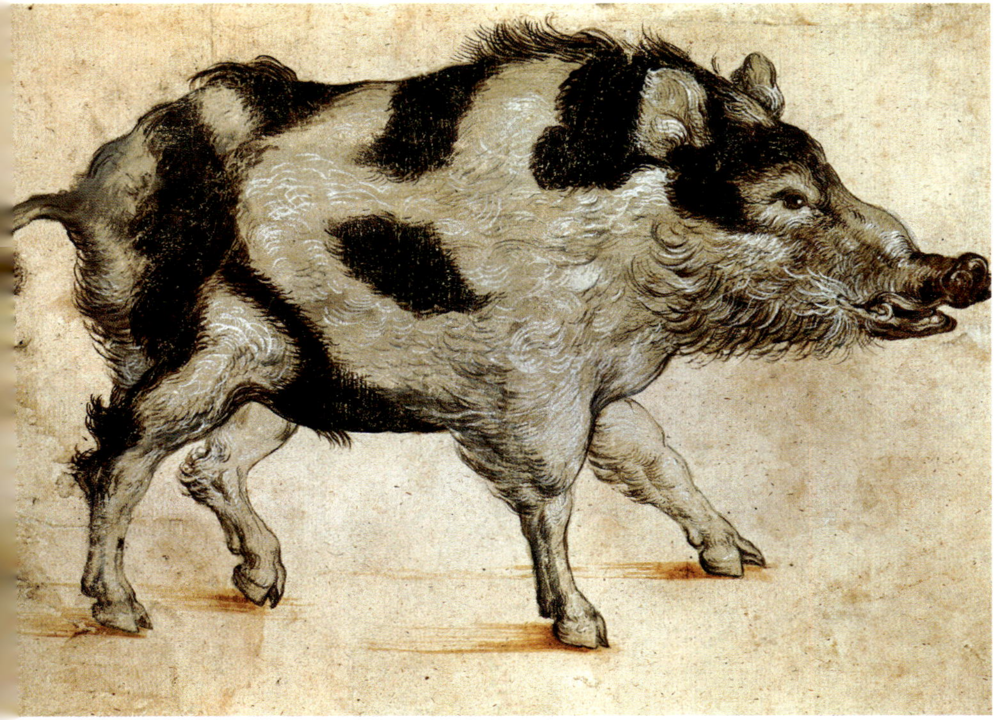

Wild Boar, approx. 1525–30.
Watercolour, 16.2 x 24.1 cm.
Dresden, Kupferstichkabinett.

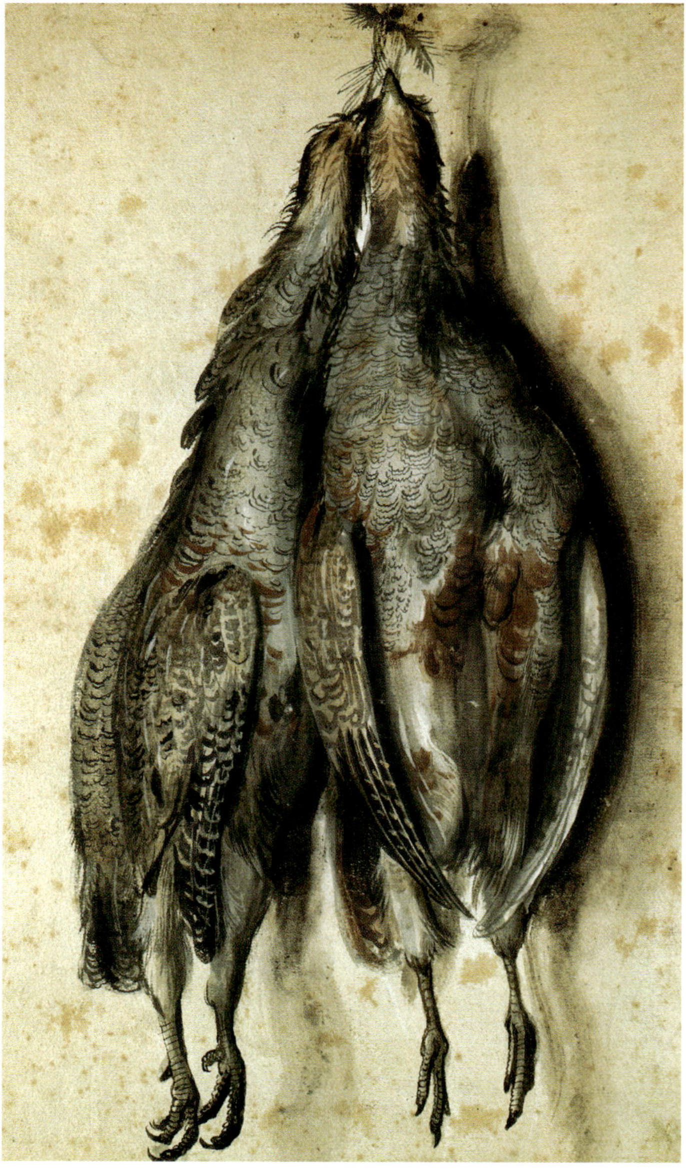

Study of Two Partridges, approx. 1525–30.
Watercolour, 41.2 x 24.7 cm.
Dresden, Kupferstichkabinett.

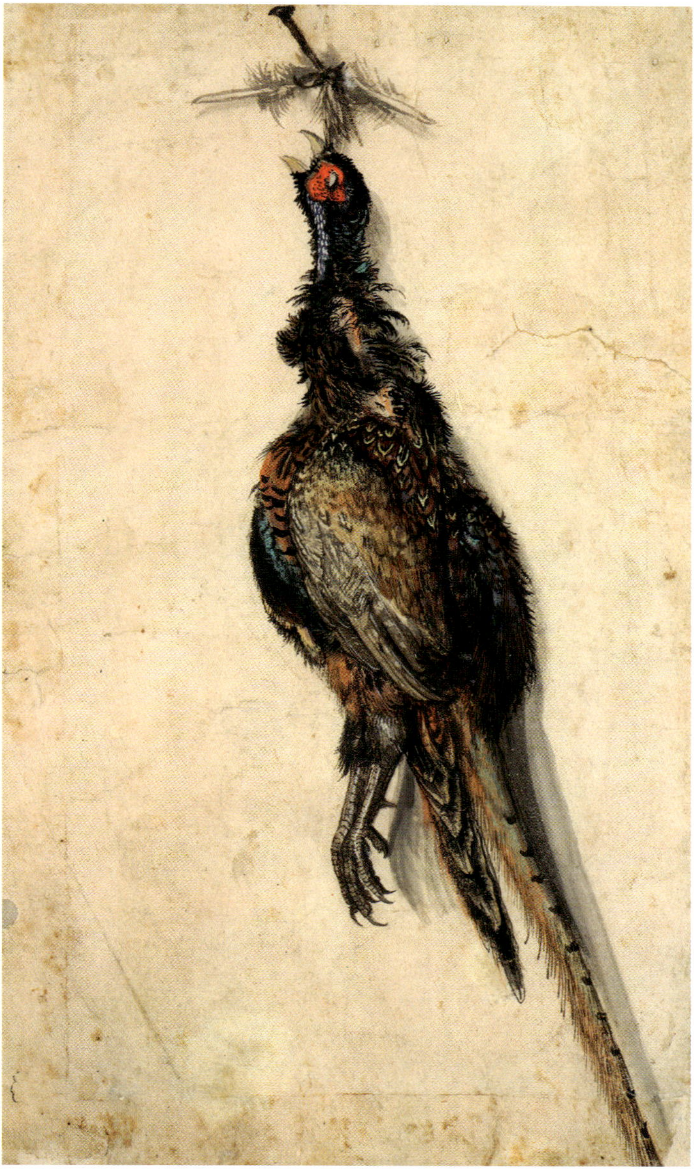

Study of a Pheasant (copy), approx. 1525–30.
Watercolour and opaque watercolour, 29.2 x 17.7 cm.
Dresden, Kupferstichkabinett.

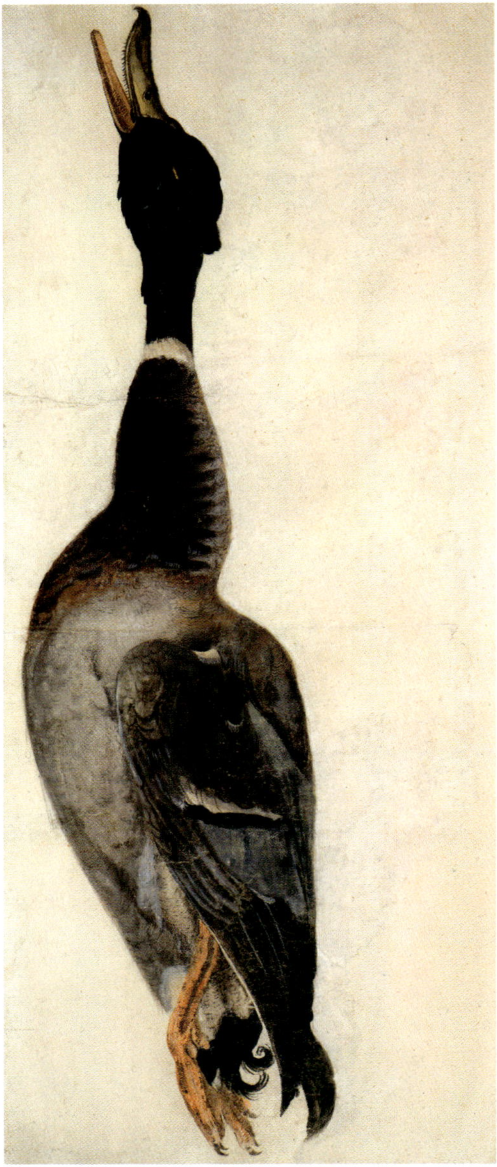

Study of a Dead Drake, approx. 1525–30.
Watercolour, 68 x 26.5 cm.
Dresden, Kupferstichkabinett.

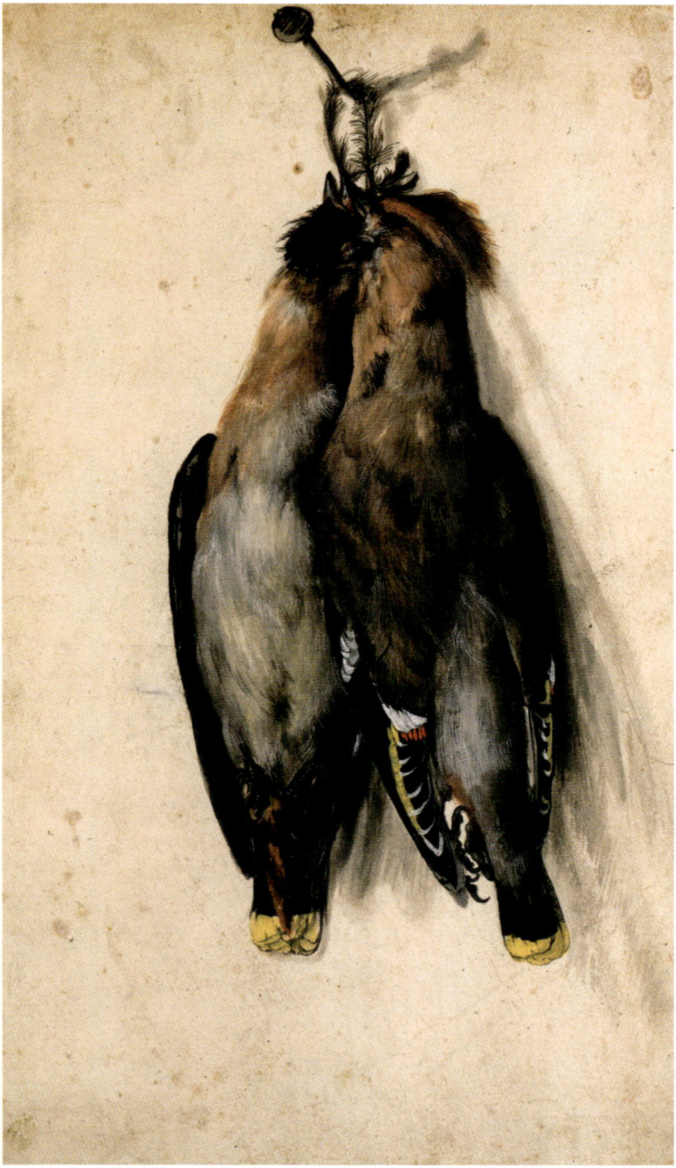

Study of Dead Waxwings Hanging on a Nail, approx. 1525–30.
Watercolour and opaque watercolour, 34.6 x 20.3 cm.
Dresden, Kupferstichkabinett.

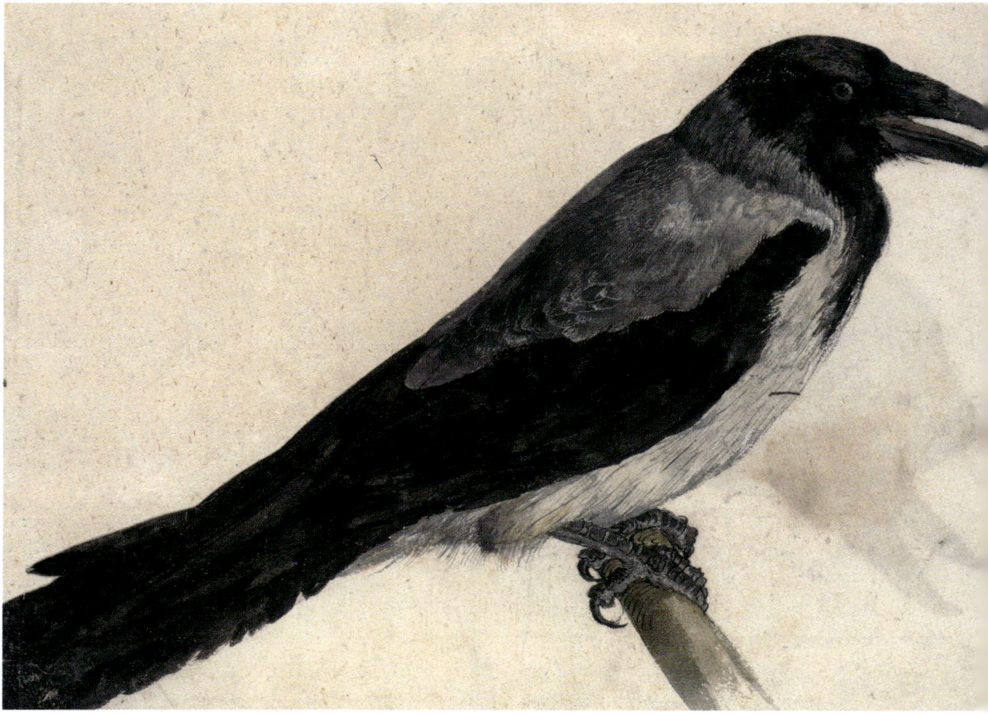

Sitting Hooded Crow, 1525–30.
Black pen and brush with watercolour, 19.1 x 28 cm.
Dresden, Kupferstichkabinett.

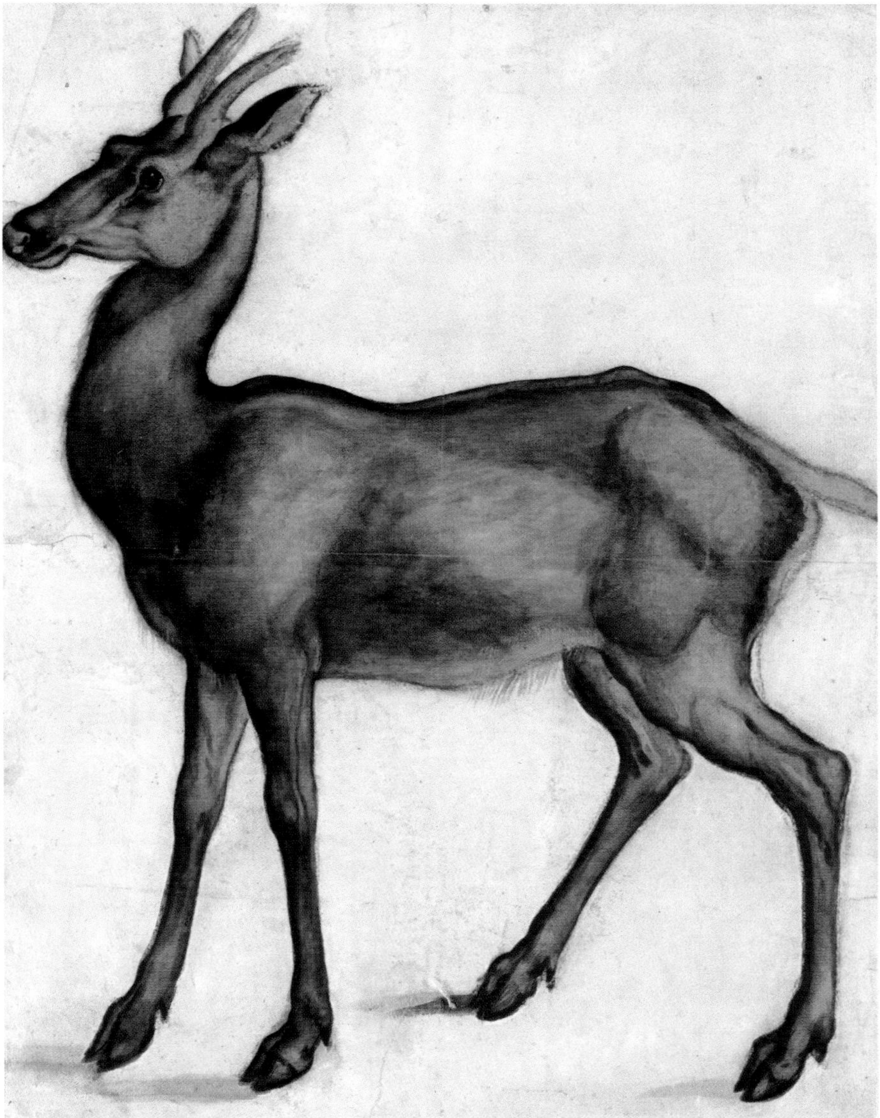

Young Deer, 1525–30.
Watercolour on charcoal, 47.9 x 37.7 cm.
Dresden, Kupferstichkabinett.

1526

□ John the Steadfast ordered from Lucas Cranach 100 copies of his 'German Mass' of which Luther had already sent him several (30.01.1526).

□ Duke Albert II of Prussia, the last Grand Master of the Teutonic Order, gave Cranach a kind of open commission to supply him with 'all the new, good and readable books' and henceforth received cases of books at his residence in Königsberg.

Albert declared his open support for the Reformation from 1525 onwards and transformed the German state into a secular hereditary dukedom under Polish suzerainty with Königsberg as the capital.

□ Lucas Cranach, along with Justus Jonas, a friend of Luther, became the godfather to Luther's first-born child. The baptism was conducted by Johannes Bugenhagen, Luther's confidant and the town priest in

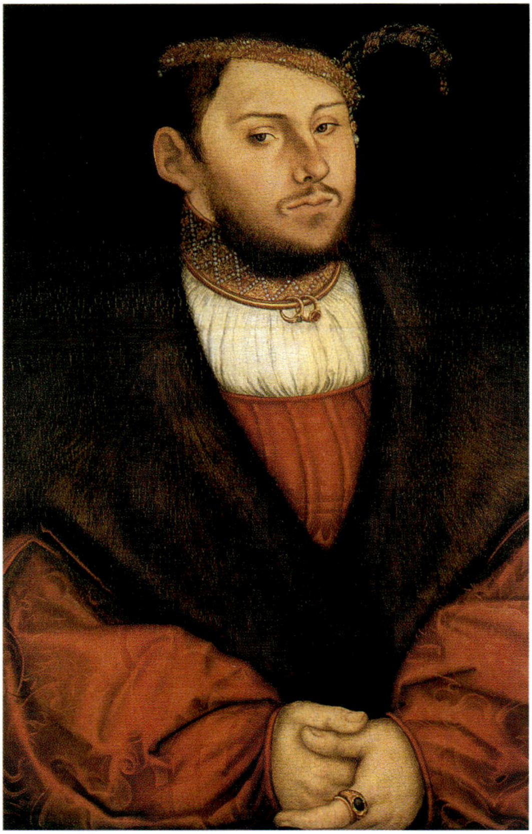

Electoral Prince John Frederick, 1526.
Oil on beech wood, 56 x 38 cm.
Weimar, Stiftung Weimarer Klassik und Kunstsammlungen.

Wittenberg. Johannes was born on 07.06.1526 (+1575, he was later the Chancellor to Duke Albert II of Prussia).

□ The Electoral Prince John Frederick I (*30.06.1503, Torgau) married Princess Sibyl (*17.07.1512, Düsseldorf), the daughter of the Duke of Jülich-Cleve-Berg. The marriage contract was signed on 08.08.1526 in Mainz; the marriage was consummated in Burg an der Wupper (before 14.09.1526, probably on 08.09.1526). The marriage produced four children: the Dukes John Frederick II of Saxe-Coburg (*08.01.1529), Johann Wilhelm of Saxe-Weimar (*11.03.1530), John Ernst II of Saxony (*05.01.1535) and John Frederick III of Saxe-Coburg (*16.01.1538).

□ At the Diet of Speyer, the estates of the Empire and the Emperor agreed on a compromise: each prince should deal with the question of faith as he wished until the matter was dealt with at a general council at some time in the future.

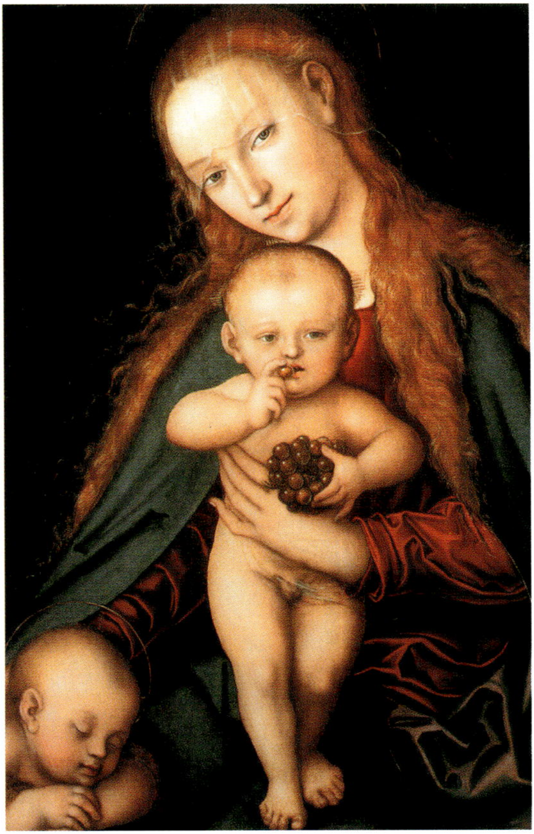

Betrothal Portrait of Princess Sybil of Cleves, 1526. Oil on beech wood, 57 x 39 cm. Weimar, Stiftung Weimarer Klassik und Kunstsammlungen.

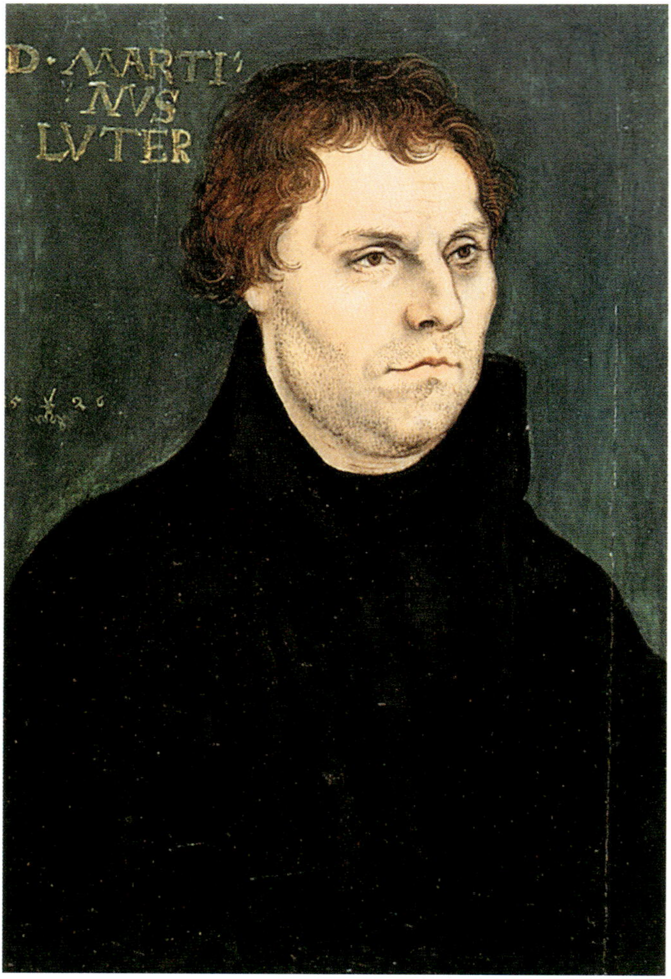

Martin Luther, around 1526.
Oil on oak wood, 21.5 x 15.5 cm.
Private collection.

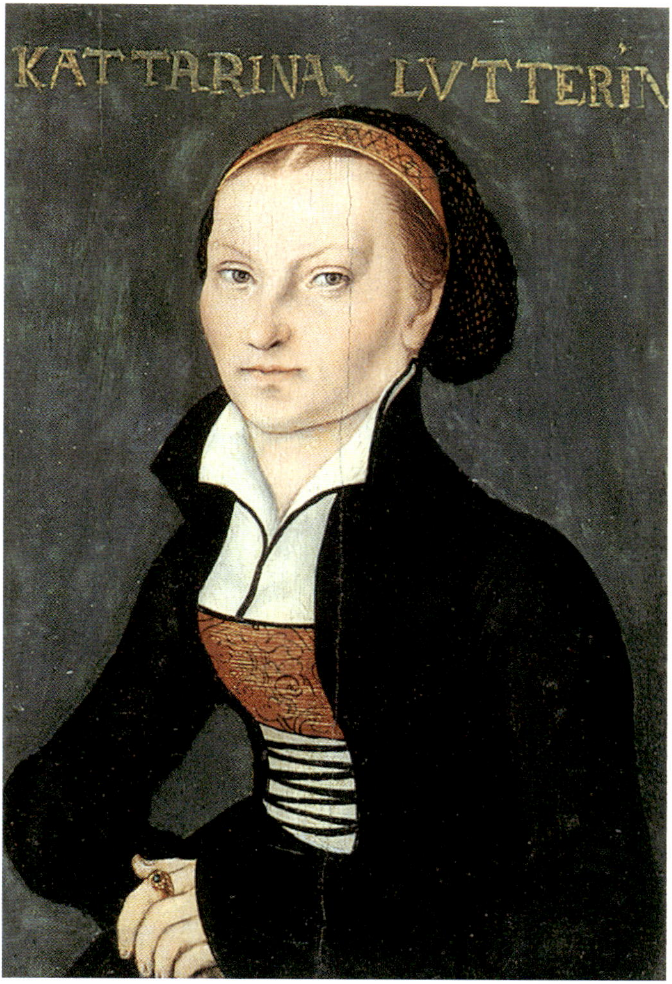

Katharina von Bora, around 1526.
Oil on oak wood, 21.5 x 15.5 cm.
Private collection.

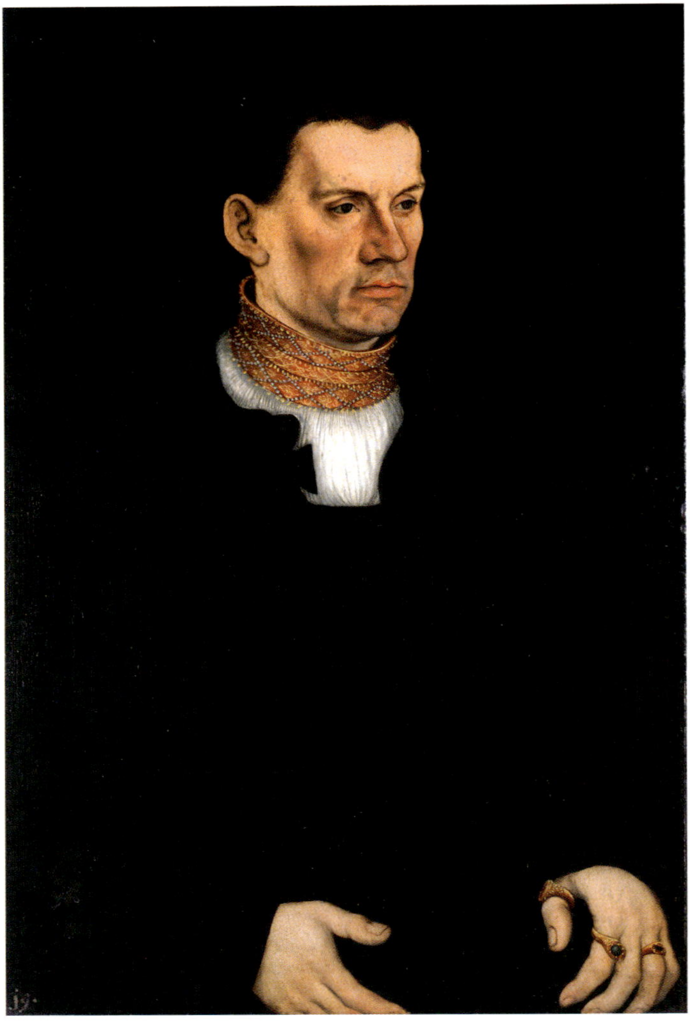

Portraits of an Unidentified Couple (Gentleman of Schleinitz?), 1526.
Oil on beech wood, 58.3 x 39.2 cm.
Weimar, Stiftung Weimarer Klassik und Kunstsammlungen.

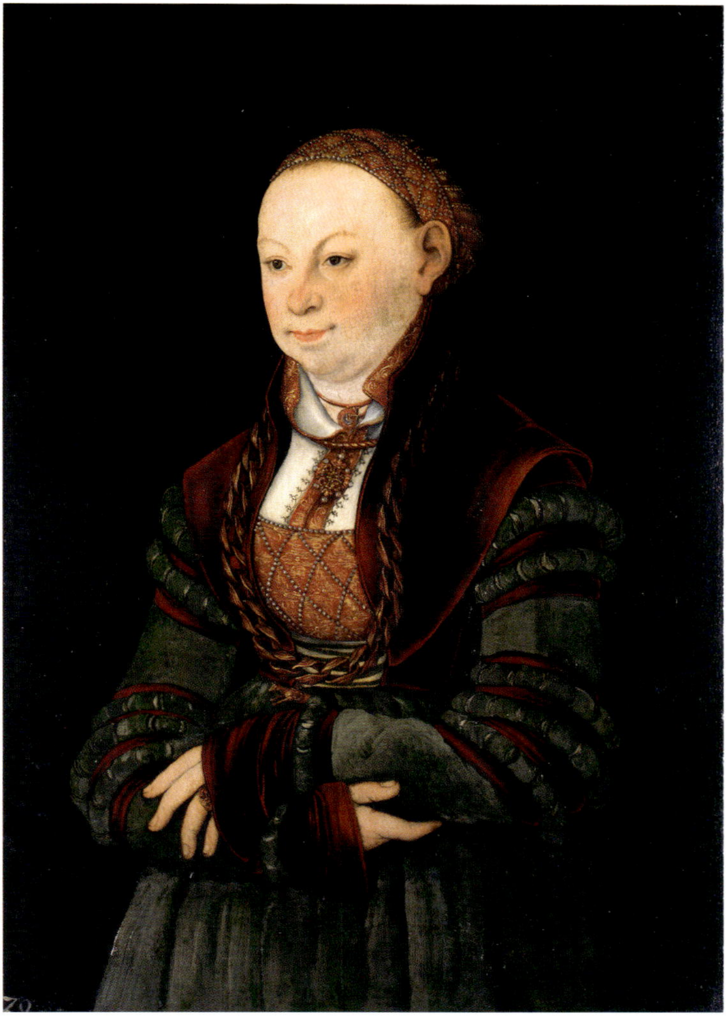

Portraits of an Unidentified Couple (Lady of Schleinitz?),
1526.
Oil on beech wood, 58.7 x 39.7 cm.
Weimar, Stiftung Weimarer Klassik und Kunstsammlungen.

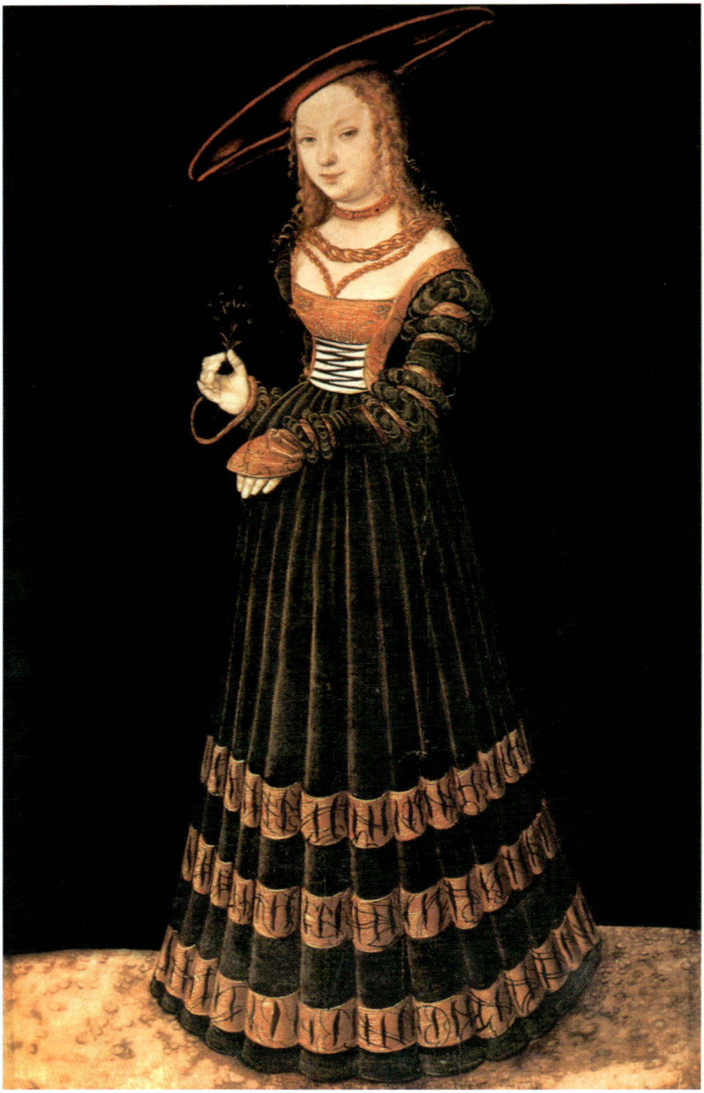

Young Lady Holding a Flower, 1526.
Oil on panel, 80 x 54 cm.
Warsaw, Nationalmuseum.

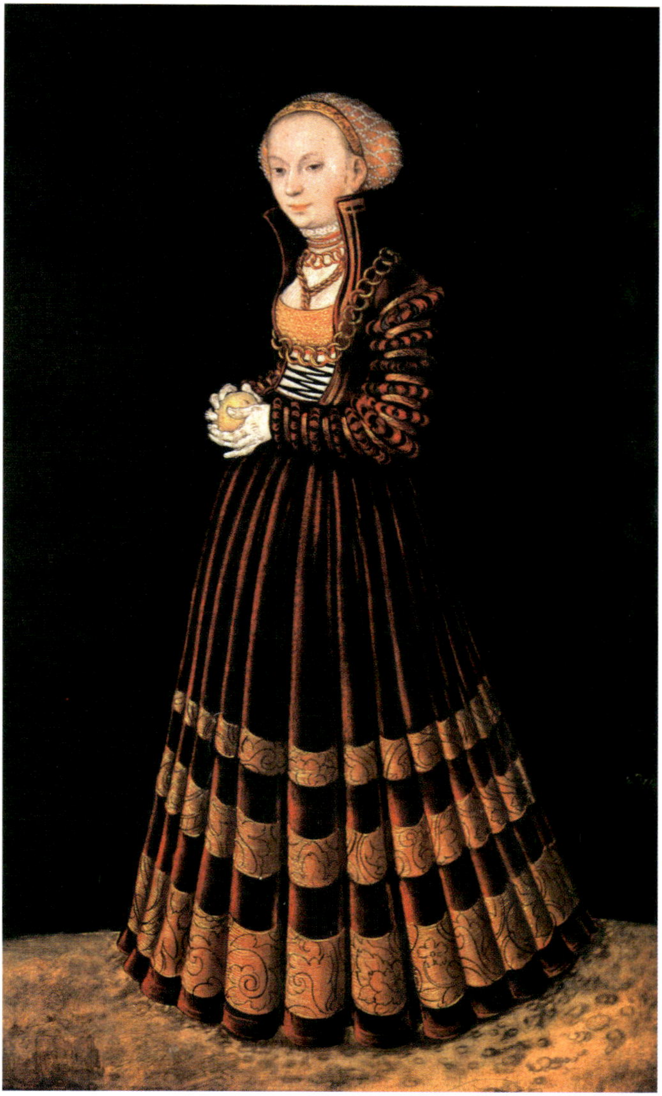

Young Lady Holding an Apple, 1526.
Oil on oak wood, 38 x 25 cm.
Prague, Nationalgalerie.

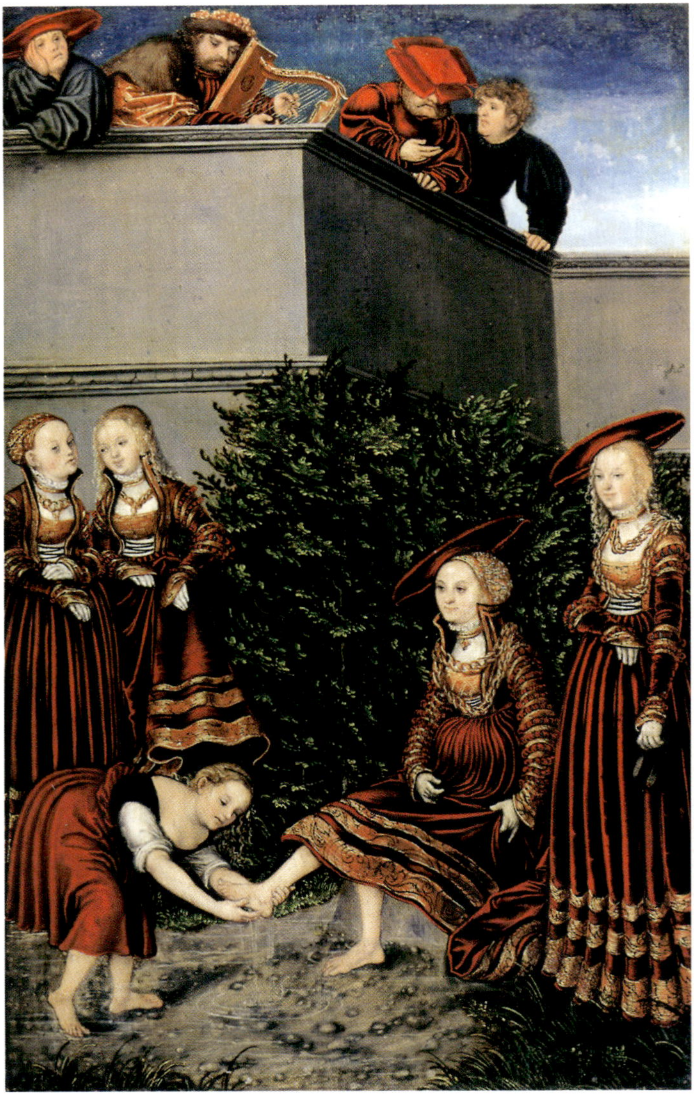

David and Bathsheba, 1526.
Oil on panel, 36 x 24 cm.
Berlin, Staatliche Museen.

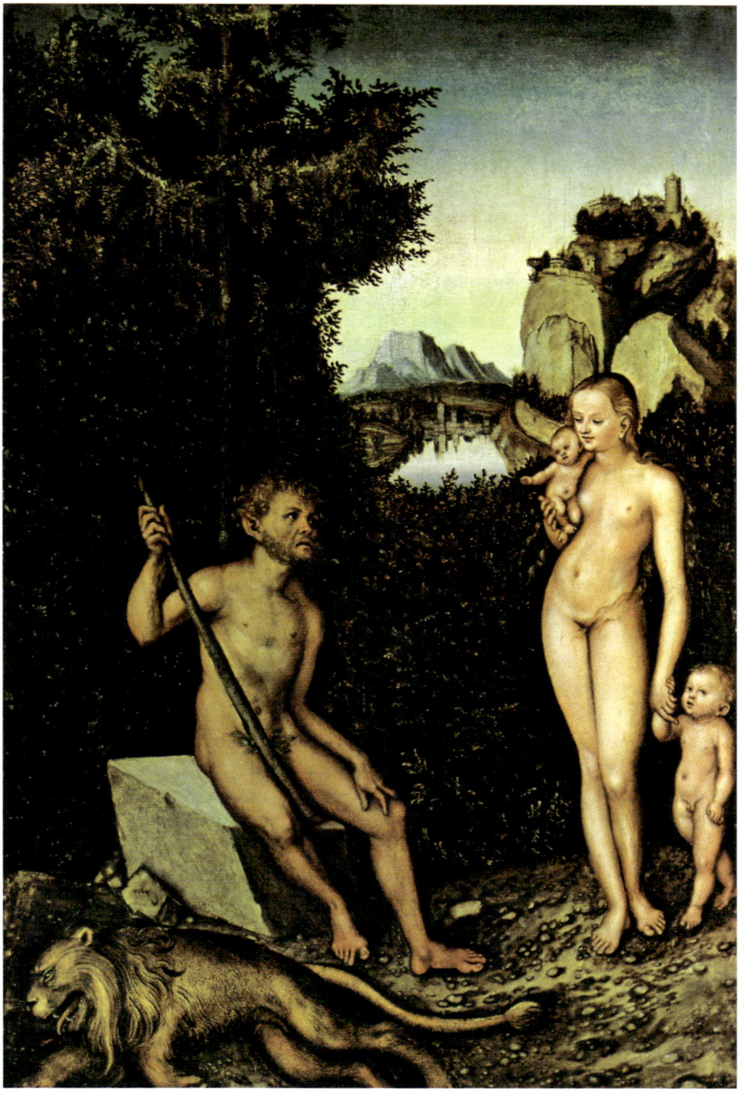

Faun with his Family, around 1526.
Oil on beech wood, 83 x 56 cm.
Private collection.

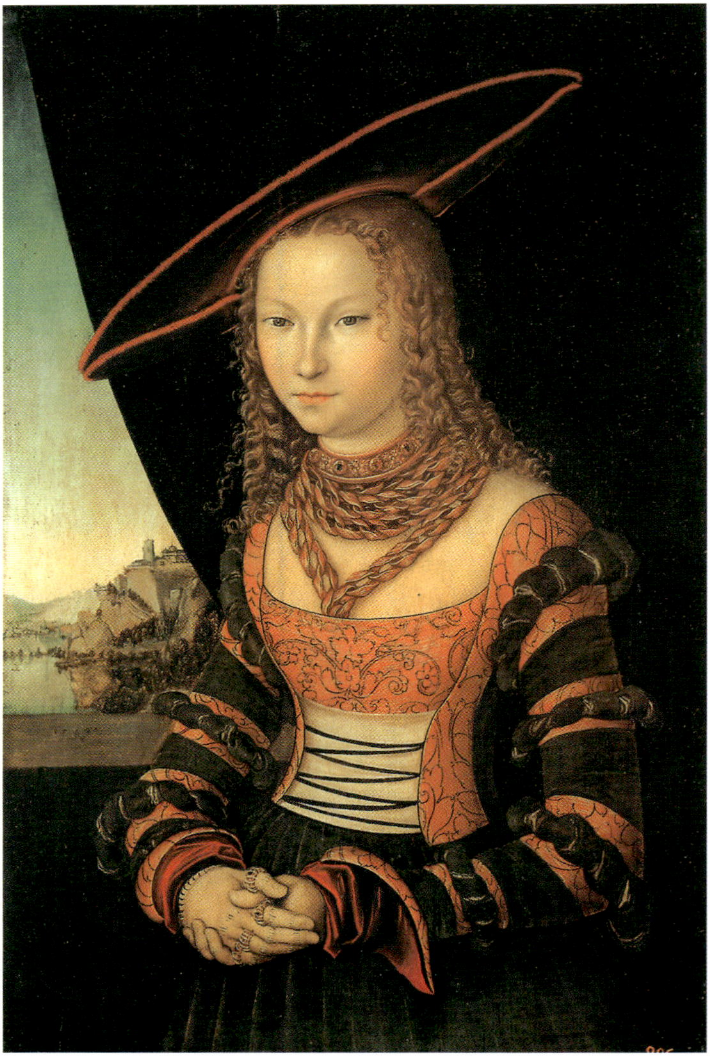

Young Woman, 1526.
Oil on beech wood, 89 x 59 cm.
St Petersburg, Hermitage.

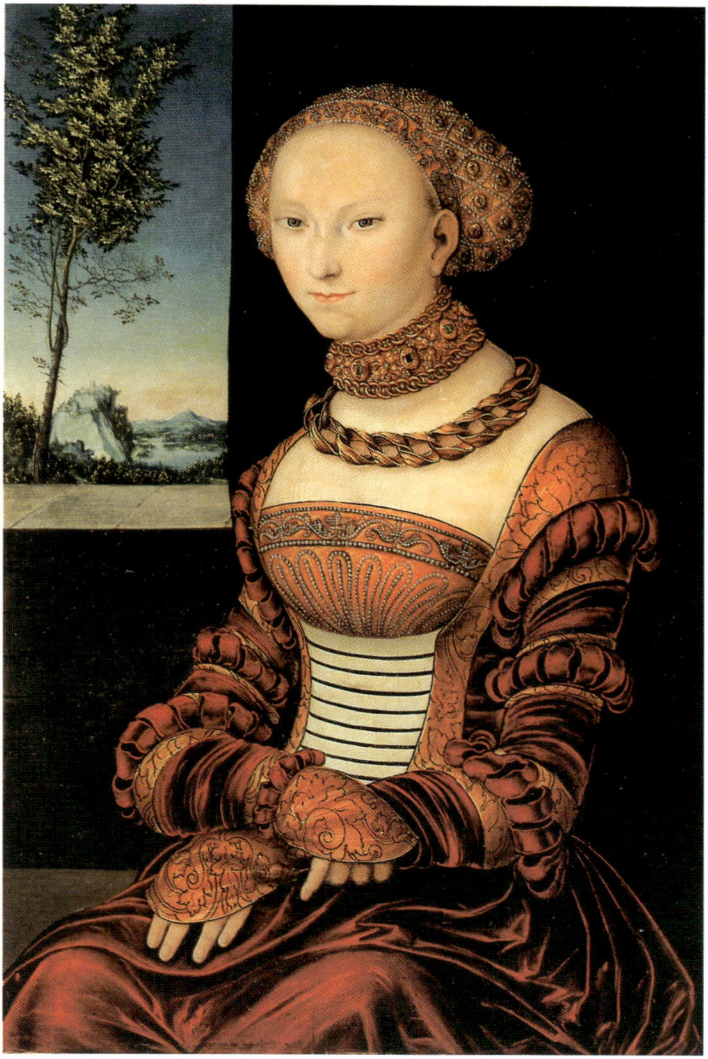

Young Woman, after 1526.
Oil on Panel, 85 x 54 cm.
Coburg, Kunstsammlungen der Veste.

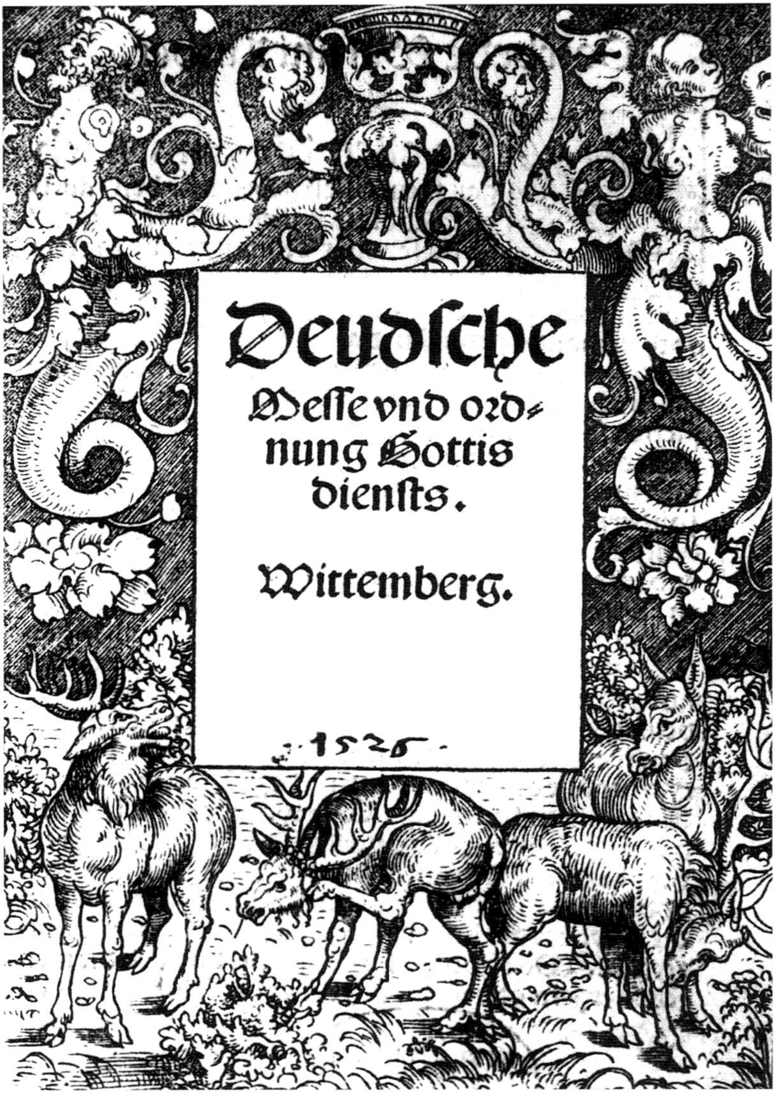

Border for the Quarto Format with Stags in the Landscape, 1526.
Martin Luther, Deutsche Messe, Wittenberg: Michael Lotter.
Woodcut, 17.2 x 12 cm.
Gotha, Stiftung Schloss Friedenstein.

1527

☐ Lucas Cranach sent a bill to the Elector's court for 221 florins for painting work carried out on the occasion of the marriage between the Electoral Prince and the Princess. The ornate and expensive festivities in Torgau from 02–06.06.1527 were to celebrate the 'journey home' of John Frederick I and Sibyl.

☐ In this year, Cranach painted portraits of Martin Luther's parents. The title above the picture of Luther's father read: '1530 on the 29th day of June [it was actually May], Hans Luther, the father of Dr Martin, passed away into God's care'. The title above the mother's picture read: '1531 on the 30th day of June, Margarethe Luther, the mother of Dr Martin, passed away into God's care'.

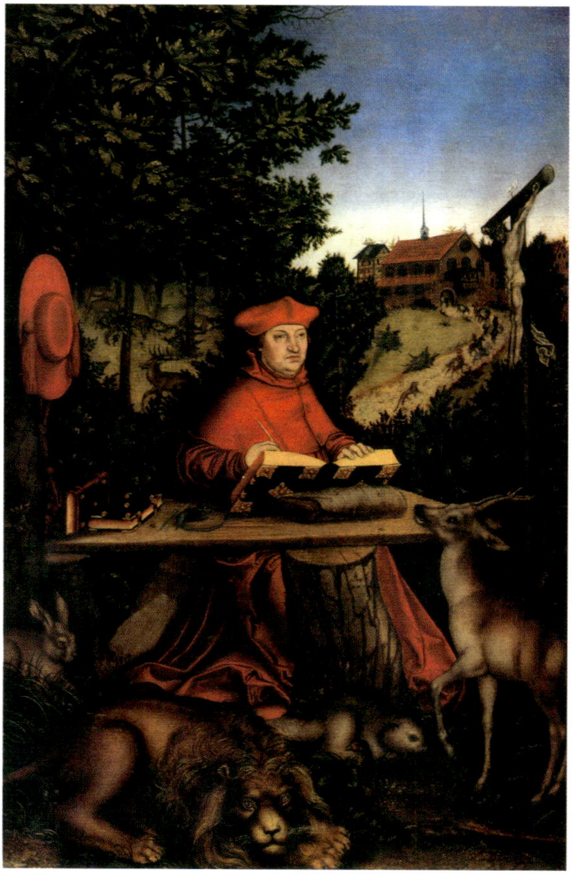

Cardinal Albert of Brandenburg as St Jerome, Outdoors, 1527.
Oil on lime wood, 57 x 37 cm.
Berlin, Staatliche Museen.

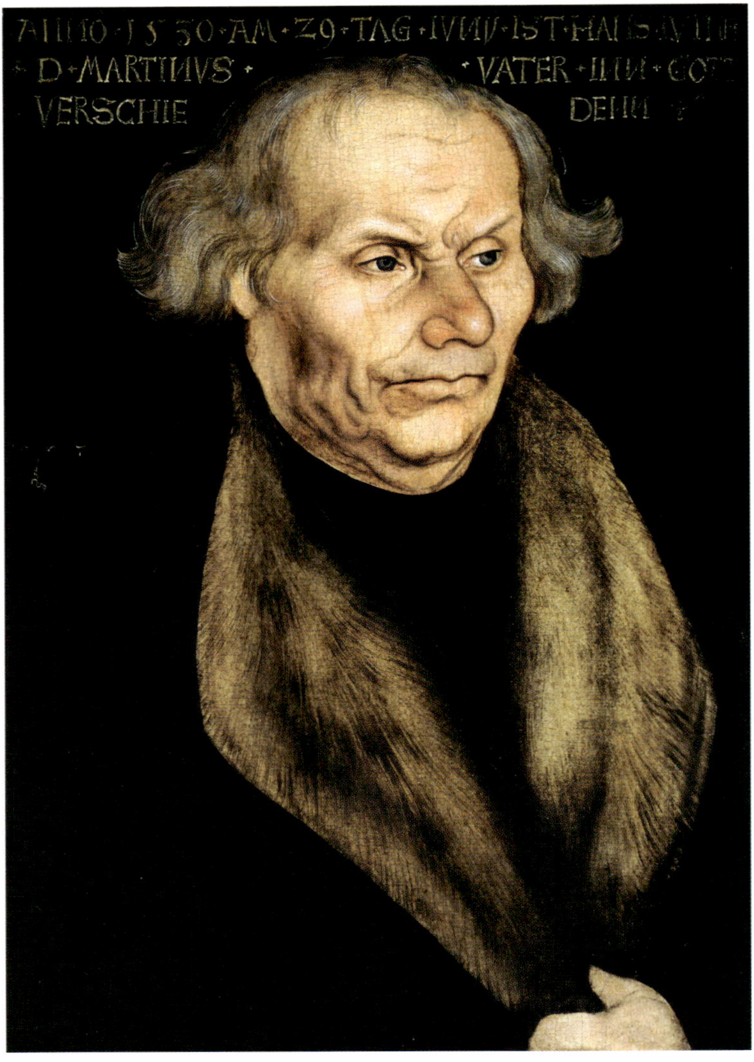

Hans Luther, 1527.
Oil on panel, 39 x 26 cm.
Eisenach, Wartburg-Stiftung.

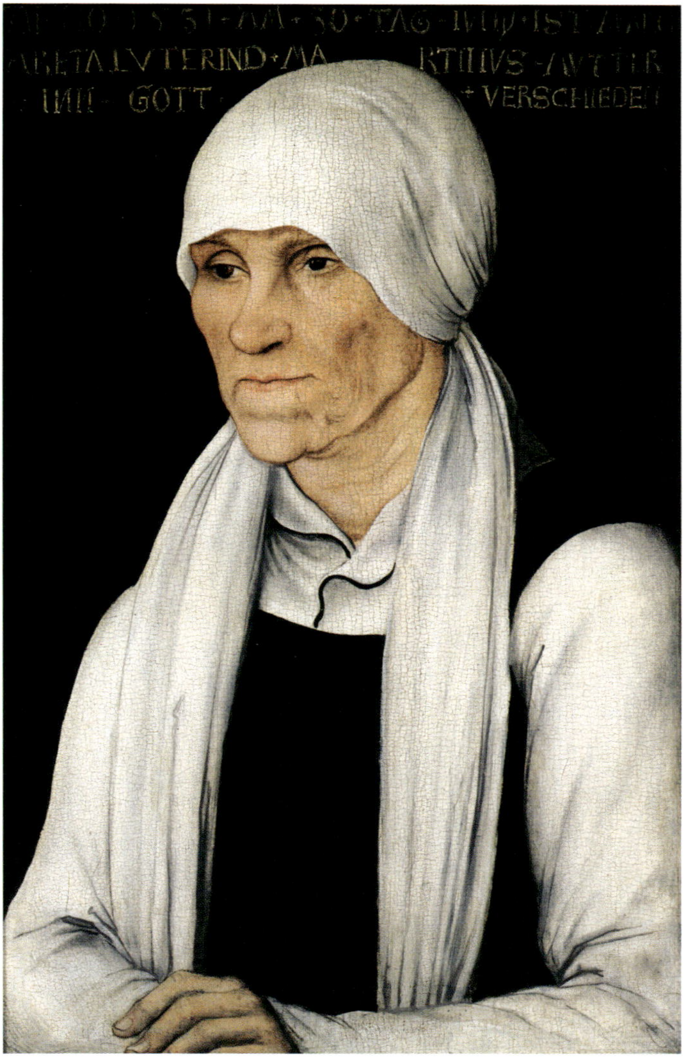

Margarethe Luther, around 1527.
Oil on panel, 39 x 26 cm.
Eisenach, Wartburg-Stiftung.

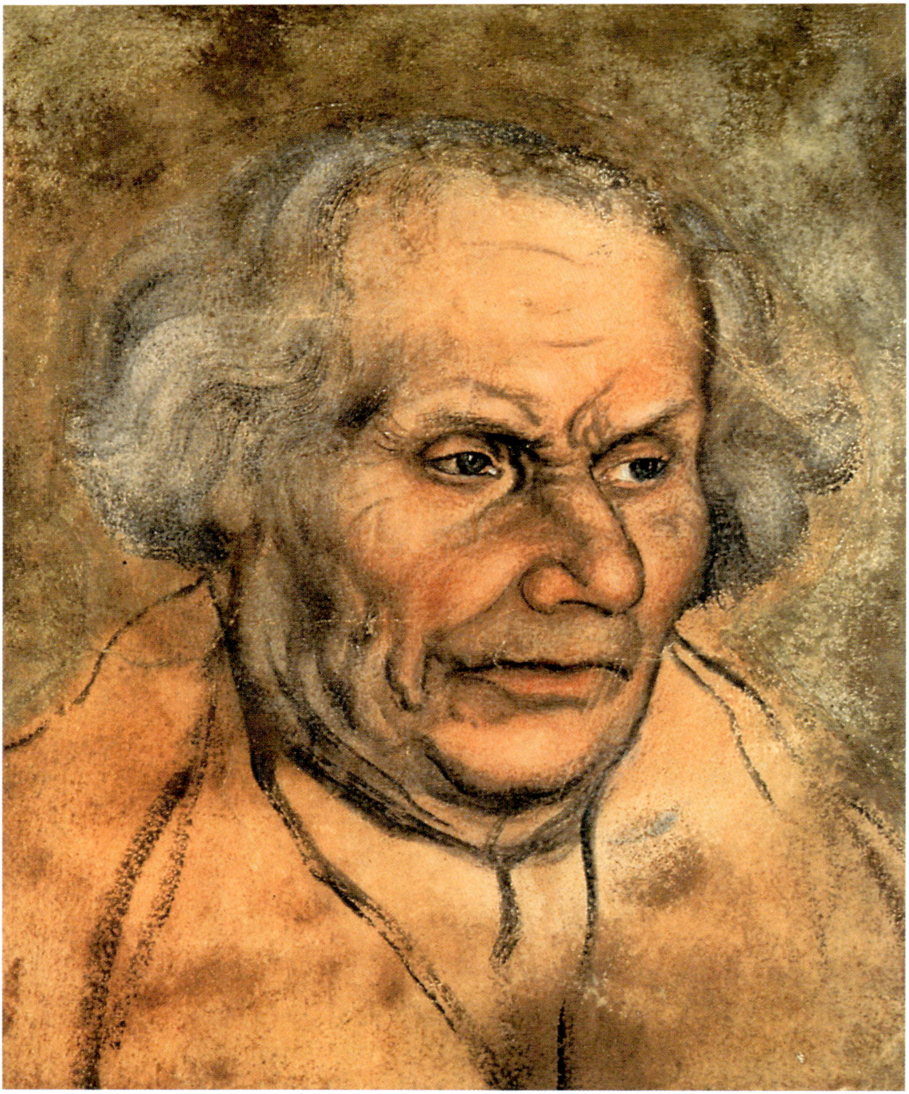

Hans Luther, 1527.
Oil and opaque watercolour on paper, 21.8 x 18.3 cm.
Vienna, Albertina.

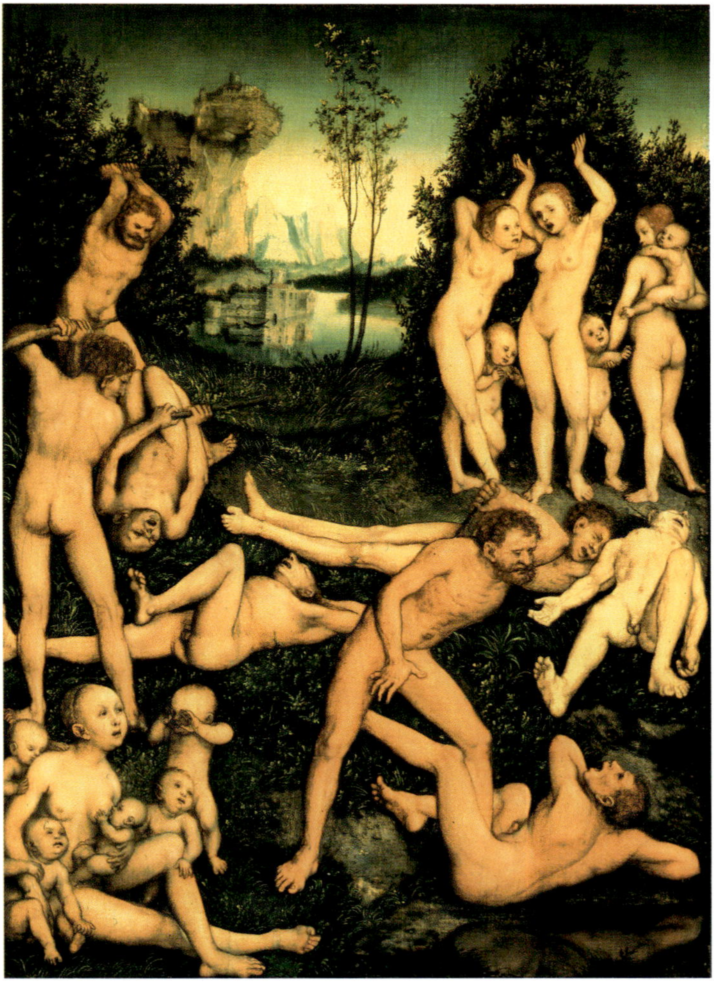

The Silver Age (Jealousy), 1527.
Oil on beech wood, 53 x 38.1 cm.
Weimar, Stiftung Weimarer Klassik und Kunstsammlungen.

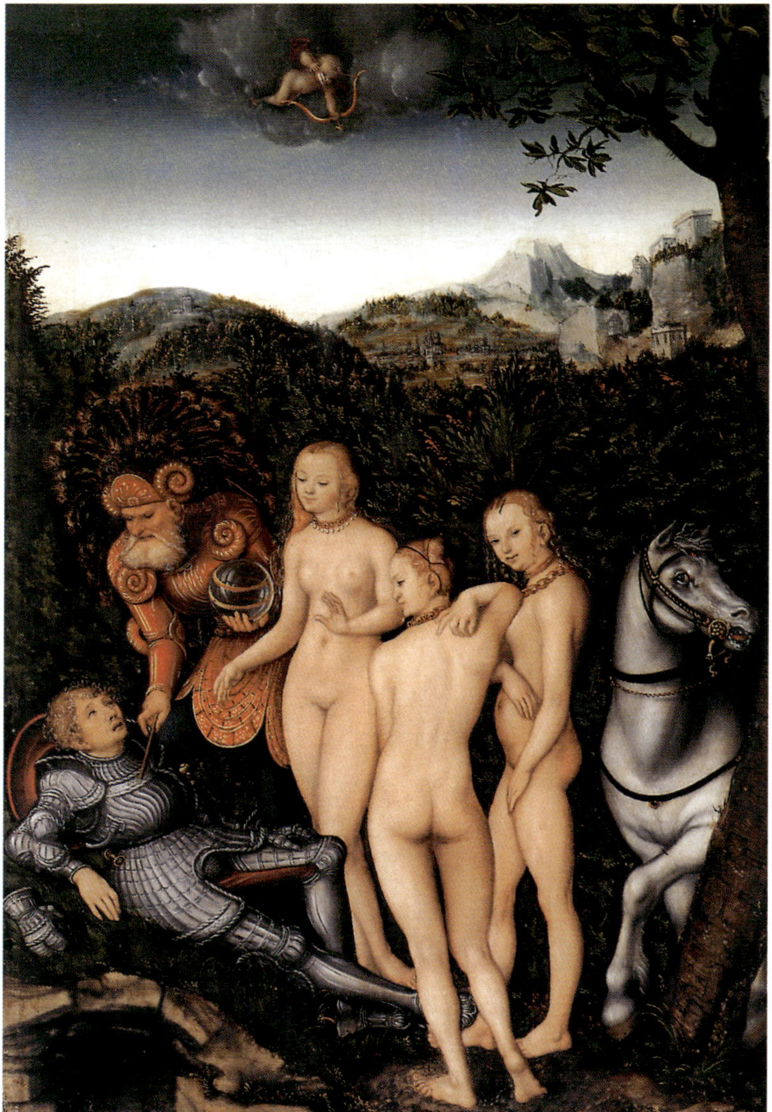

The Judgment of Paris, 1527.
Oil on panel, 50.5 x 38 cm.
Copenhagen, Statens Museum for Kunst.

1528

☐ According to his tax returns, Lucas Cranach owned land to a value of 4,016 florins and was hence the richest landowner in Wittenberg. It does not follow, however, that he was also the richest citizen in the town. He owned a large house, further houses and estates or gardens, the apothecary's privilege as well as the privilege to serve wine. Through his wife, he owned another house in Gotha. The house belonging to his wife Barbara's grandmother in Coswig, twelve kilometres upstream on the River Elbe from Wittenberg, had been signed over to him in 1529 by his relatives in Gotha.

☐ Elisabeth, the wife of the Elector of Brandenburg, born in 1485 as the daughter of King John I of Denmark, left her husband Joachim I, Elector of Brandenburg, and fled from the River Spree on 24.03.1528 to her uncle John Frederick I, Elector of Saxony. She tended towards the teachings of Luther, but had been threatened with imprisonment by her husband, who was a strong opponent of the Reformation. Elisabeth lived in turn in Torgau, Wittenberg and Weimar until Lichtenberg Castle close to Prettin on the River Elbe between Torgau and Wittenberg became her permanent residence.

Joachim I died on 11.07.1535 in Stendal without ever reconciling with his wife. Her son Joachim II (*1505) demanded that his mother return home. Since her son had just become engaged to the Catholic Polish princess Hedwig, she made her return dependent on her being allowed to freely practice her Lutheran faith. Her son did not agree to this condition, however.

Only after Joachim II had become an adherent of Luther's teachings (1539) did Elisabeth return to Brandenburg in 1545. In Spandau, she took active part in church activities. Elisabeth of Brandenburg died on 10.06.1555 at the age of 70 in Berlin.

☐ Albrecht Dürer died on 06.04.1528 at the age of 57 in Nuremberg.

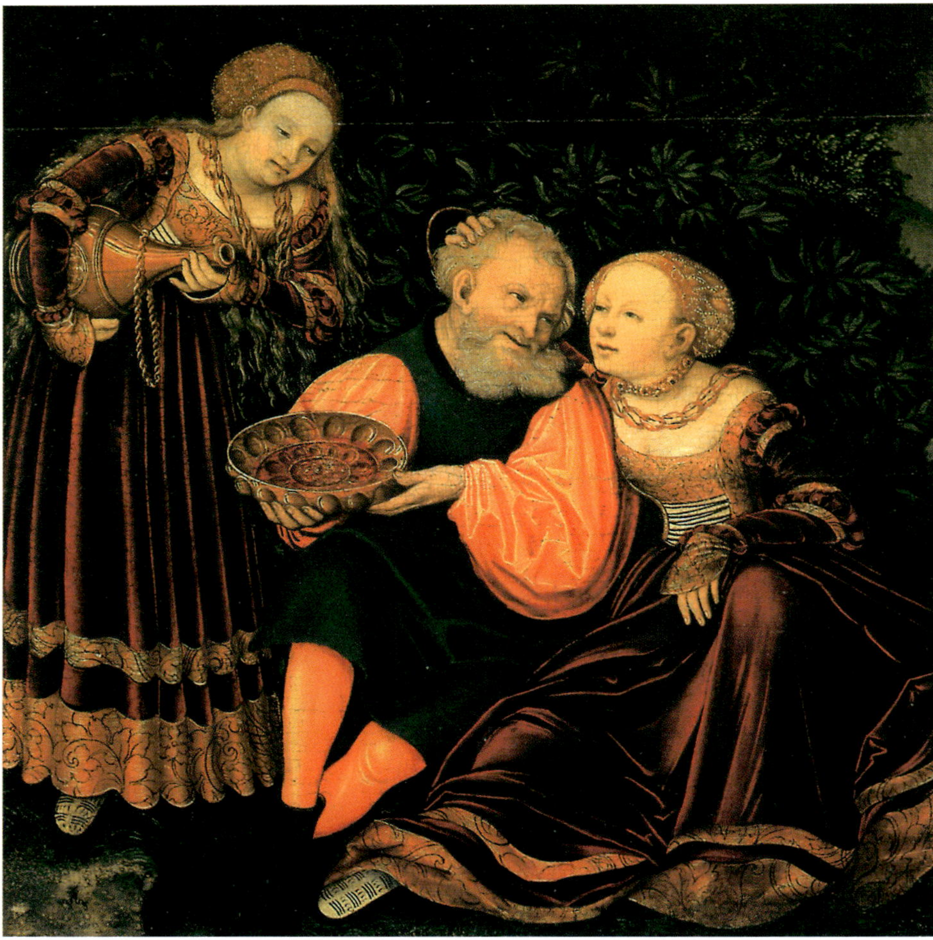

Lot and his Daughters, 1528.
Oil on panel, 37.5 x 38 cm.
Coburg, Kunstsammlungen der Veste (Oberfrankenstiftung).

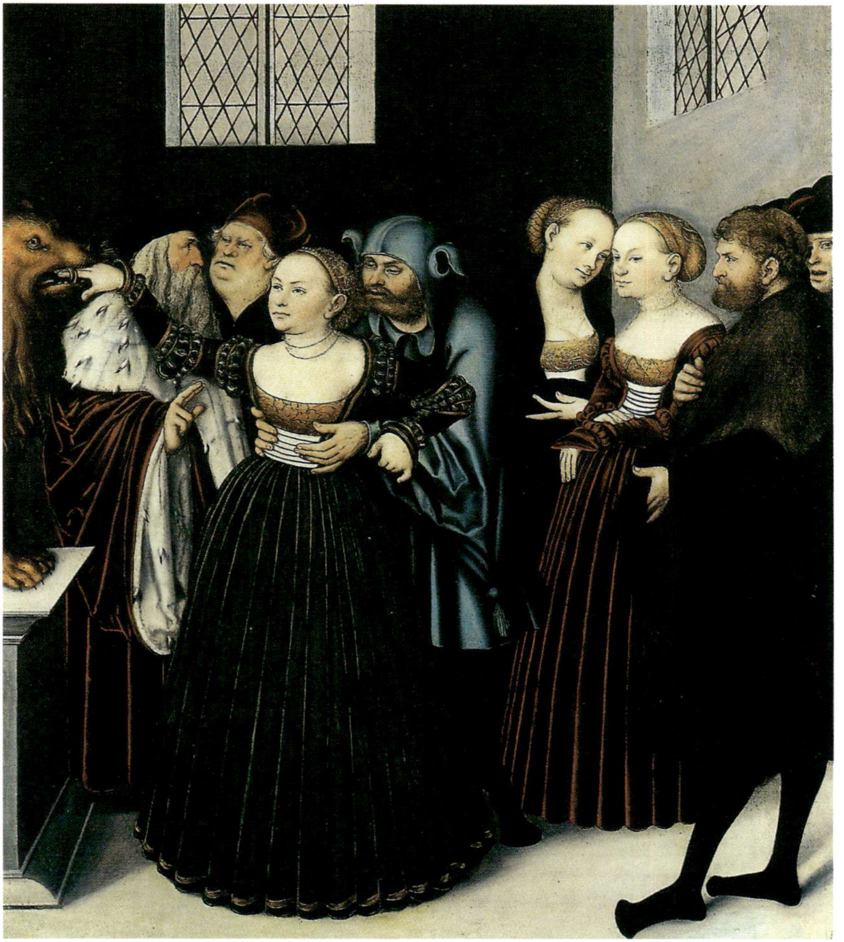

The Jaws of Truth, around 1528.
Oil on beech wood, 111 x 100 cm.
Kreuzlingen, Heinz Kisters collection.

1529

☐ At the Diet of Speyer (15.03.–22.04.1529), the estates of the Empire which were sympathetic to Luther protested against the decision of the majority from the old church to obey the Edict of Worms (1521) instead of following the compromise decided upon by Charles V at the first Diet of Speyer (1526), which was to allow each prince of the Holy Roman Empire to determine the religion of his territory until the matter was dealt with at a general council. The estates of the Empire which were sympathetic to Luther issued a formal *protestatio* against this aggravation of the situation and it is from this that the term *Protestant* derives.

☐ Johannes Cuspinian died on 19.04.1529 at the age of 56 in Vienna.

☐ The Turks, who had already overrun Hungary in 1526, were close to Vienna in September.

Elector Joachim I of Brandenburg, 1529.
Oil on panel, 52 x 35.5 cm.
Potsdam, Stiftung Preußische Schlösser und Gärten,
Berlin-Brandenburg.

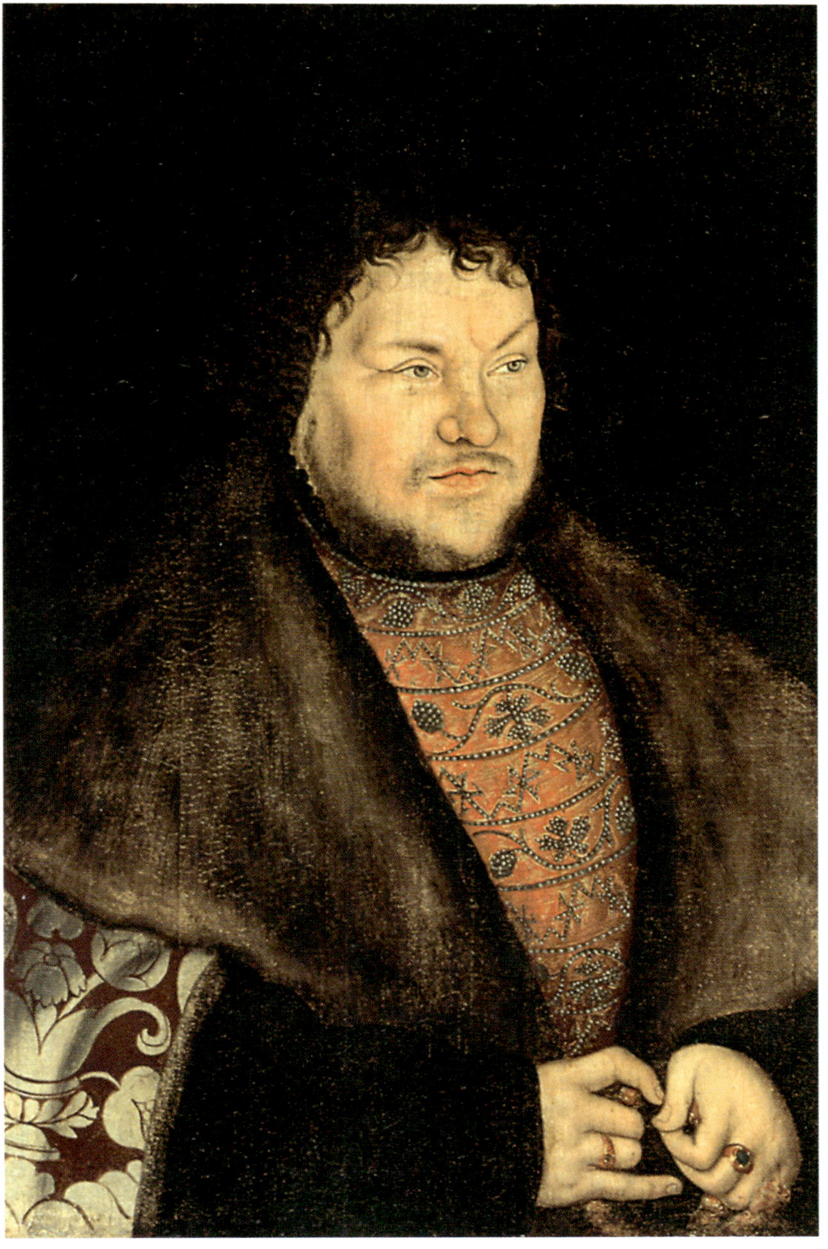

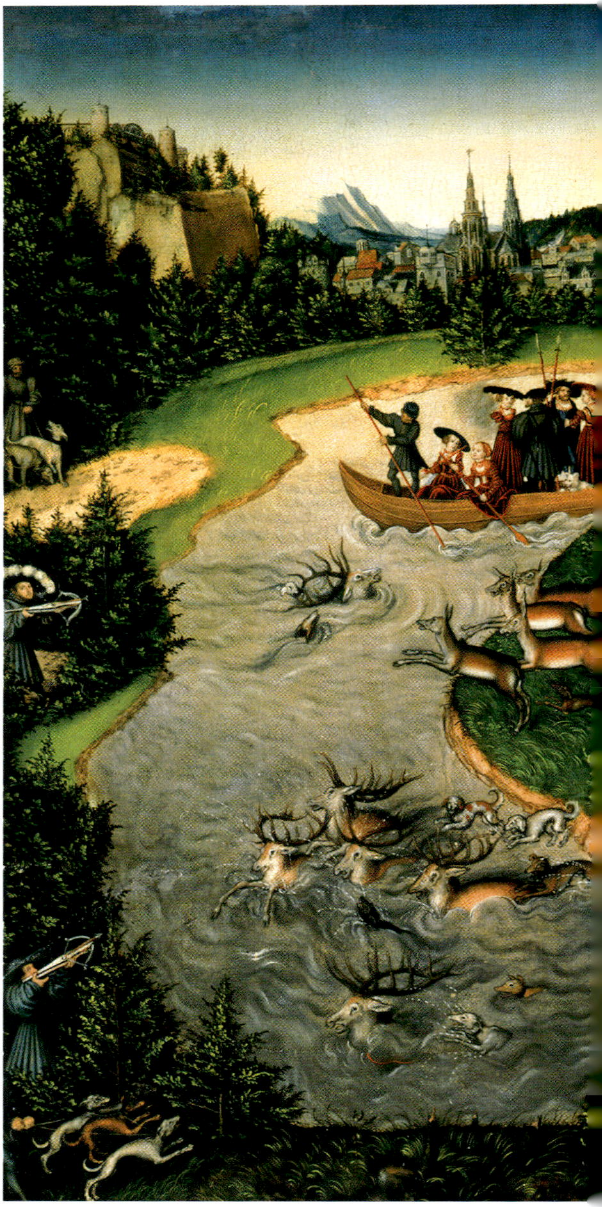

The Stag Hunt of Elector Frederick the Wise, 1529. Oil on panel, 80 x 114 cm. Vienna, Kunsthistorisches Museum.

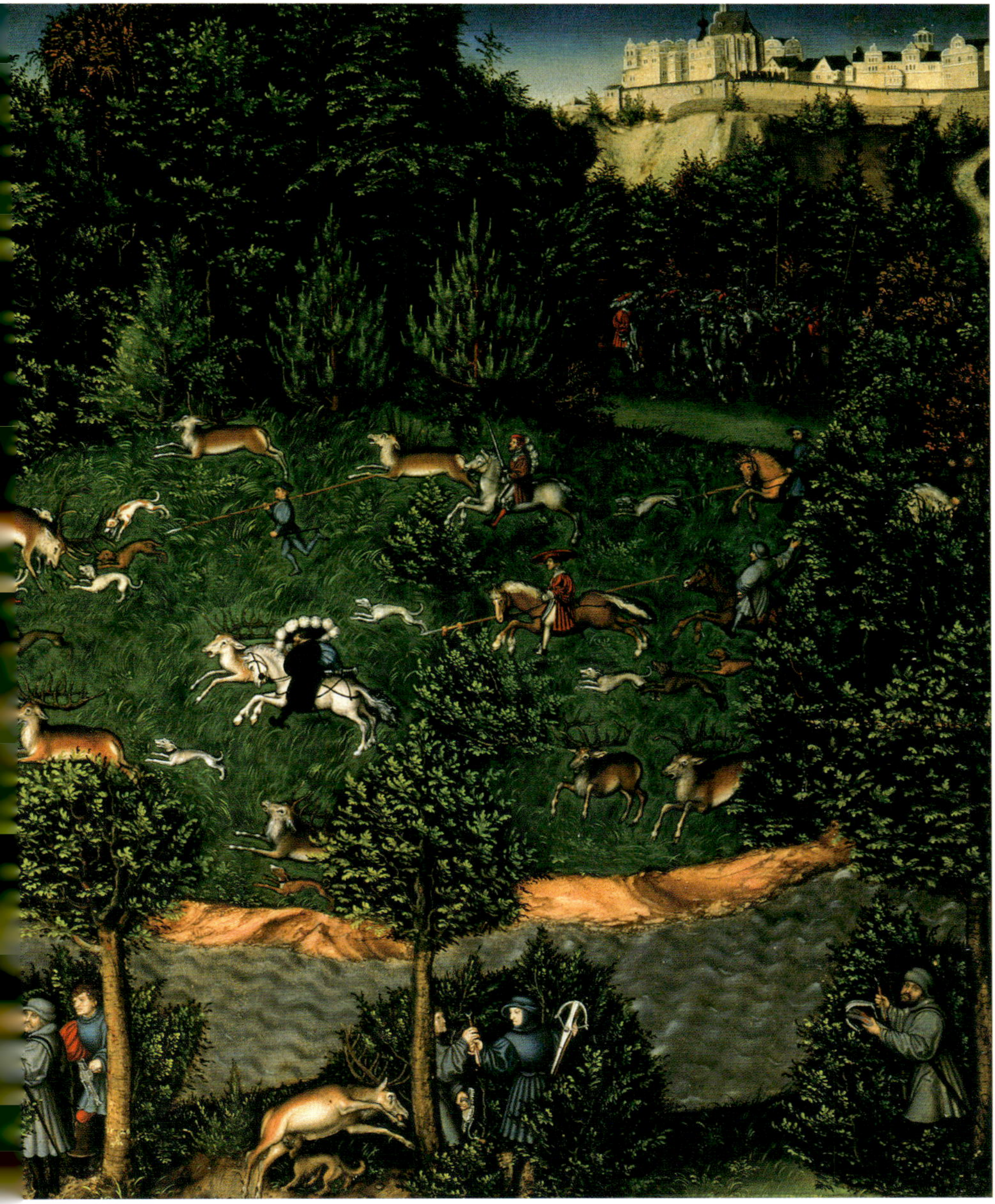

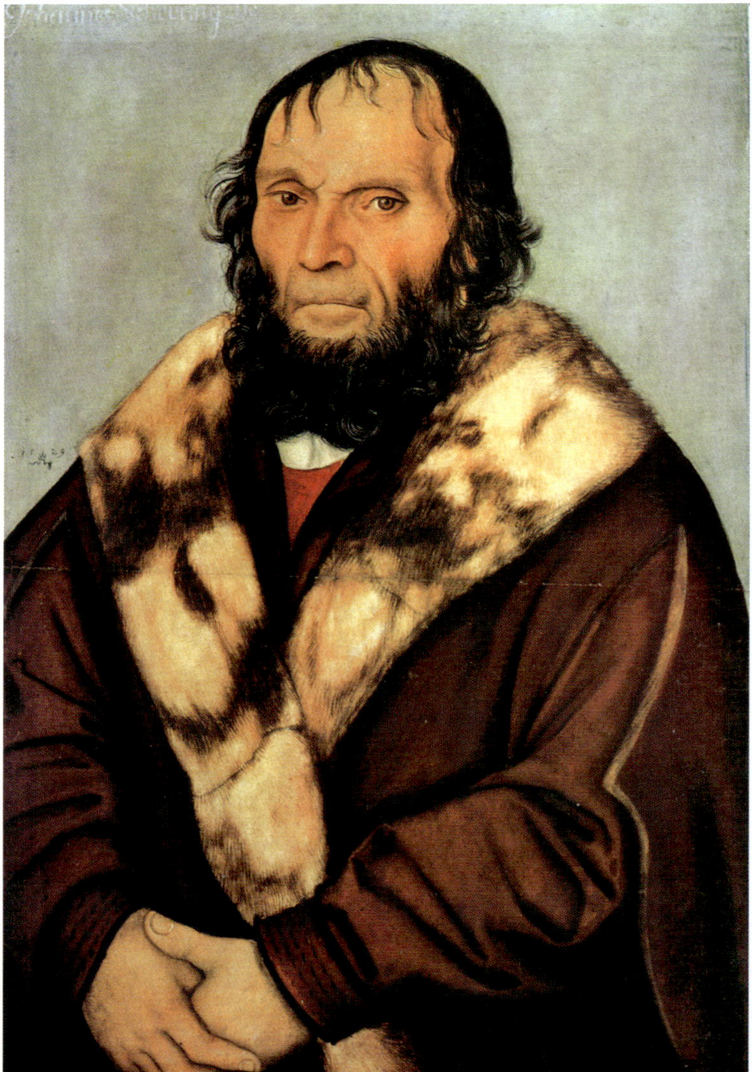

Dr Johannes Scheyring, 1529.
Oil on panel, 52 x 33 cm.
Brussels, Musee des Beaux Arts.

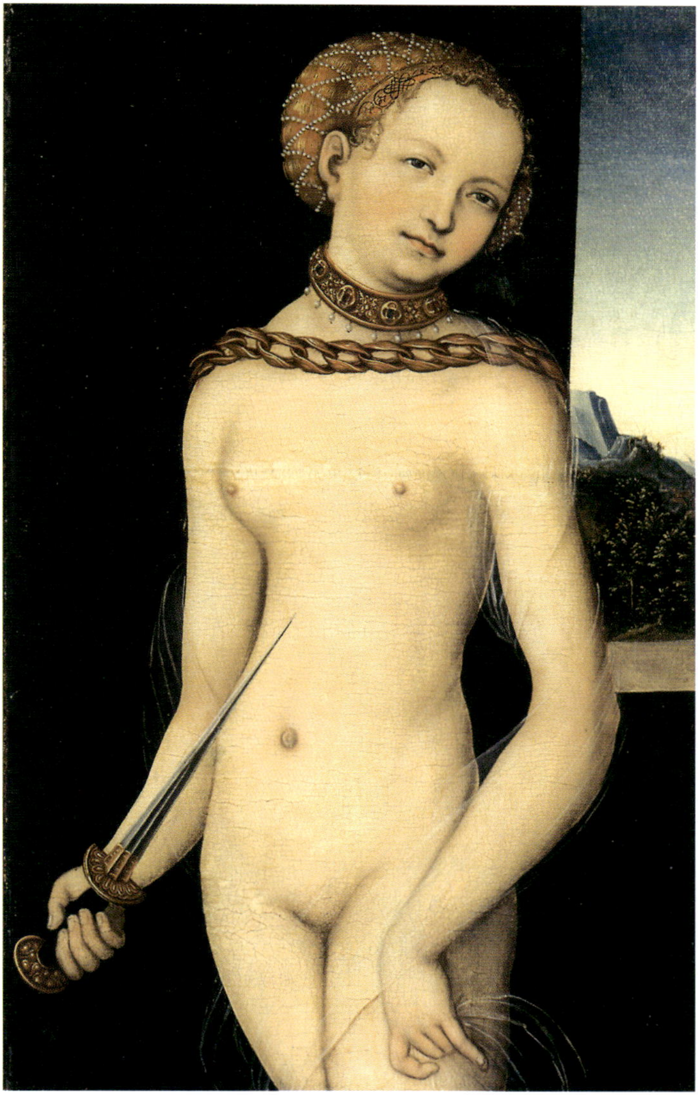

Lucretia, 1529.
Oil on panel, 56.5 x 38 cm.
Potsdam, Stiftung Preußische Schlösser und Gärten, Berlin-Brandenburg.

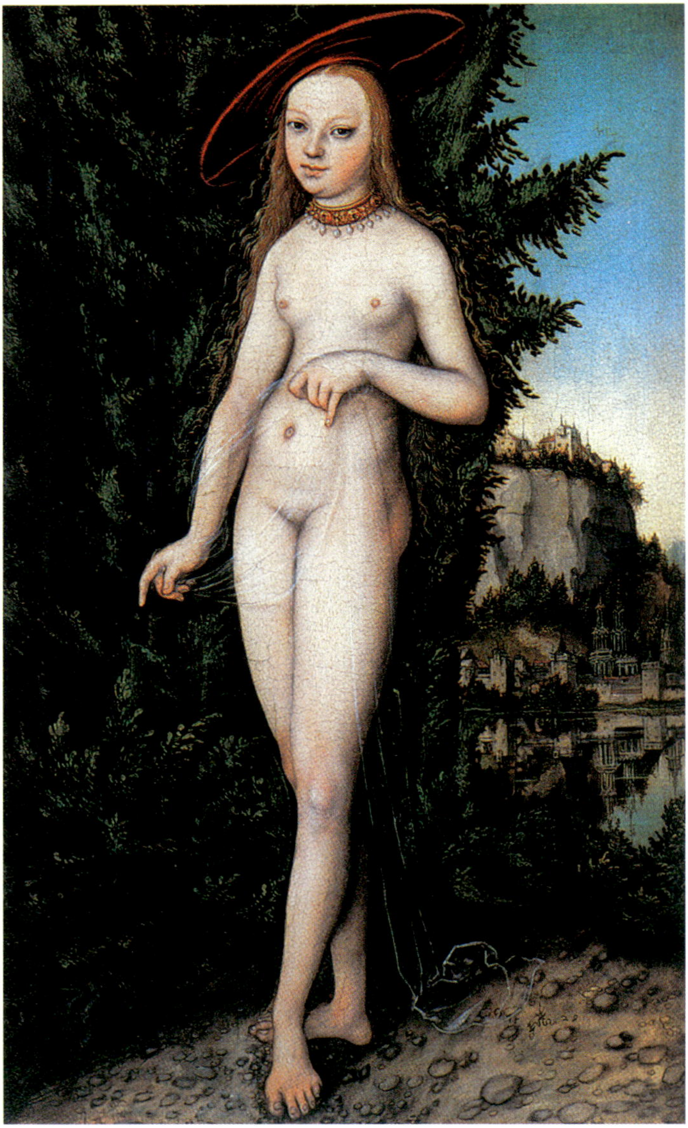

Venus, 1529.
Oil on panel, 38 x 25 cm.
Paris, Louvre.

1530

☐ For the Diet of Augsburg, which was held by Emperor Charles V in person, Philipp Melanchthon wrote a Protestant justification at the request of the future Elector of Saxony, John Frederick I, and defended the Lutheran Reformation (the 'Augsburg Confession').

Luther was not present in Augsburg as he feared for his life as a heretic who had been excommunicated and declared an outlaw; all the more so since his great supporter Frederick the Wise (+1525) had died. He spent the time between April and October at the Veste in Coburg. In that way, he was able to take part by letter in the discussions in Augsburg from the southernmost point of the Elector's territories.

However, the Emperor condemned Protestant teachings, reaffirmed the Edict of Worms and demanded that the estates of the Empire enforce the edict.

☐ Around 1530, approximately 500 people belonged to the full court of the Elector of Saxony.

☐ *The Chronicle of the Saxons and Thurinigians*, written by Georg Spalatin around 1530 and illustrated by artists from Cranach's workshop, probably in Wittenberg, was one of the last illustrated manuscripts from the heyday of Old German art. In addition to his duties as tutor to the princes and librarian, Spalatin, as a court historiographer, had been given the long-term task by the Elector of researching into the history of Saxony.

☐ The Latin inscription on the painting *Venus with Cupid Stealing Honey* reads in translation: 'The young Cupid was stealing honey from a hive when he was stung on his finger by a bee. Such is the situation for us: the brief and transient pleasures for which we strive are accompanied by miserable pain which hurts us'.

In a poem entitled *The Honey Thief* from the 3rd century, the Greek poet Theocritus described how Cupid complained to his mother Venus about the bee stings he had received after stealing honey from a beehive. Cupid asked how such a small creature could hurt him so much. Venus laughed and explained that the effect was comparable to the wounds that he himself had inflicted on others when he had shot at them with his arrows and caused pain to them.

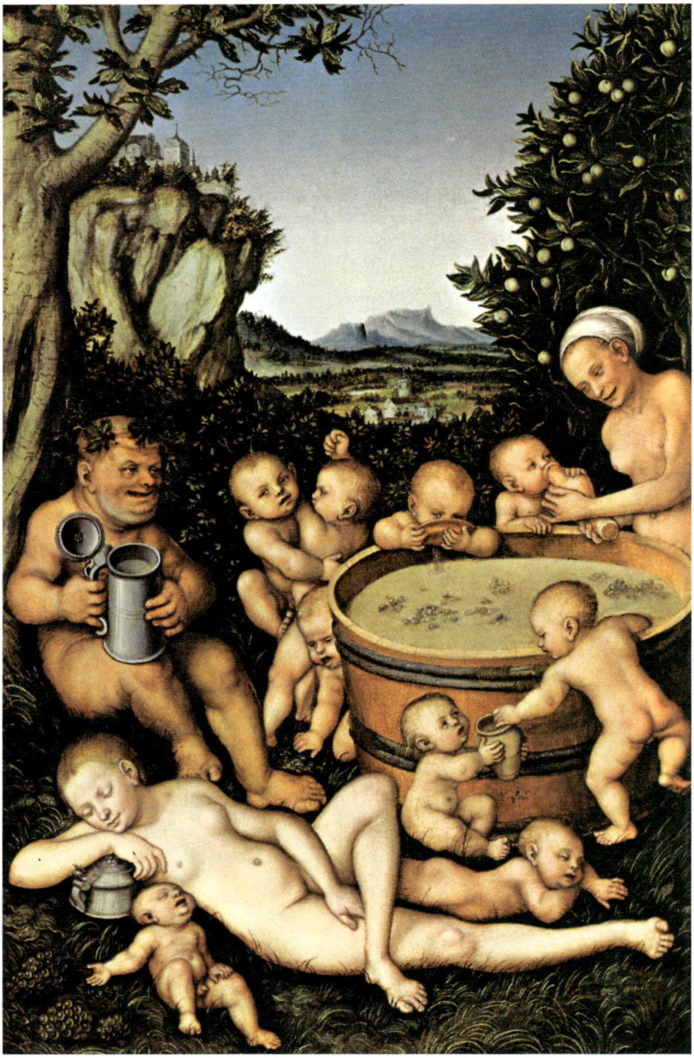

Bacchus at the Wine Tub,
1530.
Oil on beech wood,
59 x 39.5 cm.
Private collection.

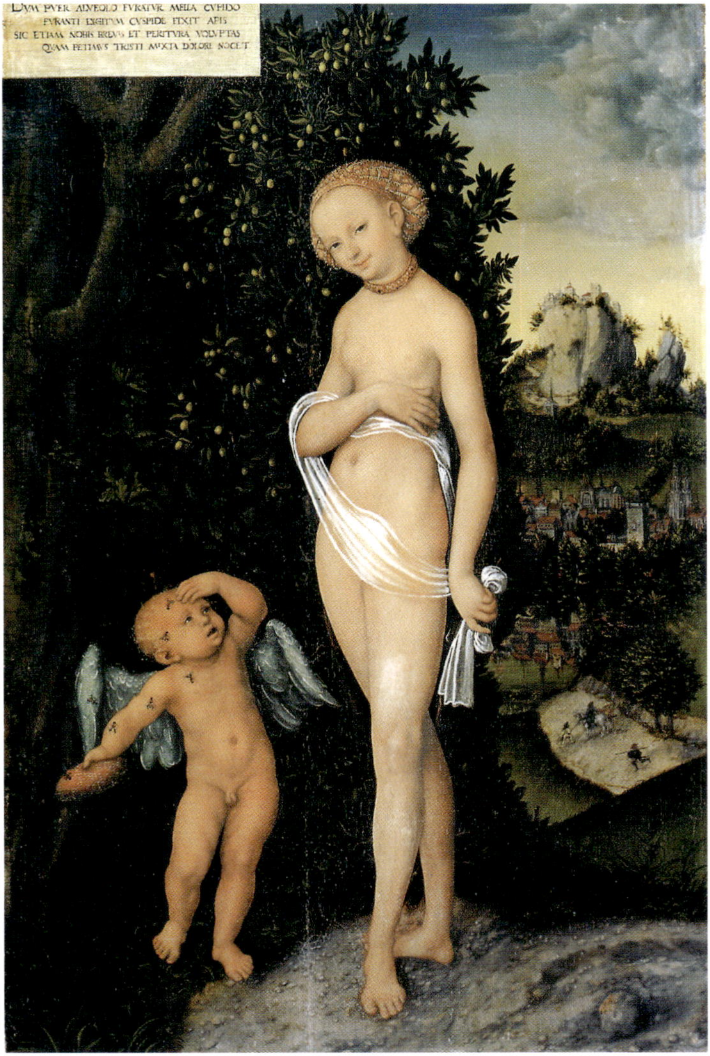

Venus with Cupid Stealing Honey, 1530.
Oil on panel, 58 x 38 cm.
Copenhagen, Statens Museum for Kunst.

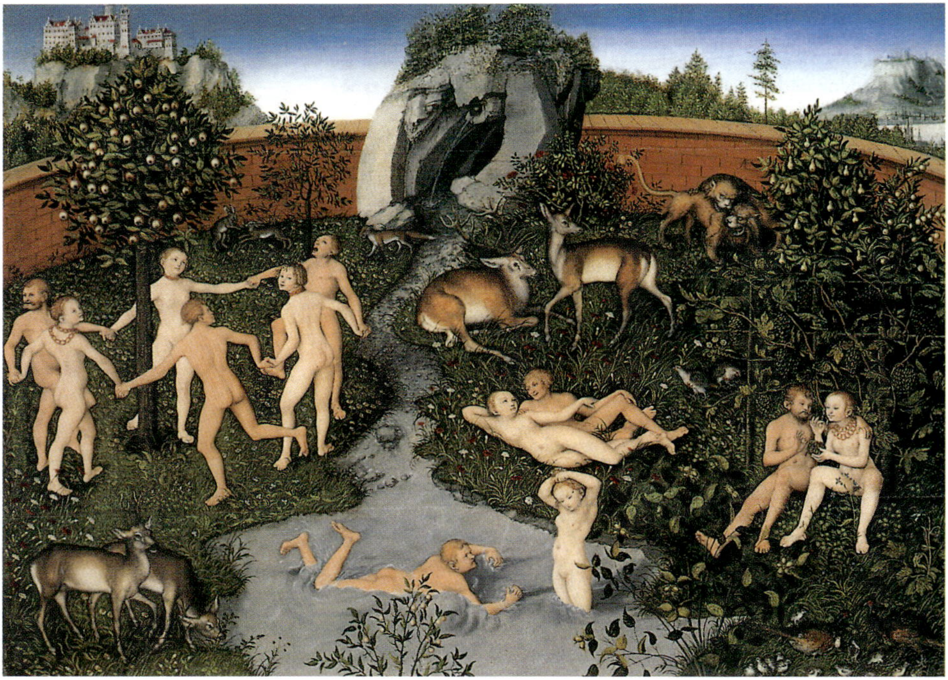

The Golden Age, around 1530.
Oil on panel, 75 x 105 cm.
Oslo, Nationalgalerie.

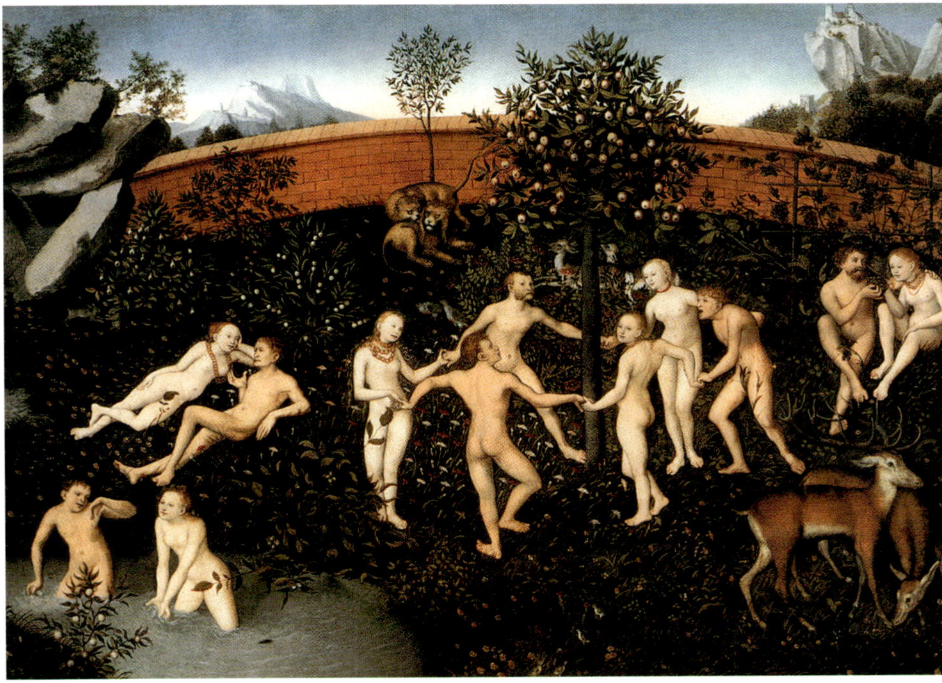

The Golden Age, around 1530.
Oil on panel, 73.5 x 105.5 cm.
Munich, Bayerische Staatsgemäldesammlungen.

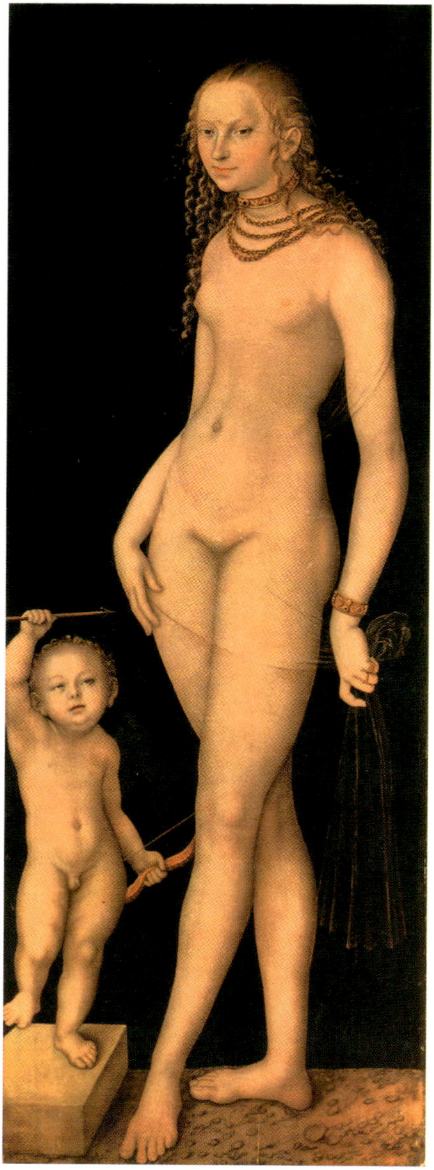

Venus and Cupid, around 1530.
Oil on lime wood, 165 x 60 cm.
Berlin, Staatliche Museen.

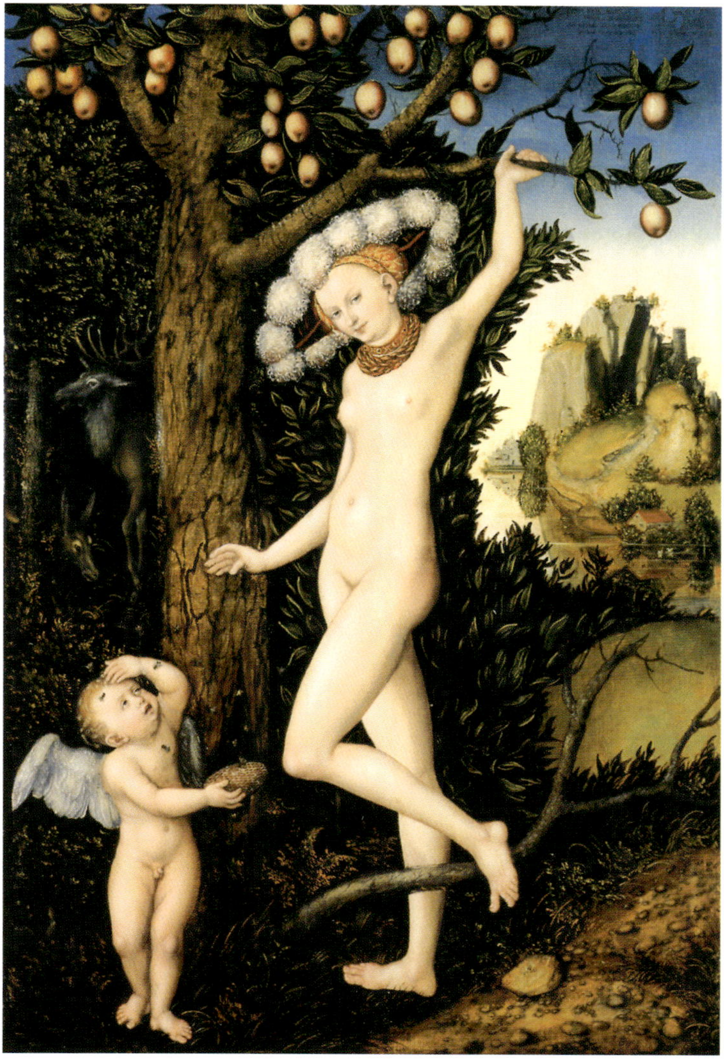

Venus and Cupid, around 1530.
Oil on panel, 82 x 55.8 cm.
London, The National Gallery.

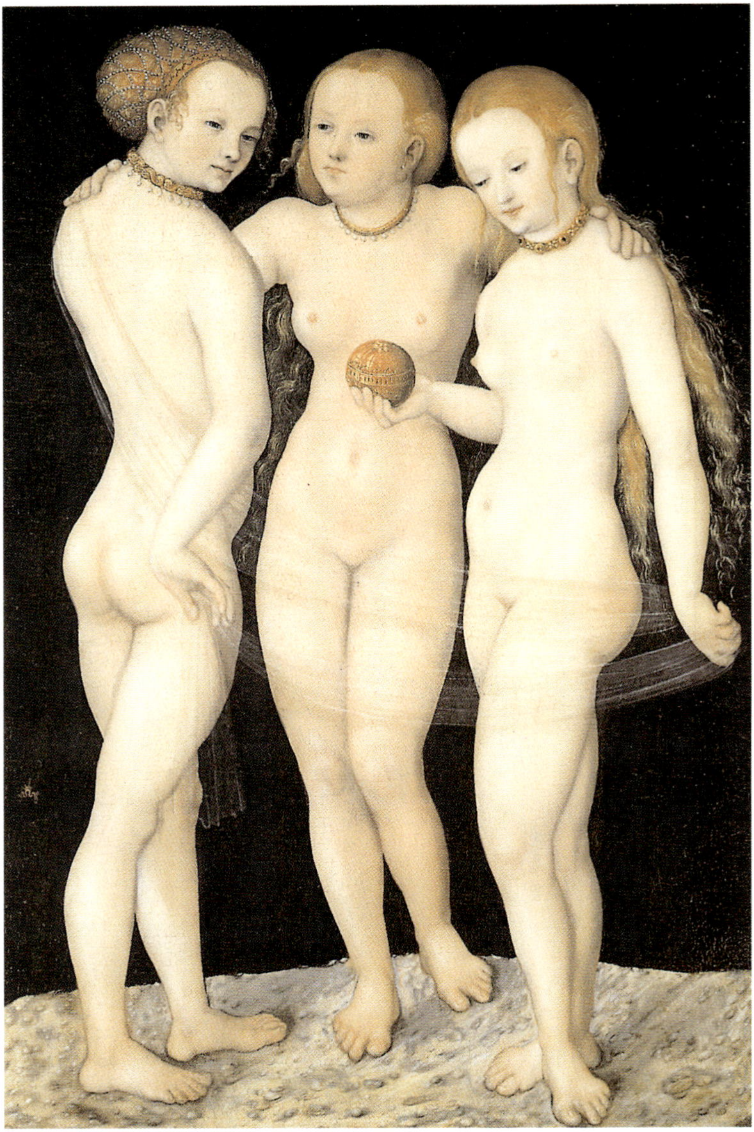

The Three Graces, around 1530.
Oil on panel, 57.5 x 38 cm.
Private collection.

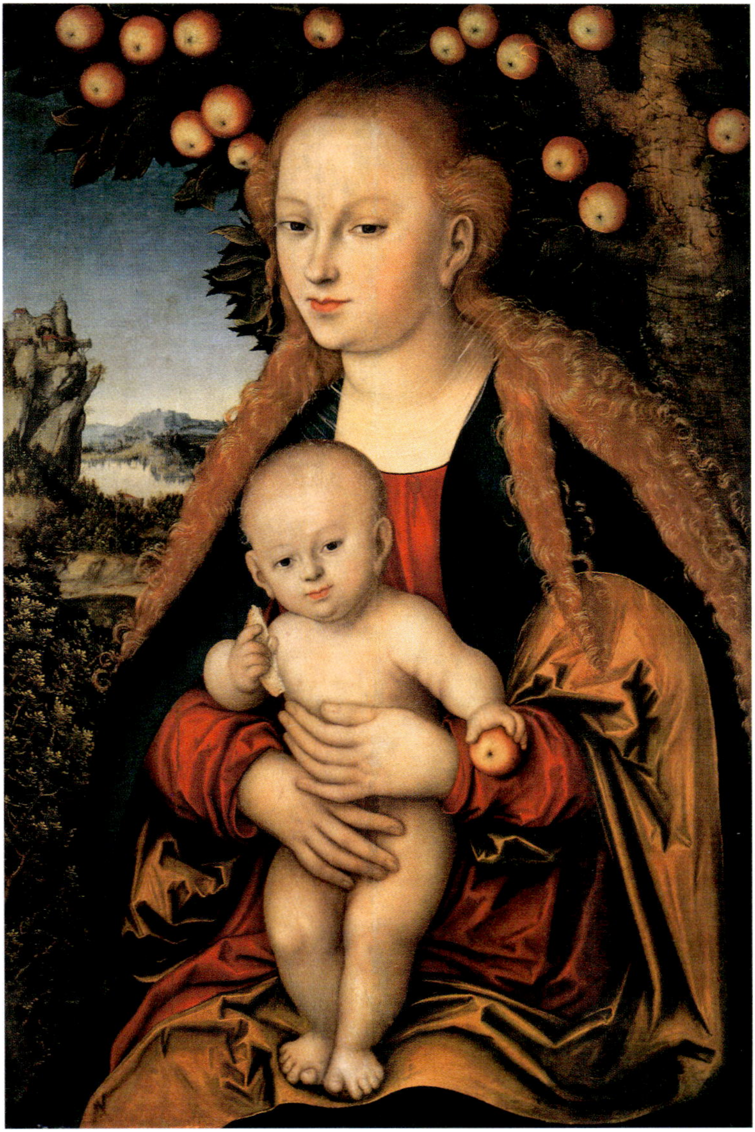

Virgin and Child under an Apple Tree, around 1530.
Panel transferred to canvas, 87 x 59 cm.
St Petersburg, Hermitage.

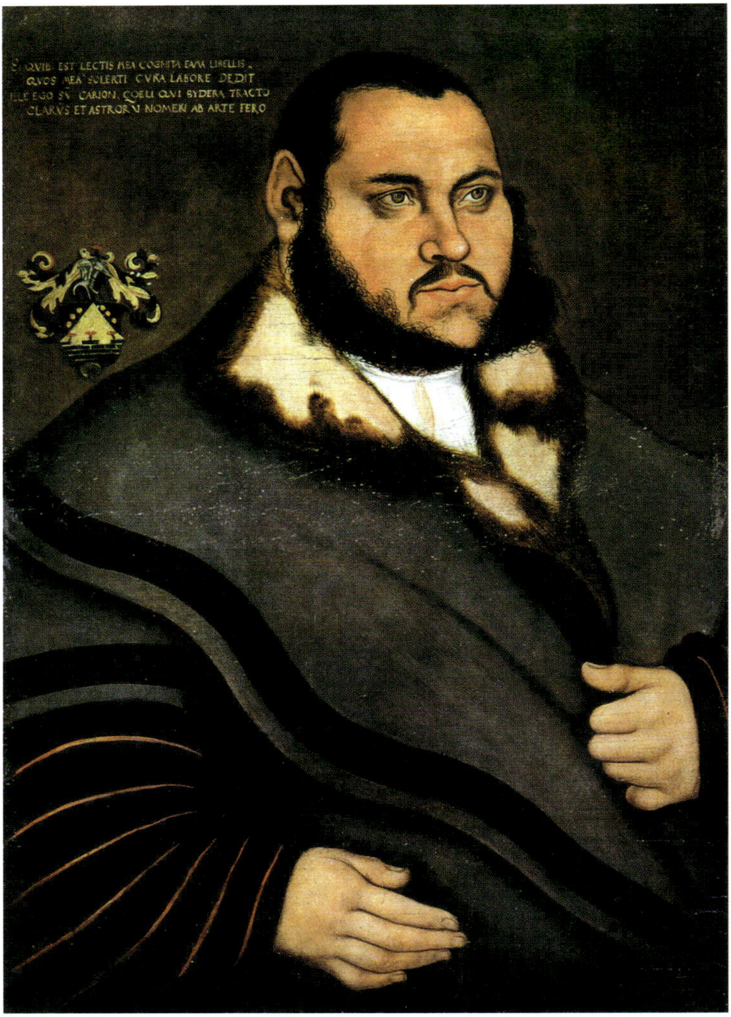

Johannes Carion, around 1530.
Oil on beech wood, 52 x 37 cm.
Berlin, Deutsche Staatsbibliothek.

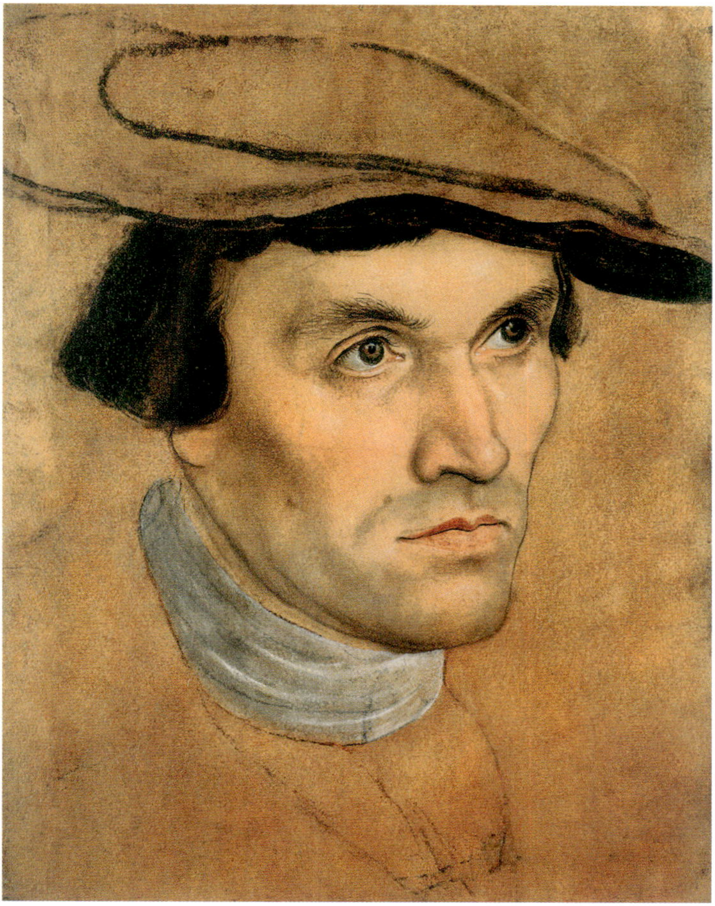

Clean-Shaven Man with a Broad-Rimmed Beret, approx. 1530–40.
Oil on paper, 26.2 x 19.9 cm.
Malibu, J. Paul Getty Museum.

1531

□ Lucas Cranach was paid for work carried out on the fortifications of Wittenberg.

□ Melanchthon fostered contact with Johannes Carion, the astronomer and advisor to the Elector Joachim I of Brandenburg.

□ On 27.02.1531, the mainly Protestant dukes and towns formed an alliance known as the Schmalkaldic League. The purpose of the alliance was to defend the Protestant cause against the threat to stamp out Lutheranism (the imperial summation of the Diet of Augsburg 1530). Those involved in the League were Landgrave Philipp I of Hesse, Elector John Frederick I of Saxony, the Dukes Philipp of Brunswick-Grubenhaben and Ernst of Brunswick-Lüneburg, the Counts of Anhalt-Bernburg and Mansfeld, as well as three Lower and eight Upper German imperial cities. The constitution of 1533 declared the Landgrave of Hesse and the Elector of Saxony to be their leaders who, according to the decision of the League, were to lead the forces of the alliance into battle to defend the faith.

The political importance of the Schmalkaldic League grew as Württemberg was re-conquered and Duke Ulrich was returned to office (1534). The Schmalkaldic League became a power factor in Europe and grew into a partner in negotiations with the Emperor, the Pope and foreign powers.

However, the League was not united: the Electorate of Saxony shared the reluctance of Martin Luther to go to war and Hesse was weakened from 1540 onwards by the bigamy of Landgrave Philipp I and the difficulties which resulted from this bigamy for the legality of the Empire.

□ In the decree of Grimma on 17.07.1531, the Ernestine and Albertine lines agreed on a mutual use of the mines and confirmed at the same time that there would be a common currency for all the territories of Saxony.

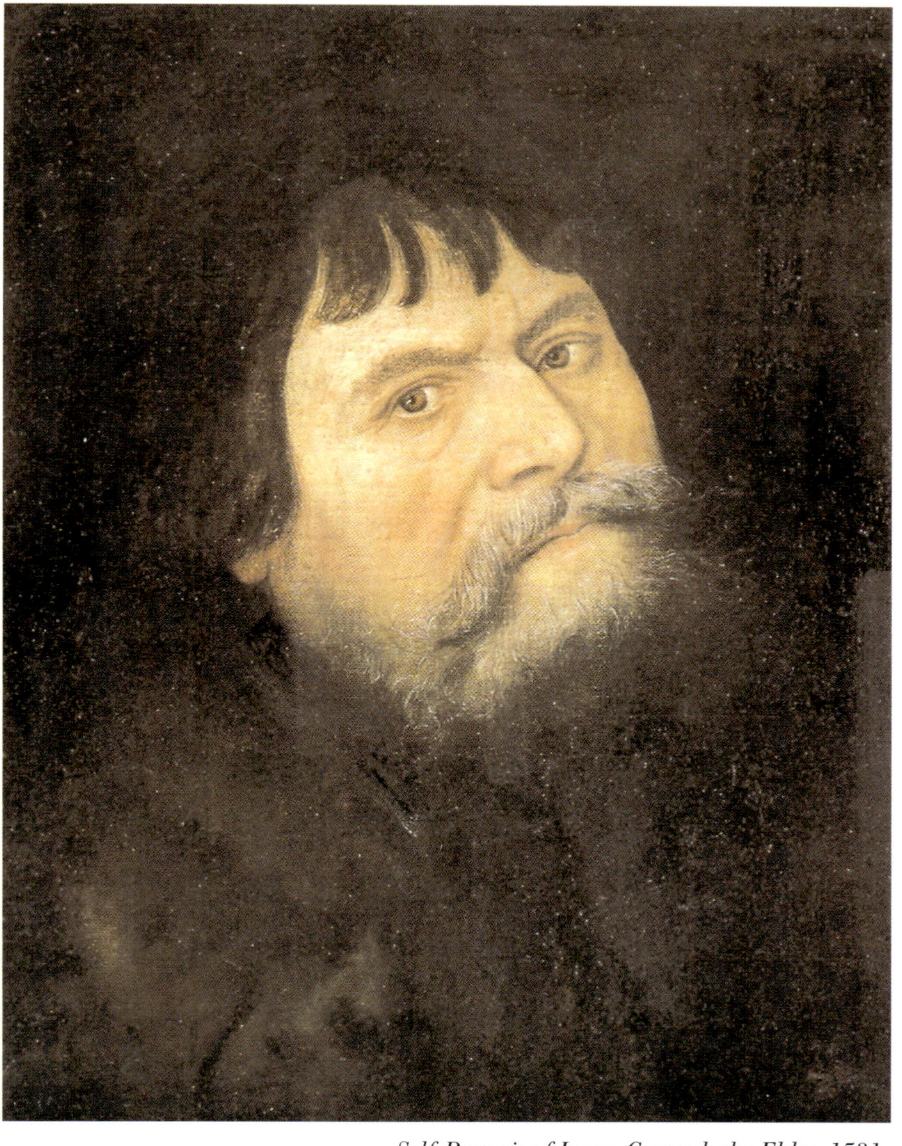

Self-Portrait of Lucas Cranach the Elder, 1531.
Oil on panel, 45.2 x 36 cm.
Koblenz, Schloss Stolzenfels.

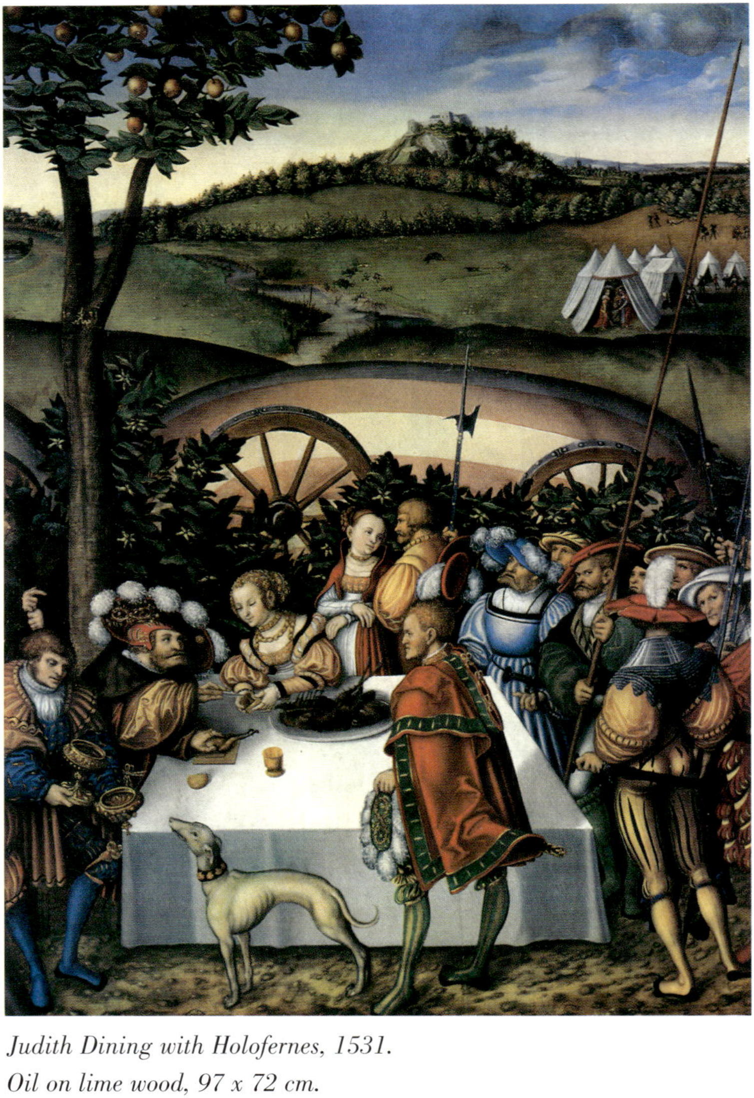

Judith Dining with Holofernes, 1531.
Oil on lime wood, 97 x 72 cm.
Gotha, Stiftung Schloss Friedenstein.

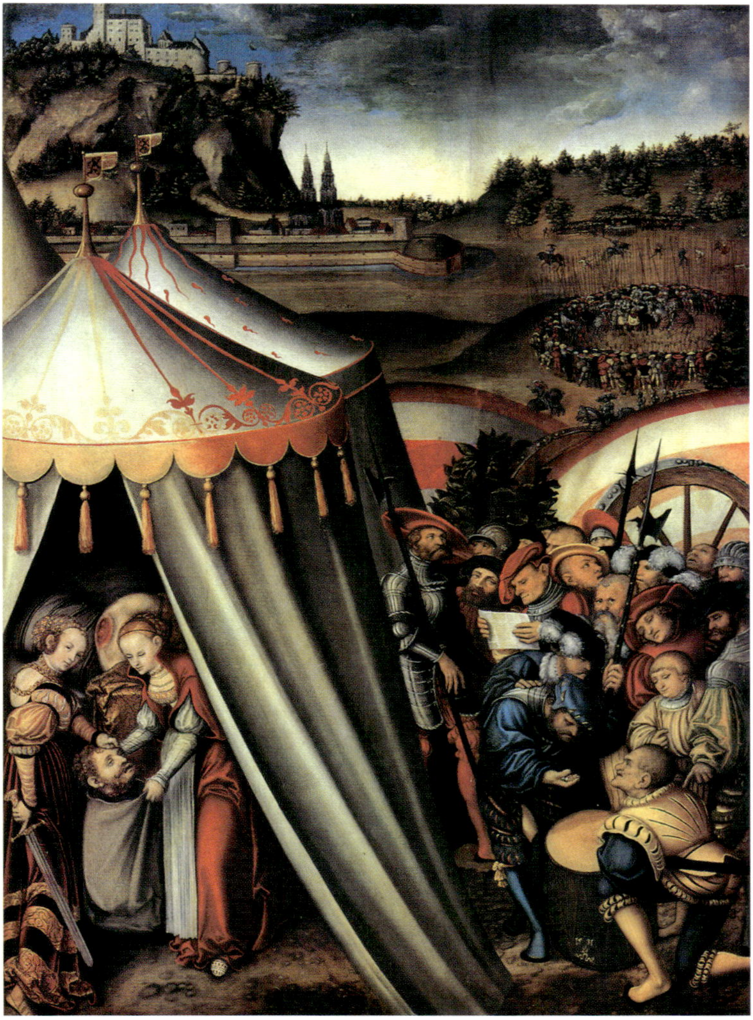

The Death of Holofernes, 1531.
Oil on lime wood, 97 x 72 cm.
Gotha, Stiftung Schloss Friedenstein.

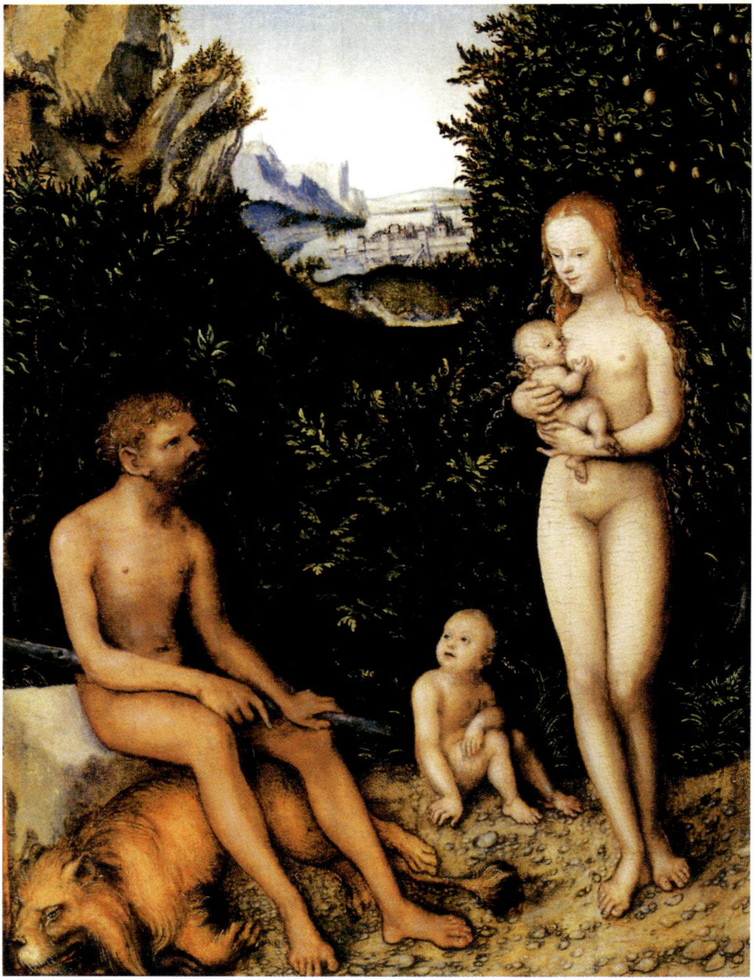

Faun and his Family with a Slain Lion, 1531.
Oil on panel, 44 x 34 cm.
Private collection.

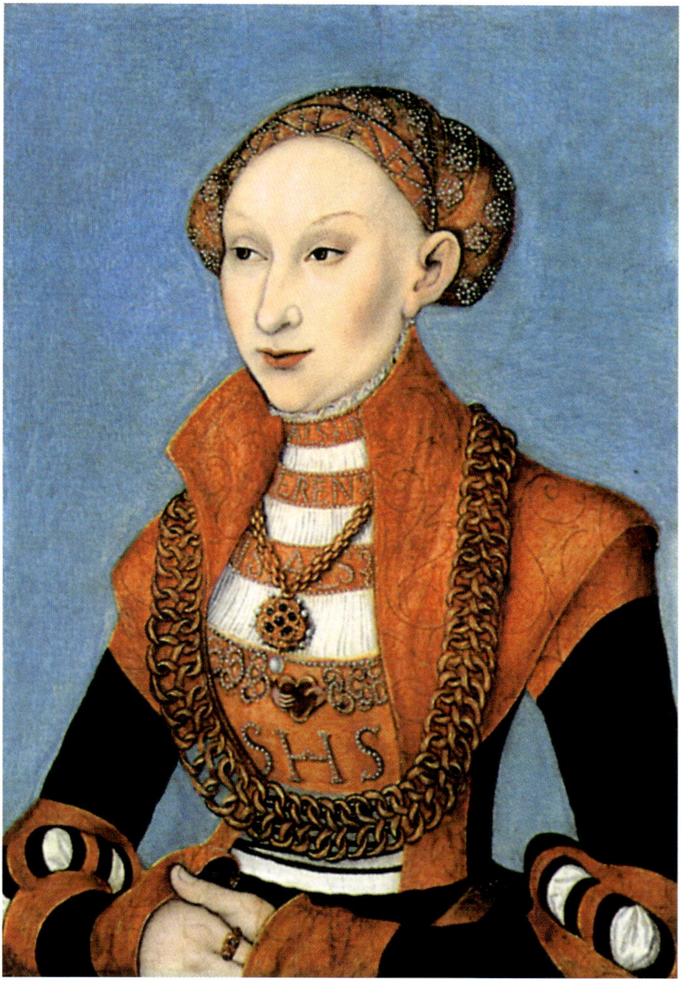

Electress Sybil of Saxony, Consort of John Frederick the Magnanimous, around 1531.
Oil on panel, 51.5 x 36 cm.
Private collection.

1532

□ Lucas Cranach was paid for painting work carried out on the arsenal and on the arrow slits and gates on the fortifications in Wittenberg.

□ Neither Emperor Charles V nor his brother King Ferdinand was willing to assert the Edict of Worms by force. When the Turks again attacked Hungary in 1532, they needed the help of the Protestant estates of the Empire and, by means of the religious Peace of Nuremberg (23.07.1532), bought themselves a ceasefire until the next general council, which was, however, only to take place in 1545 in Trent. The Peace of Nuremberg granted the freedom of religion until then.

An unusually large army of both Catholics and Protestants forced the Turks in the areas around Graz and Budapest to withdraw.

□ John the Steadfast, Elector of Saxony, died on 16.08.1532 at the age of 64 in Schweinitz Castle on the Schwarzer Elster river, 26 kilometres east of Wittenberg and 8 kilometres north of Lochau. He was laid to rest, like his brother Frederick the Wise had been, in the Castle Church in Wittenberg. The new Elector of Saxony was his 29-year-old son from his first marriage, John Frederick I the Magnanimous.

□ The 60-year-old Lucas Cranach was retained in his position as court painter. In the context of the new generation at court, the picture *Hercules with Omphale* was painted which was intended to inspire virtue in the new ruler.

□ The change of ruler in the person of Duke John Frederick I was accompanied by a flood of pictures: in 1533, a payment was made for the delivery of 60 pendants bearing portraits of his two predecessors, the Electors Frederick the Wise and John the Steadfast.

Portraits of Luther and Melanchthon were also produced in great numbers by Cranach's workshop. Cranach was in a position to respond to the demand; his accounts, as well as the large number of existent versions from his workshop, reveal that pictures such as *Charity* or *Lucretia* were produced in series.

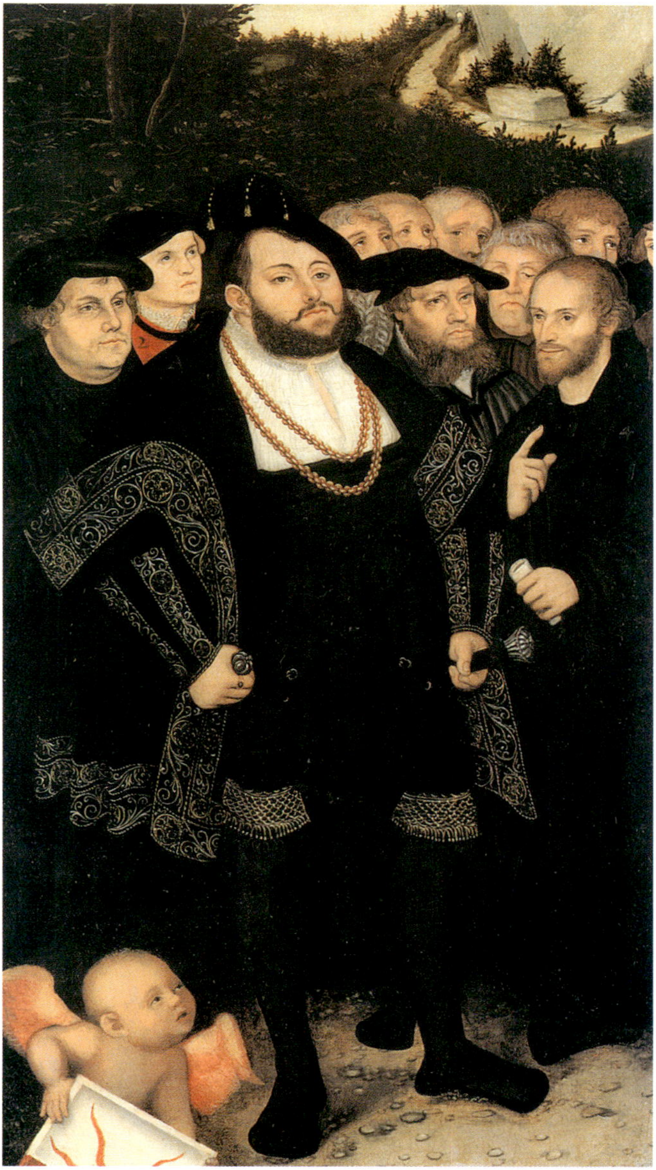

Elector John Frederick the Magnanimous with the Reformers, approx. 1532–39. Oil on panel, 72.8 x 39.7 cm. Toledo, Museum of Art.

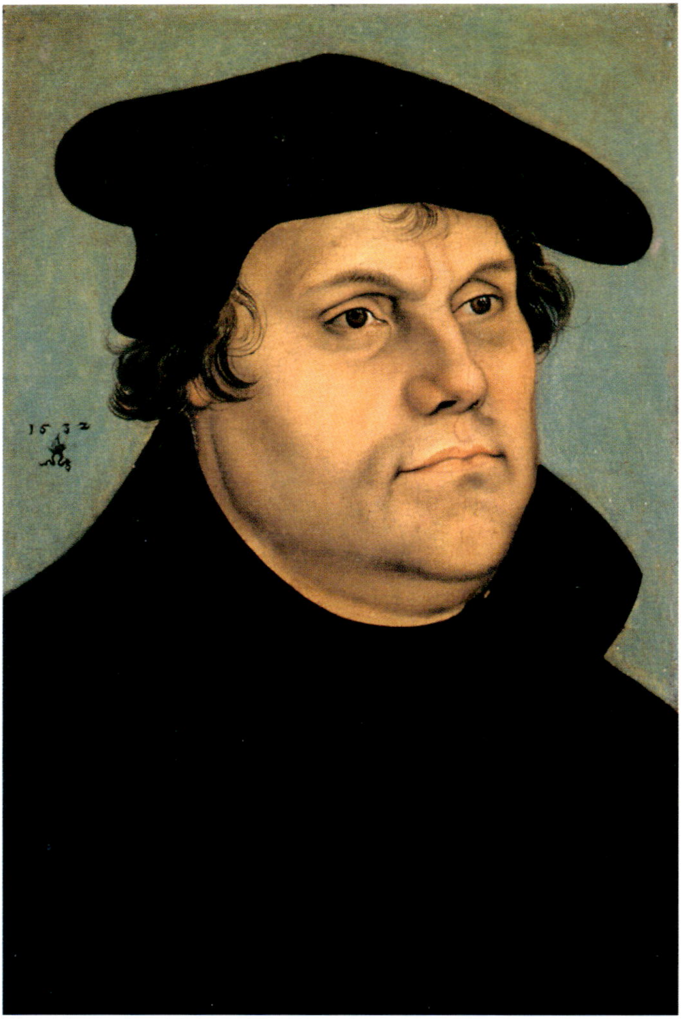

Martin Luther, 1532.
Oil on panel, 37 x 23.5 cm.
Copenhagen, Statens Museum for Kunst.

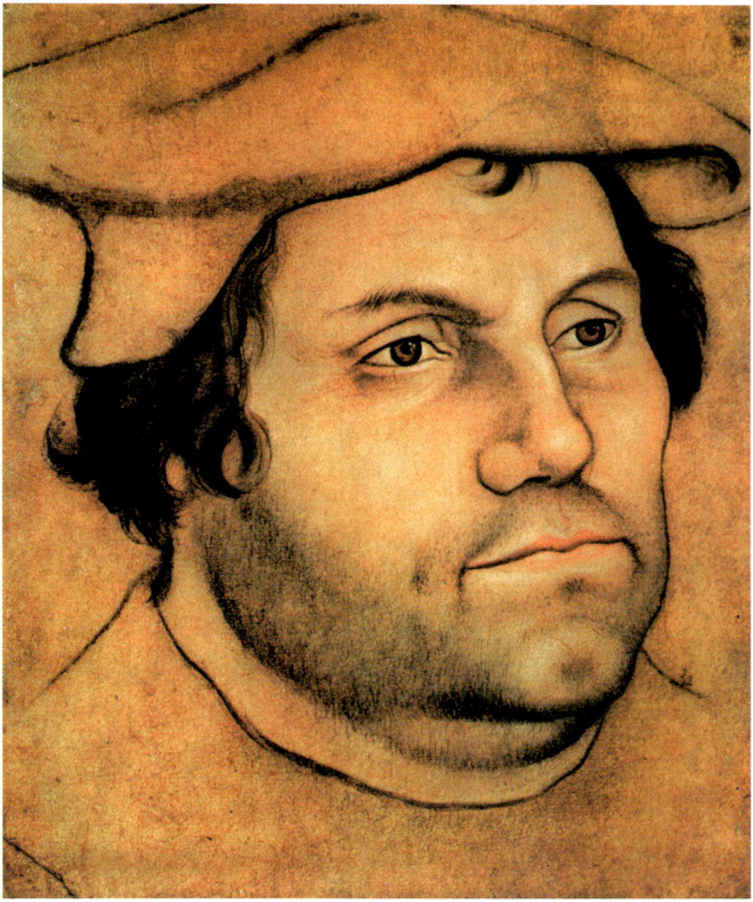

Martin Luther, around 1532.
Watercolour on vellum, 22 x 19 cm.
Private collection.

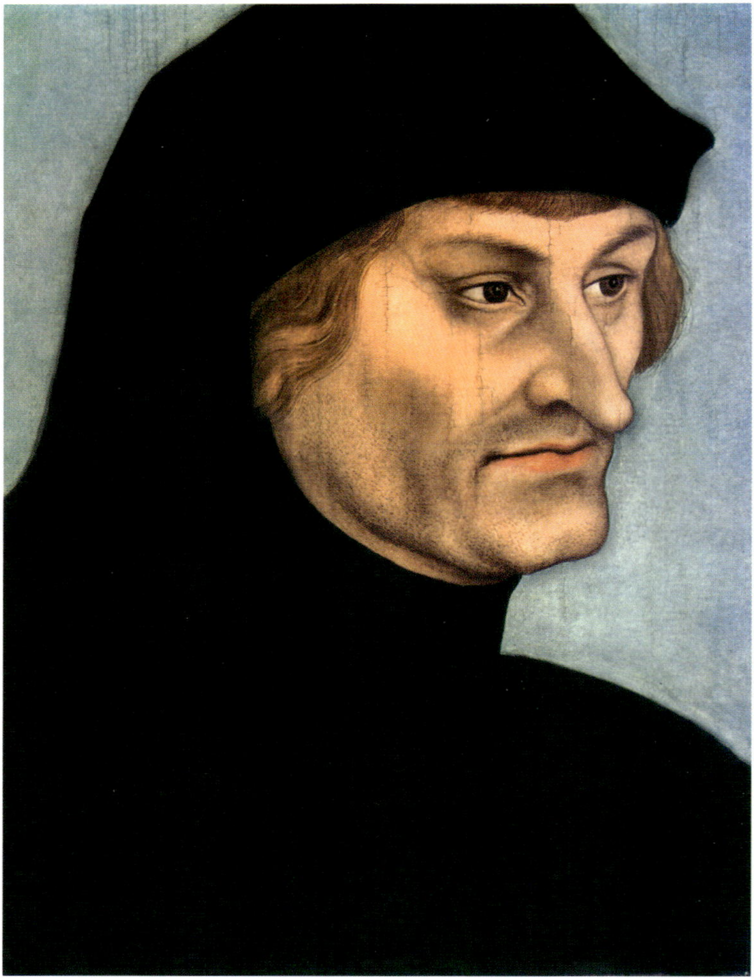

Rudolph Agricola, around 1532.
Oil on beech wood, 30 x 23 cm.
Munich, Bayerische Staatsgemäldesammlungen.

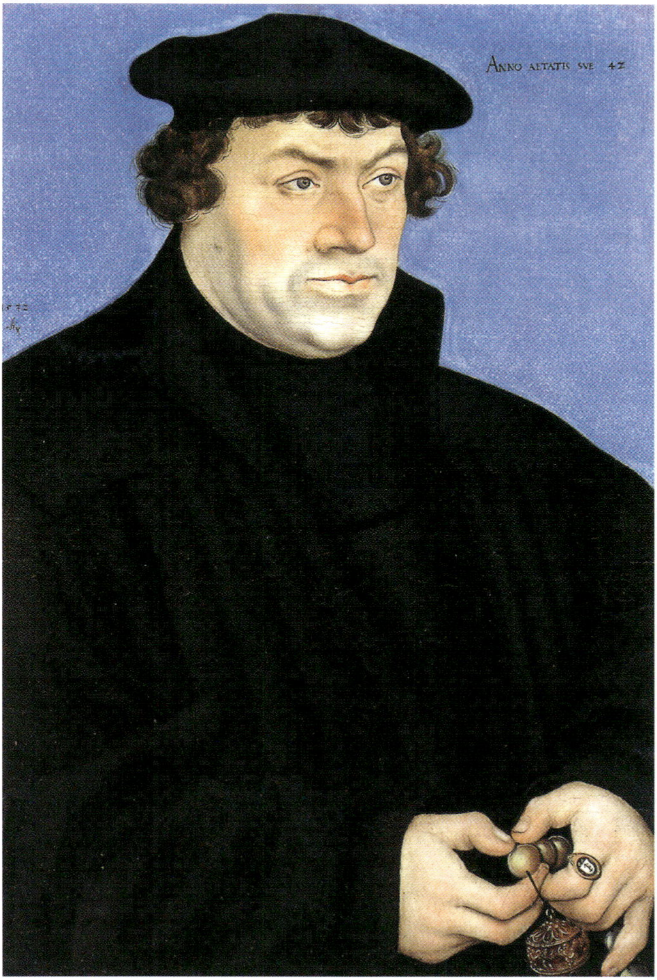

Johannes Bugenhagen, 1532.
Oil on panel, 54 x 38.5 cm.
Hamburg, Kirchenkreis Alt-Hamburg.

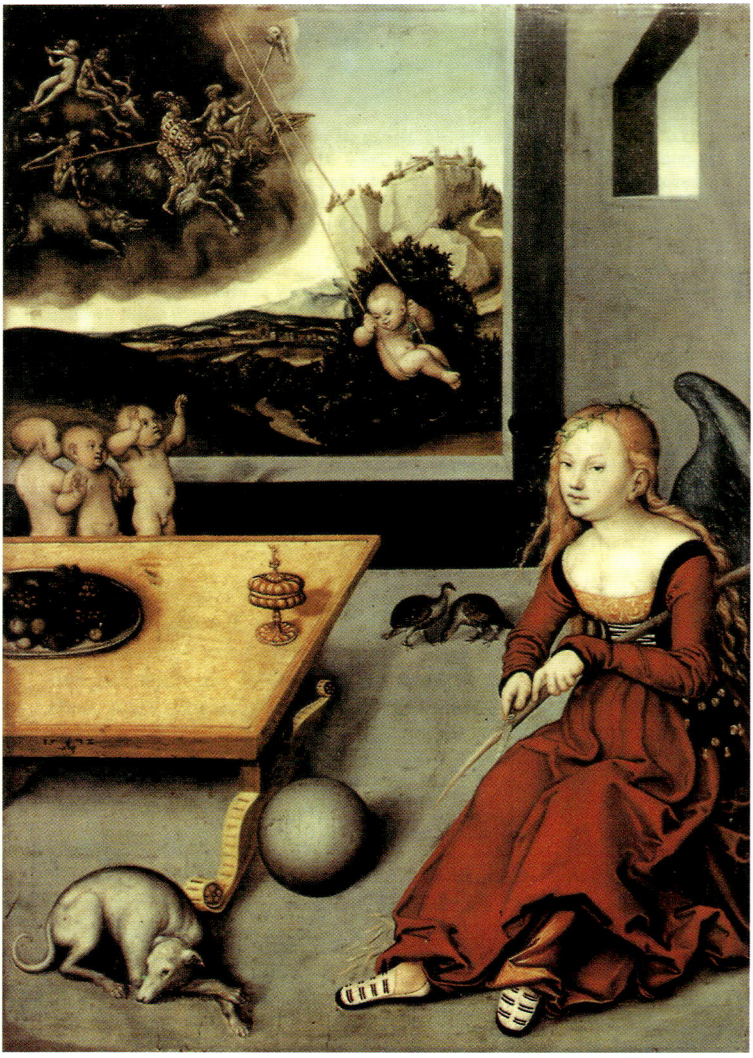

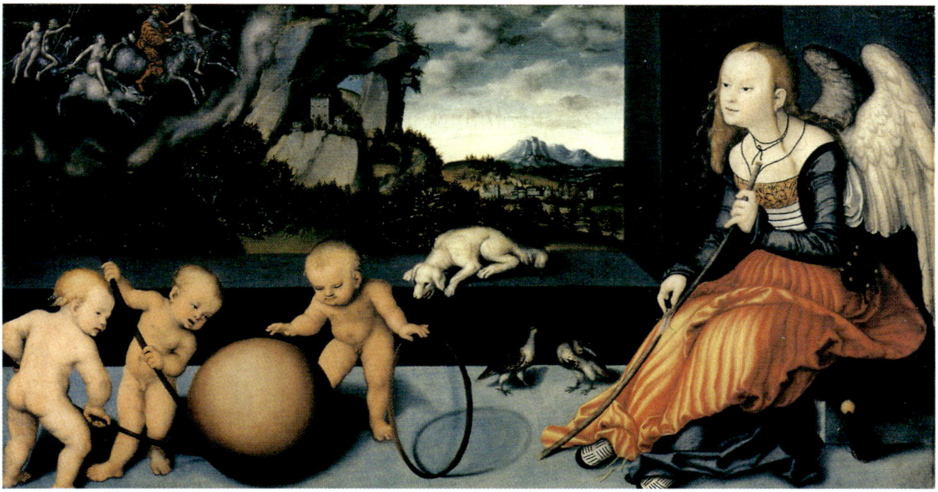

Melancholy, 1532.
Oil on panel, 51 x 97 cm.
Copenhagen, Statens Museum for Kunst.

Melancholy, 1532.
Oil on panel, 76.5 x 56 cm.
Private collection.

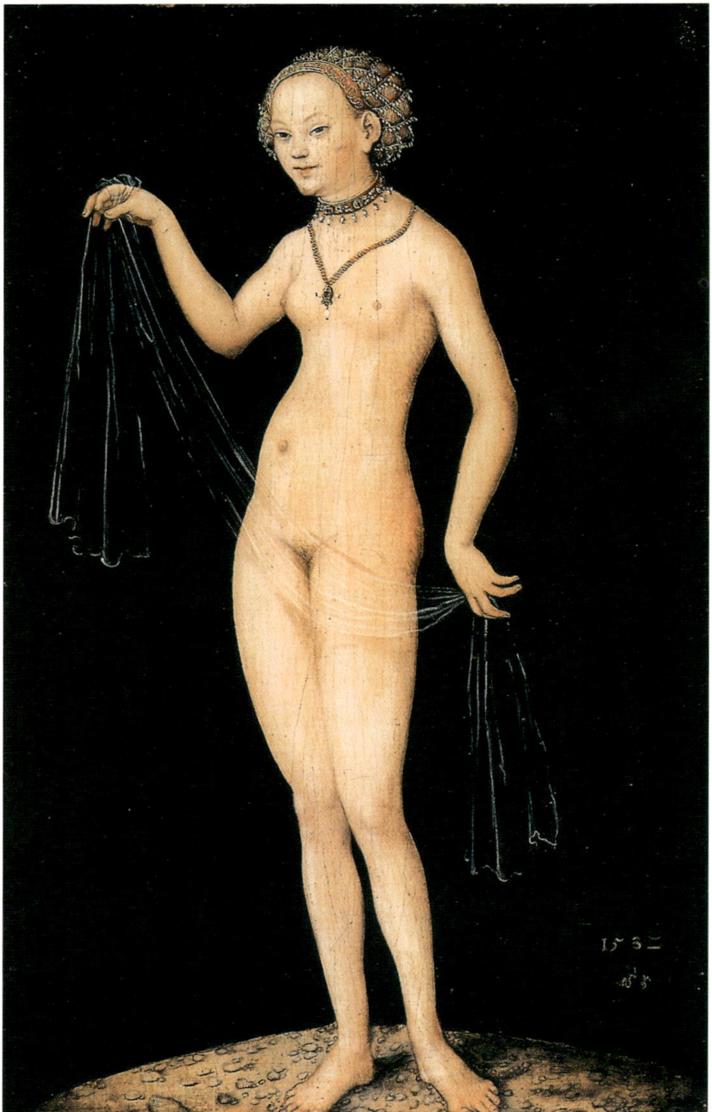

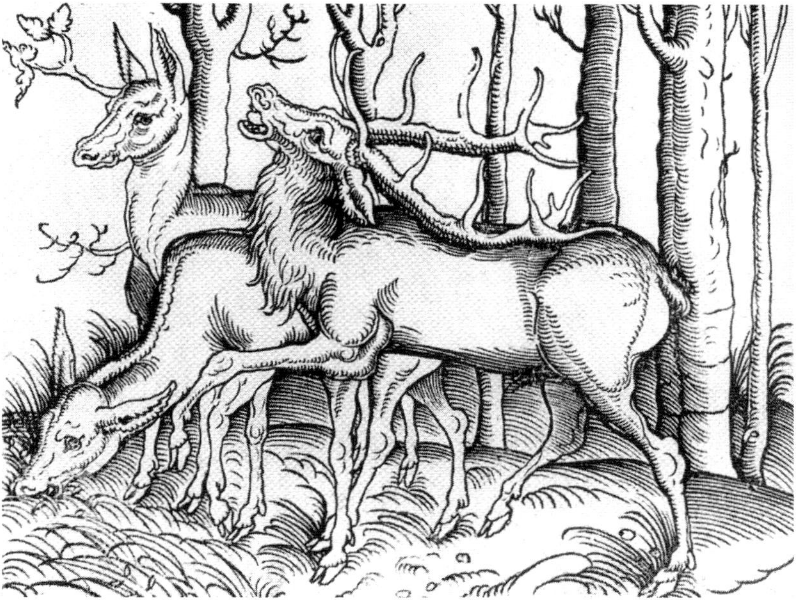

Stag with Two Deer, 1532.
Woodcut, 17.3 x 22.8 cm.
Gotha, Stiftung Schloss Friedenstein.

Venus, 1532.
Oil on panel, 37.9 x 24.6 cm.
Frankfurt, Städelsches Kunstinstitut.

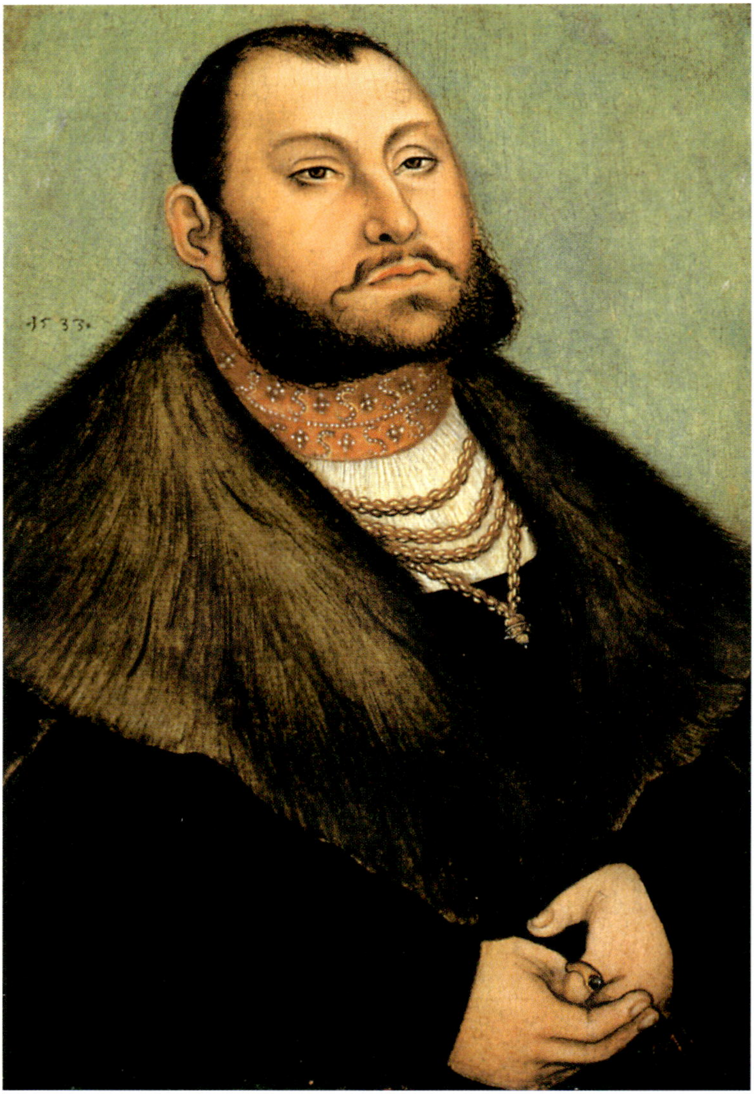

Elector John Frederick of Saxony, 1533.
Oil on panel, 20 x 14 cm.
Copenhagen, Statens Museum for Kunst.

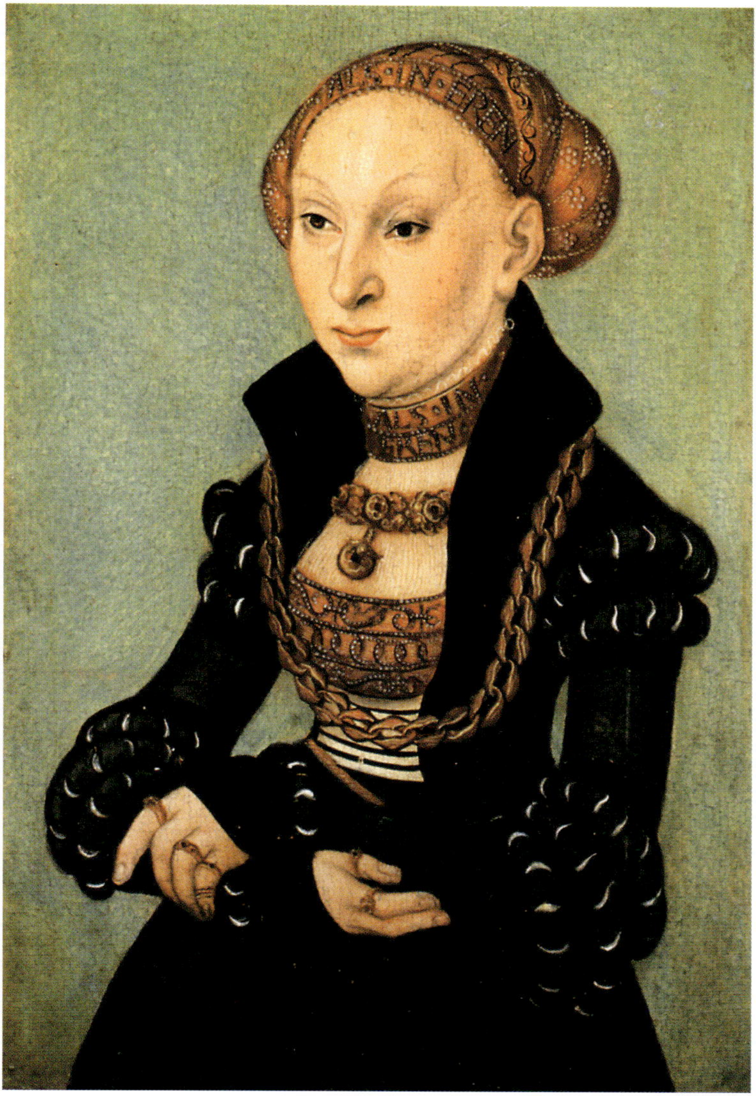

Electress Sybil of Saxony, around 1533.
Oil on panel, 20 x 14 cm.
Copenhagen, Statens Museum for Kunst.

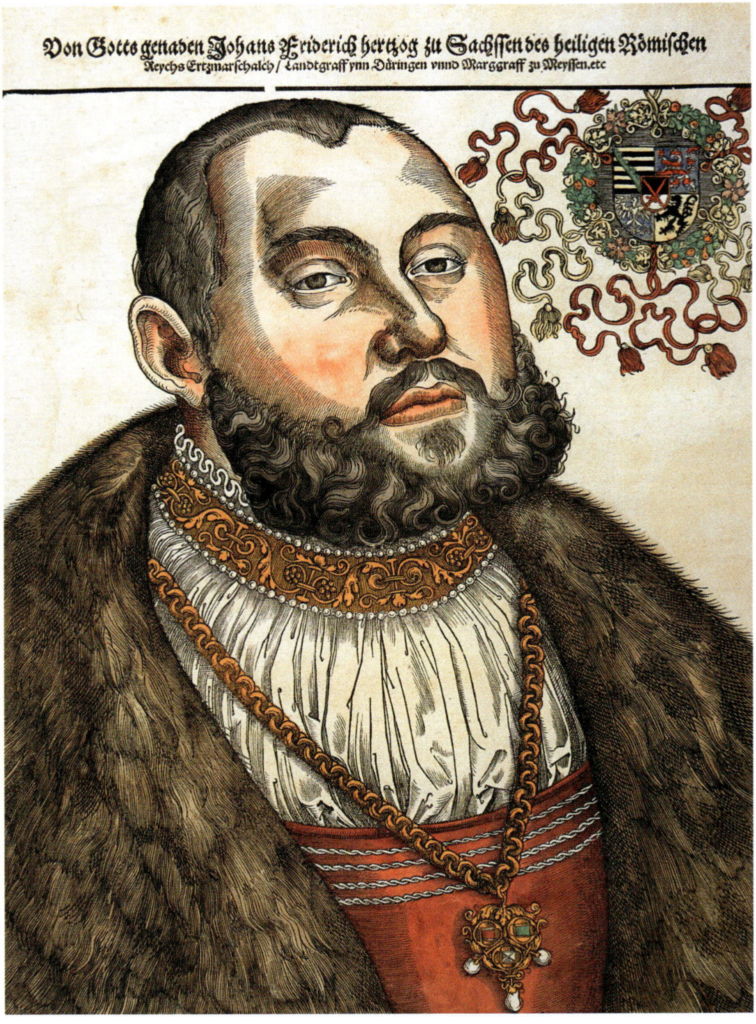

Elector John Frederick the Magnanimous of Saxony, around 1533.
Woodcut, 33 x 26.7 cm.
Gotha, Stiftung Schloss Friedenstein.

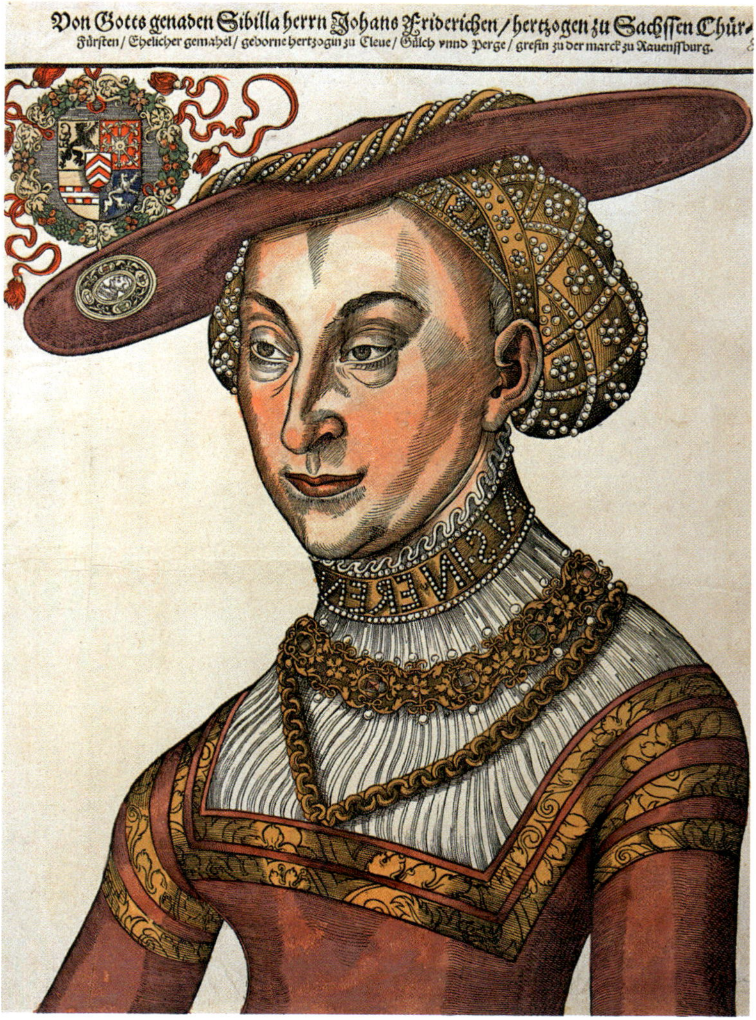

Electress Sybil of Saxony, around 1533.
Woodcut, 32.9 x 26.9 cm.
Gotha, Stiftung Schloss Friedenstein.

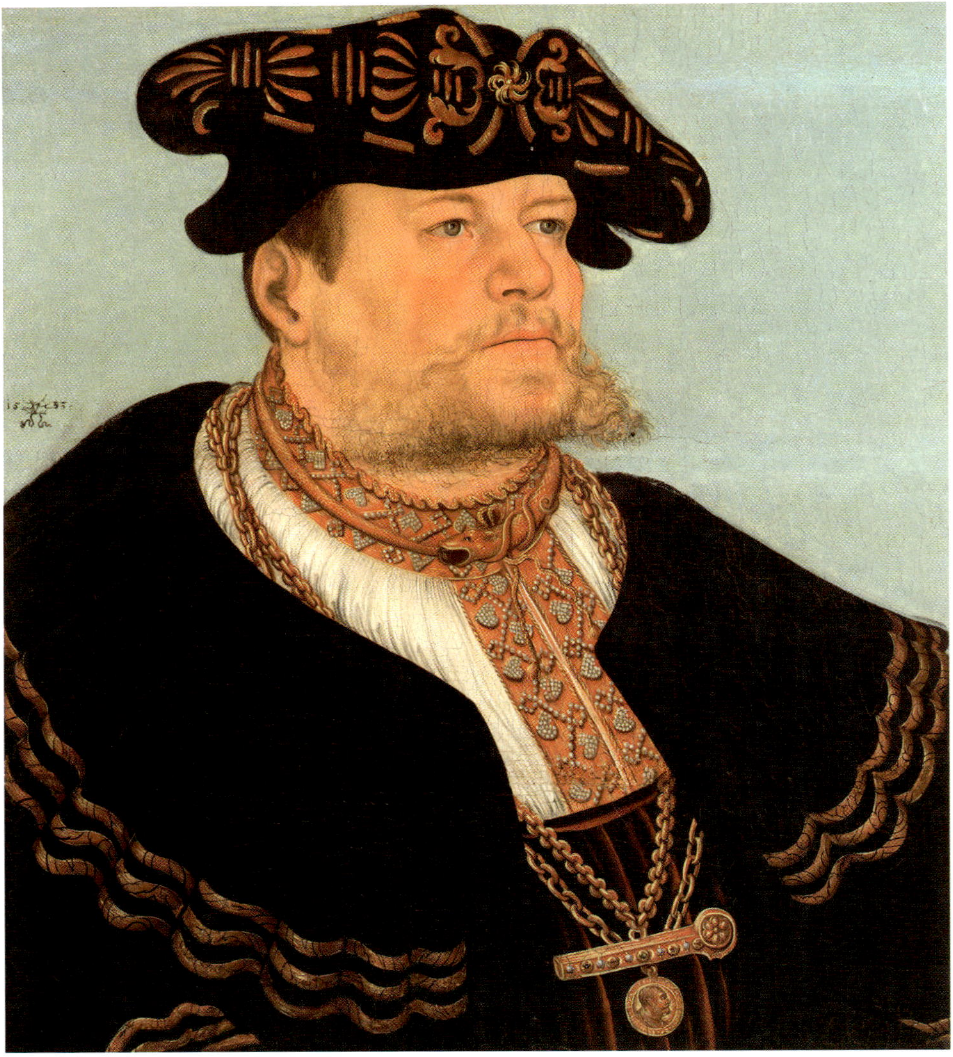

Chancellor Gregor Brück, 1533.
Oil on panel, 41 x 38 cm.
Nuremberg, Germanisches Nationalmuseum.

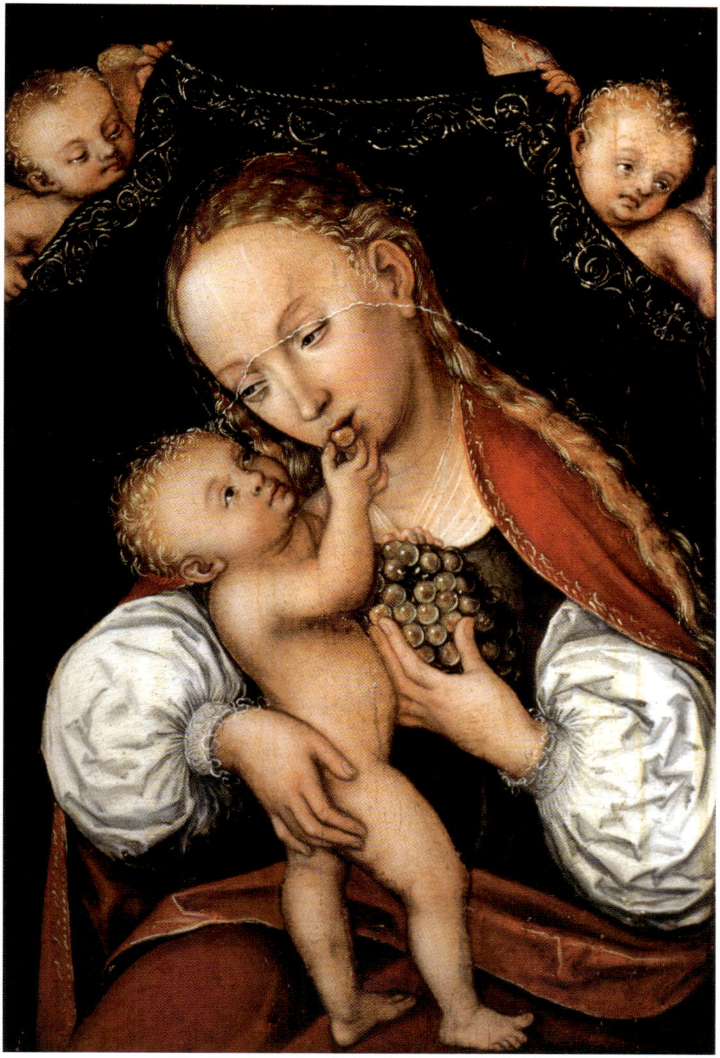

The Virgin in a Grape Arbour, (late 16th cent.).
Oil on panel, 34.3 x 50.8 cm.
Eisenach, Wartburg-Stiftung.

1534

□ Duke George of Saxony and Cardinal Albert summoned Philipp Melanchthon and others to Dresden to take part in a religious discussion. The Elector John Frederick I travelled there as well, as did Lucas Cranach. On this occasion, the Duke once again availed himself of the artist's services. A year later, Cranach painted a picture for Cardinal Albert with the motif *Hercules with Omphale*.

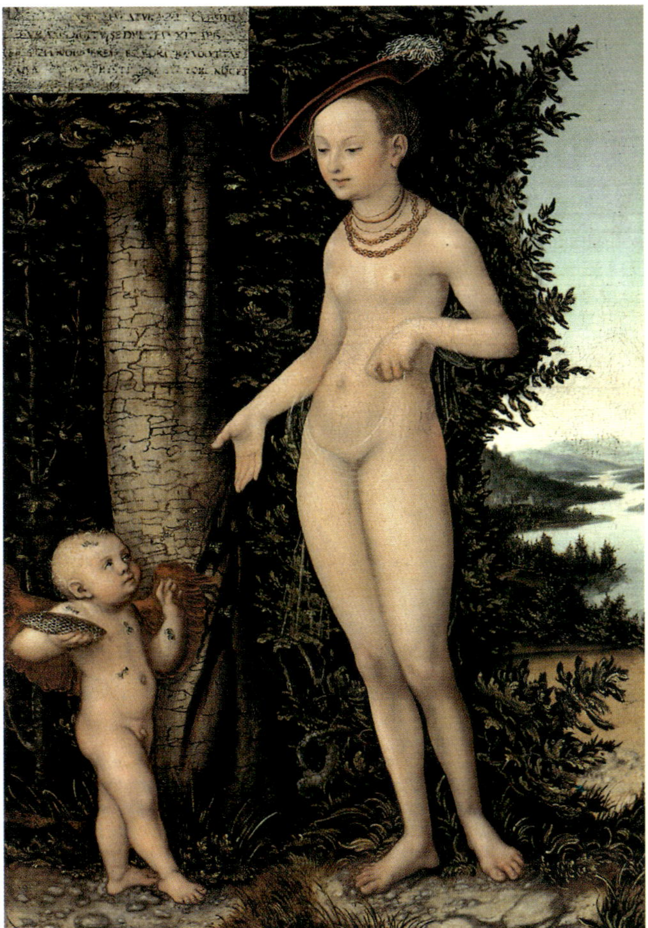

Venus with Cupid Stealing Honey, 1534. Oil on panel, 49.5 x 34 cm. Munich, Bayerische Staatsgaleriesammlungen.

1535

□ Between 1535 and 1540, Cranach worked with up to six co-workers at Hartenfels Castle above Torgau on the new buildings erected between 1533 and 1536 by the master builder Konrad Krebs.

□ Joachim I, Elector of Brandenburg, died on 02.07.1535 at the age of 51 in Stendal.

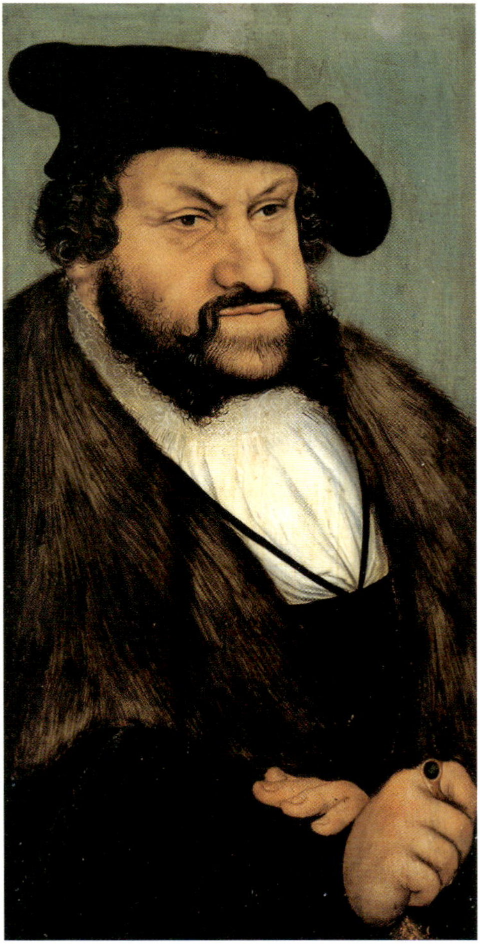

Elector John the Steadfast of Saxony, around 1535.
Oil on panel, 46.5 x 24.5 cm.
Copenhagen, Statens Museum for Kunst.

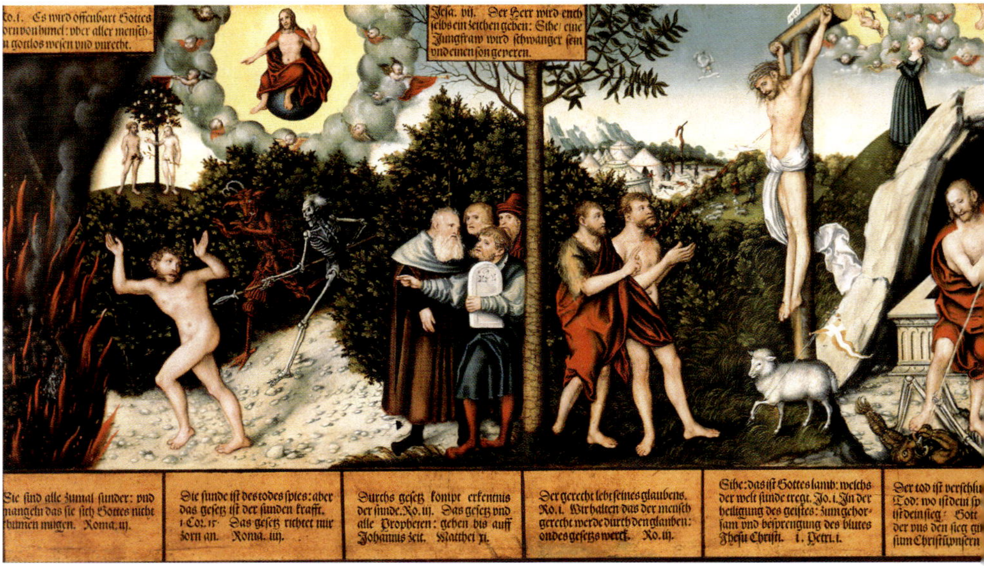

The Fall and Salvation of Man, approx. 1535–40.
Mixed media on beech wood, 54 x 102 cm.
Weimar, Stiftung Weimarer Klassik und Kunstsammlungen.

Young Woman, before 1537.
Oil on panel, 41.5 x 25.5 cm.
Copenhagen, Statens Museum for Kunst.

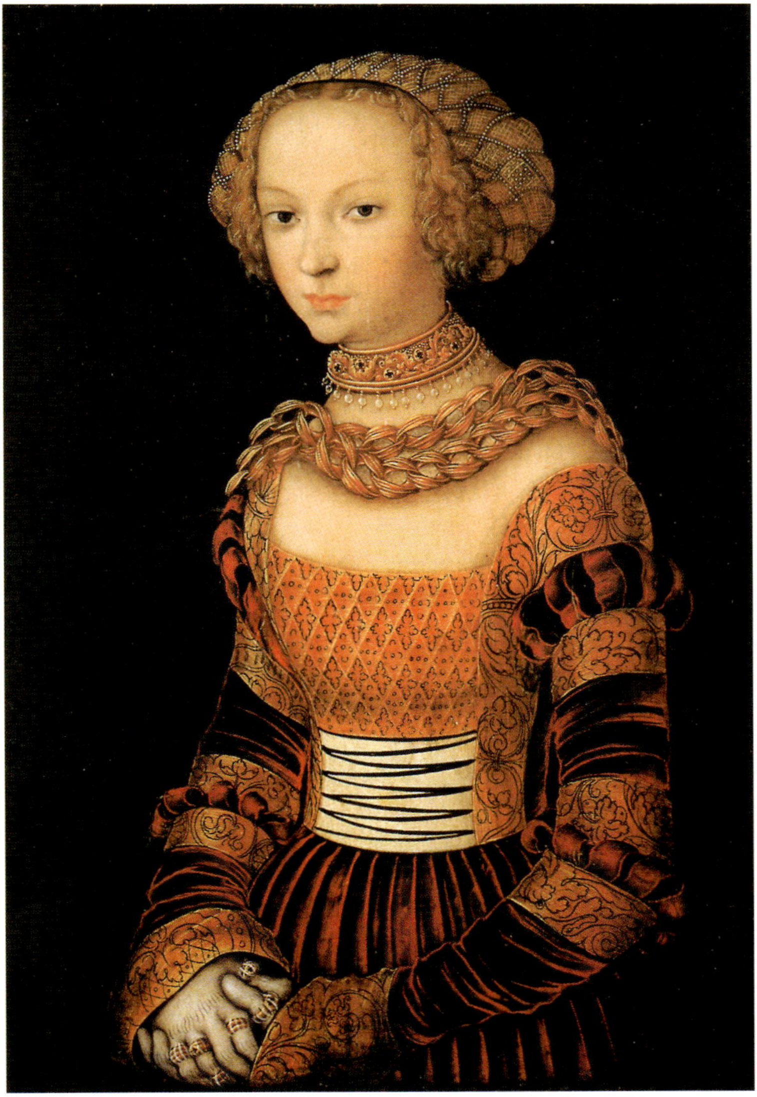

1536

☐ The 19-year-old Marie of Saxony, daughter of the Elector John the Steadfast, married the 20-year-old Philipp I, Duke of Pomerania, in Torgau on 27.02.1536. The marriage produced ten children.

1537

☐ The painter Hans Cranach, the eldest son of Lucas Cranach, died on 09.10.1537 at the age of 24 in Bologna. Between 1534 and 1536, he had been involved in the furnishing of Hartenfels Castle above Torgau. He was said to have painted 'many thousands of copies' of Luther's portrait. Hans Cranach was largely responsible for the volume of production in the workshop in the mid-1530s.

☐ The 65-year-old councillor Lucas Cranach, who had been a member of the council since 1519, was elected mayor of Wittenberg for the first time in this year. He also served in this office in 1540 and 1543.

☐ In this year, the coat of arms or the workshop insignia changed. The serpent's body, instead of having the spread wings of a bat, now had the closed wings of a bird, which was probably the occasionally seen monogram of Lucas Cranach's son. The monogram now became the trademark for Cranach's productions as a whole.

It is probable that Cranach's second son, who was also called Lucas and who had long since became a master in his own right, but had not been able to develop any style of his own, became the co-owner or manager of the workshop. Lucas Cranach the Elder remained the court painter, however.

☐ After 1537 the works are only rarely dated. The workshop had become a manufactory, the production in which was marked by a high degree of routine and production in series.

In addition to a polished practice of variation (replicas were avoided), an extension of the repertoire can be detected from time to time. The style, subject matter, iconography and colouring seemed to have been standardised to an otherwise unknown degree. Work was carried out with exchangeable set pieces and motif groups with a universally acknowledged degree of perfection in the production.

Instead of attaching importance to the authenticity of the individual artist, the supply of paintings with a constant guarantee of quality was preferred. A reason for this uniformity and constancy was probably due to the fact that Cranach's position in central eastern Germany, in contrast to the situation in the south and west German centres of art, was largely without competition. As inspiration and competition were not present as reasons for further developments, the need for renovation and change was lacking, too.

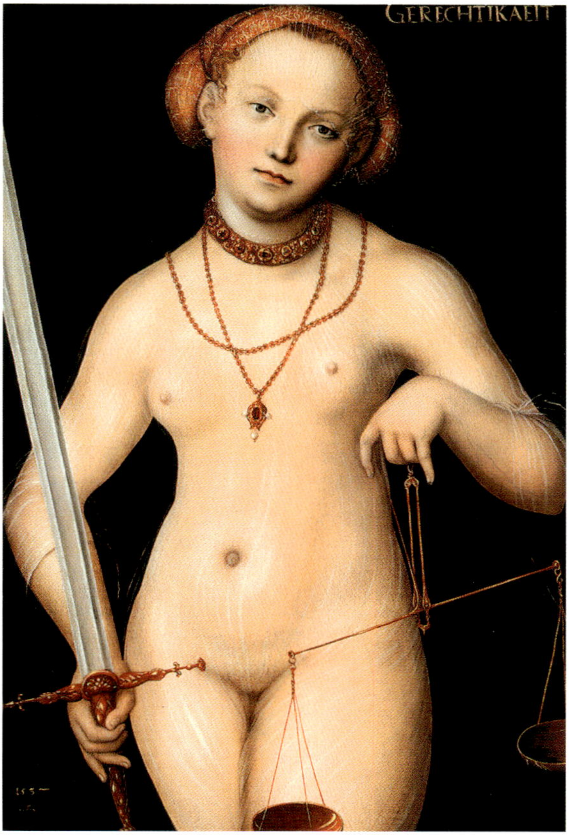

Justice, 1537.
Oil on panel, 72 x 49.6 cm.
Amsterdam, Fridart-Stichting.

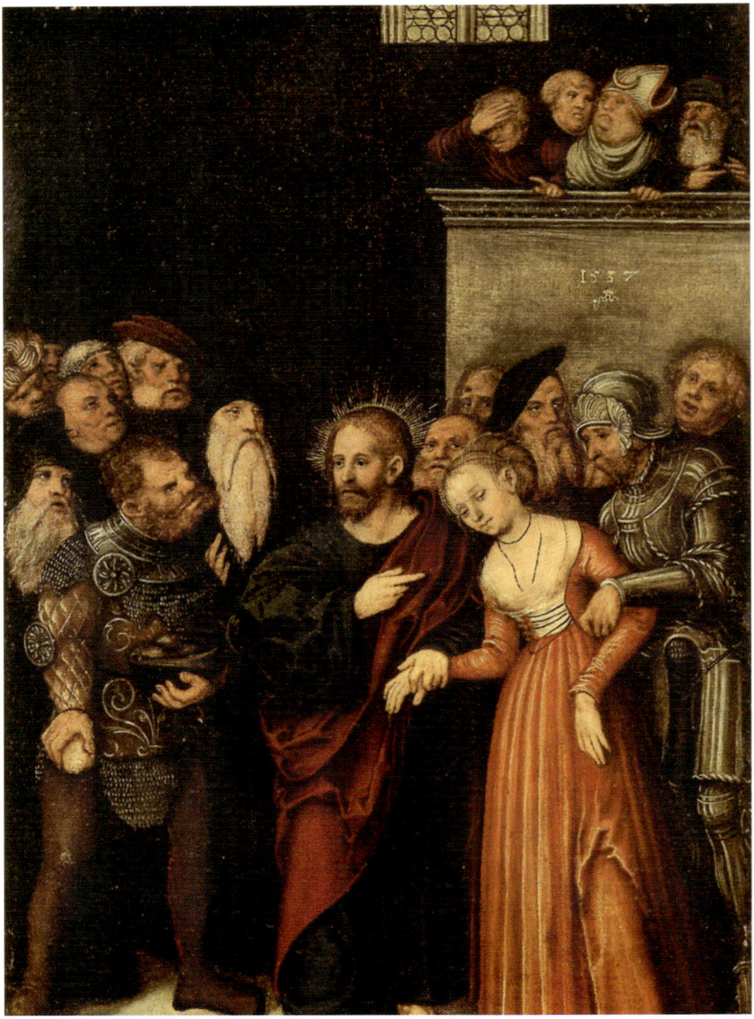

Jesus and the Woman Caught in Adultery, 1537.
Oil on panel, 36 x 24 cm.
Lucerne, Galerie Fischer.

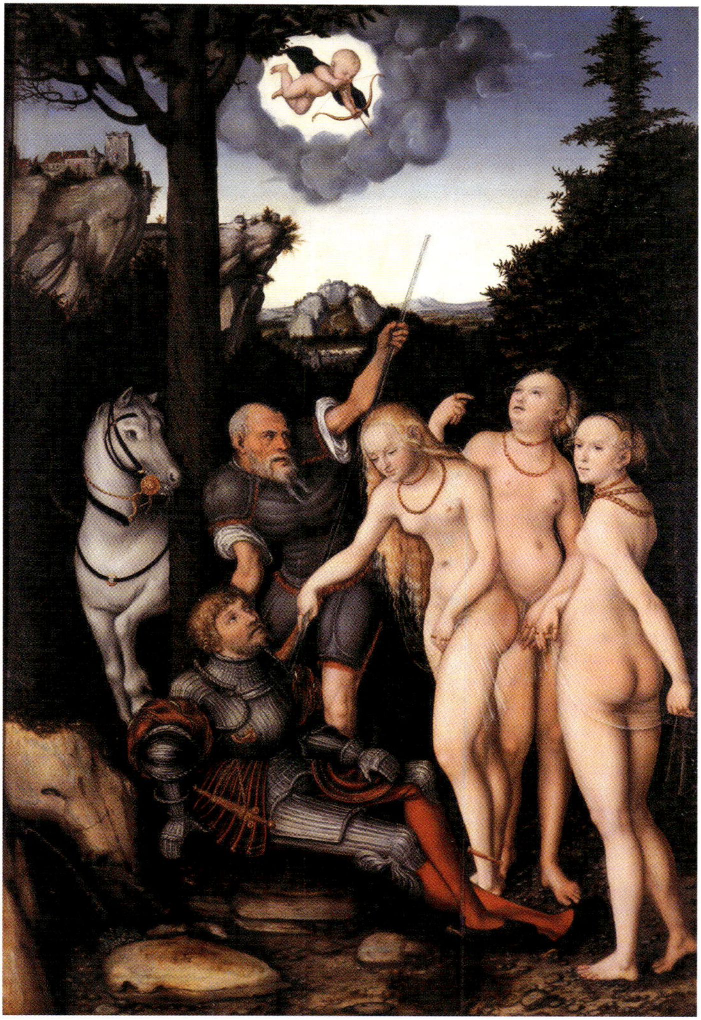

The Judgment of Paris, after 1537.
Oil on panel, 119 x 85 cm.
Gotha, Stiftung Schloss Friedenstein.

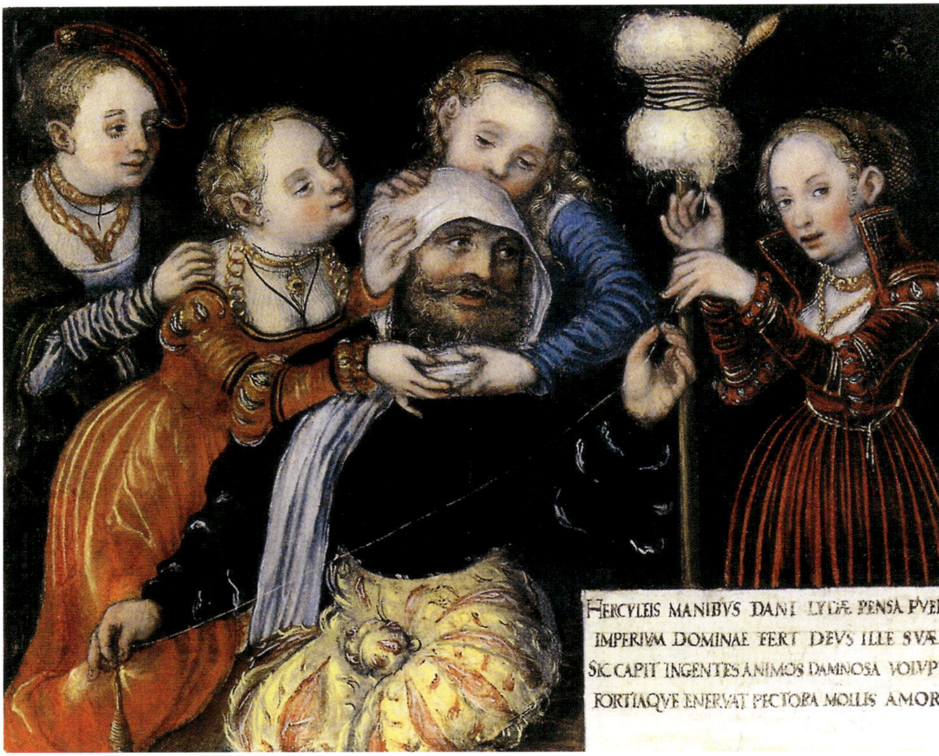

Hercules with Omphale, around 1537.
Oil on panel, 14.4 x 19.2 cm.
Gotha, Stiftung Schloss Friedenstein.

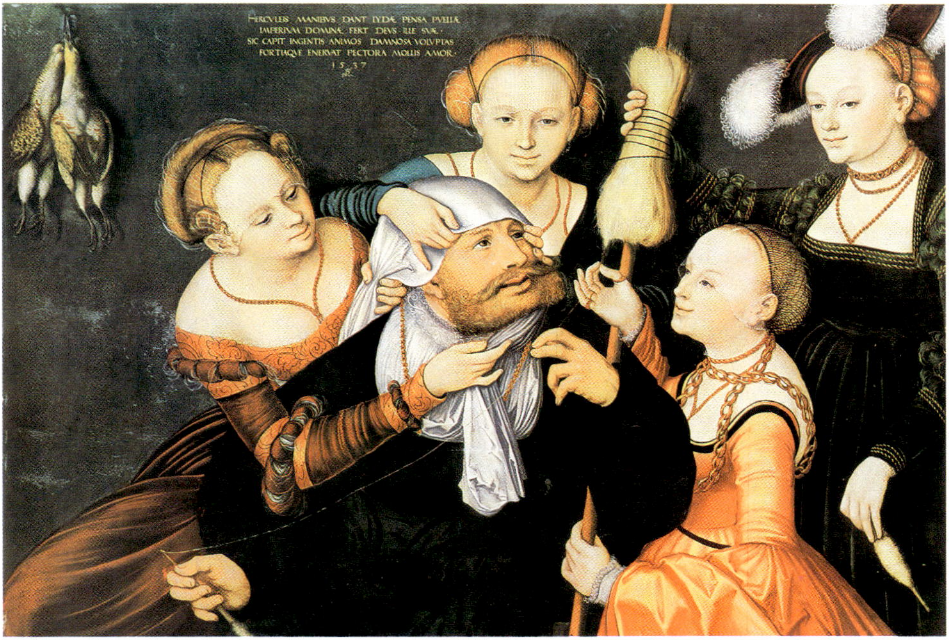

Hercules with Omphale, around 1537.
Oil on beech wood, 82 x 119 cm.
Brunswick, Herzog Anton Ulrich-Museum.

1539

☐ If the documents are interpreted correctly, Lucas Cranach spent this year in Nuremberg, seeking refuge from the plague. He received permission from the city council to 'carry on working on his art' for six months.

☐ George the Bearded, Duke of Saxony and son of Albert III the Courageous, the founder of the Albertine line of the House of Wettin, died at the age of 68 on 17.04.1539 in Dresden. He died without a legal heir. His successor was his brother, the 66-year-old Duke Henry V the Pious. It was Henry V who, from 1539 onwards, introduced the Reformation to all territories belonging to the Albertine line.

☐ The negotiations carried out by Emperor Charles V with the German estates of the Empire led to the signing of the 'Frankfurt *Anstand*', as it is known (10.04.1539). In this agreement, the religious Peace of Nuremberg of 1532 (the limited tolerance of the Reformation) was confirmed.

1540

☐ Barbara Brengbier, the wife of the 68-year-old Lucas Cranach, died in December at the age of 63 in Wittenberg. There is no known picture of Barbara, nor a gravestone nor an inscription on a tombstone.

☐ On 04.03.1540, the 36-year-old Philipp I, Landgrave of Hesse, married, with the consent of his 35-year-old consort Christine of Saxony, the 18-year-old unmarried noblewoman Margarete von der Saale. This new marriage produced eight children; the Landgrave had already had six children with Christine of Saxony. After this marriage, Philipp fathered a further three children with Christine (1541, 1543, 1547).

This act of bigamy was preceded by an absolution from Wittenberg. Although it went against all manner of conventions, including that of Reformation theology, Melanchthon and Luther wrote, 'If your Grace decides once and for all to take another wife, then we think it best to keep such a consort secret'. The matter did not remain secret, however.

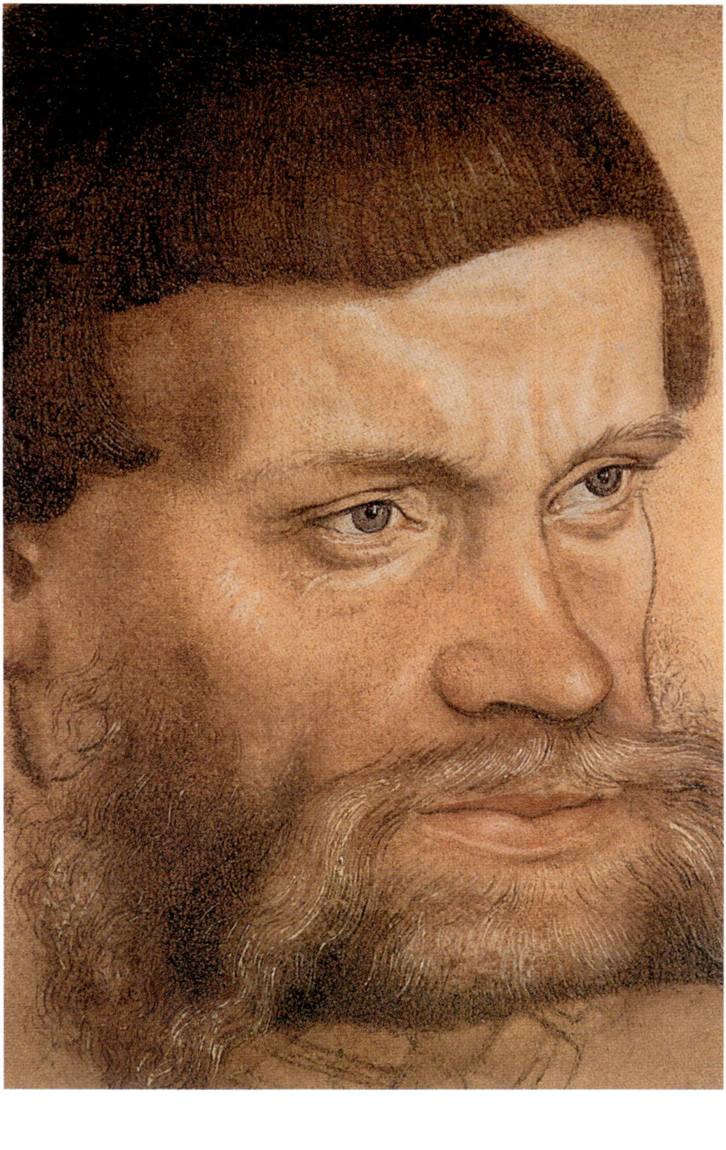

Portrait of a Bearded Man, around 1540. Oil on paper, 31 x 23.5 cm. Reims, Musée des Beaux Arts.

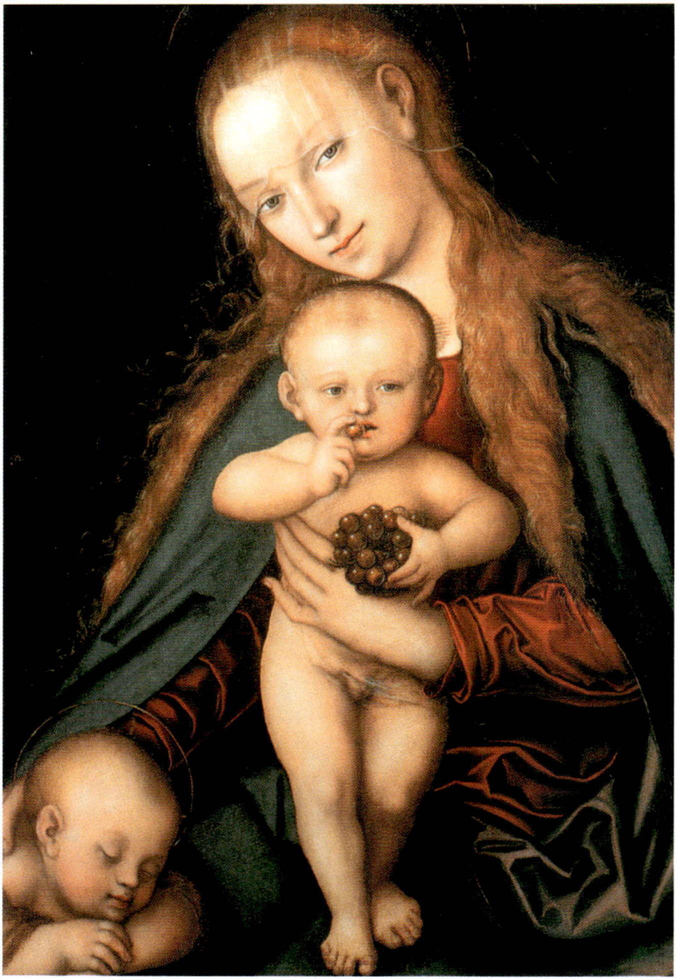

Virgin and Child with the Boy St John Asleep,
approx. 1540–50.
Oil on panel, 77.5 x 57 cm.
Private collection.

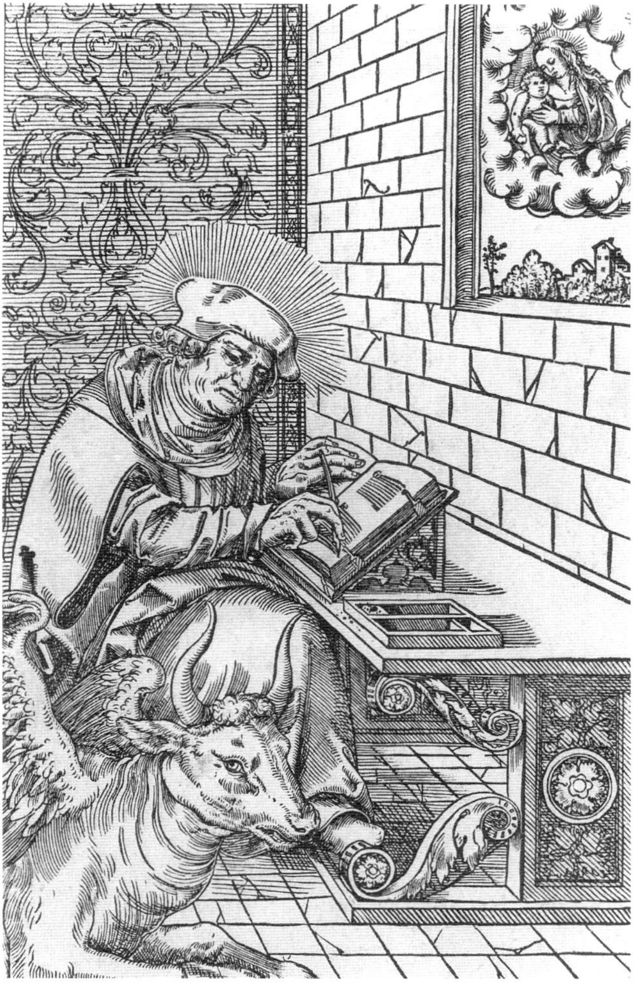

St Luke, from the series:
'The Four Apostles and St Paul', 1540.
Woodcut, 25.2 x 15.8 cm.
Gotha, Stiftung Schloss Friedenstein.

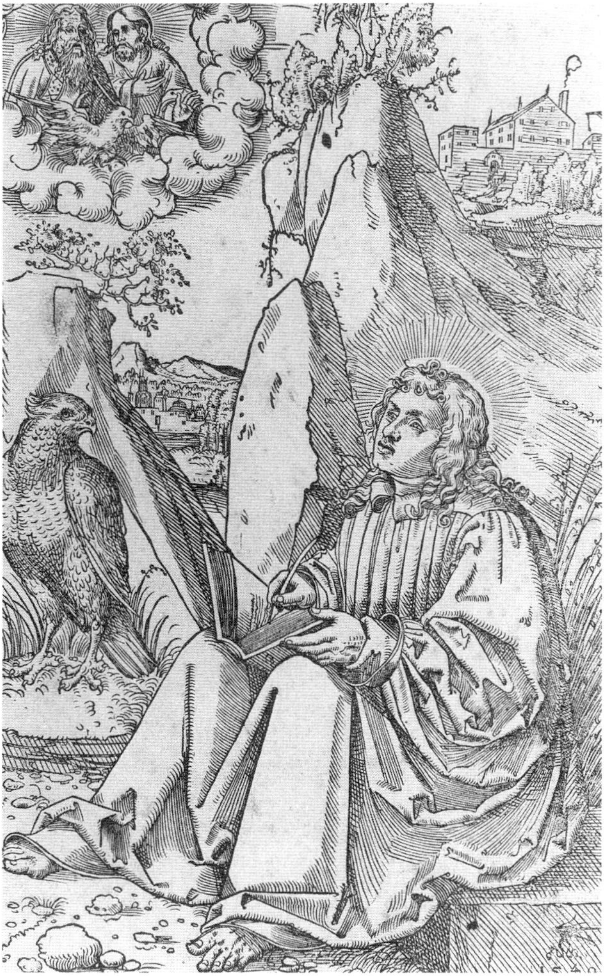

St John, from the series:
'The Four Apostles and St Paul', 1540.
Woodcut, 24.5 x 15.4 cm.
Gotha, Stiftung Schloss Friedenstein.

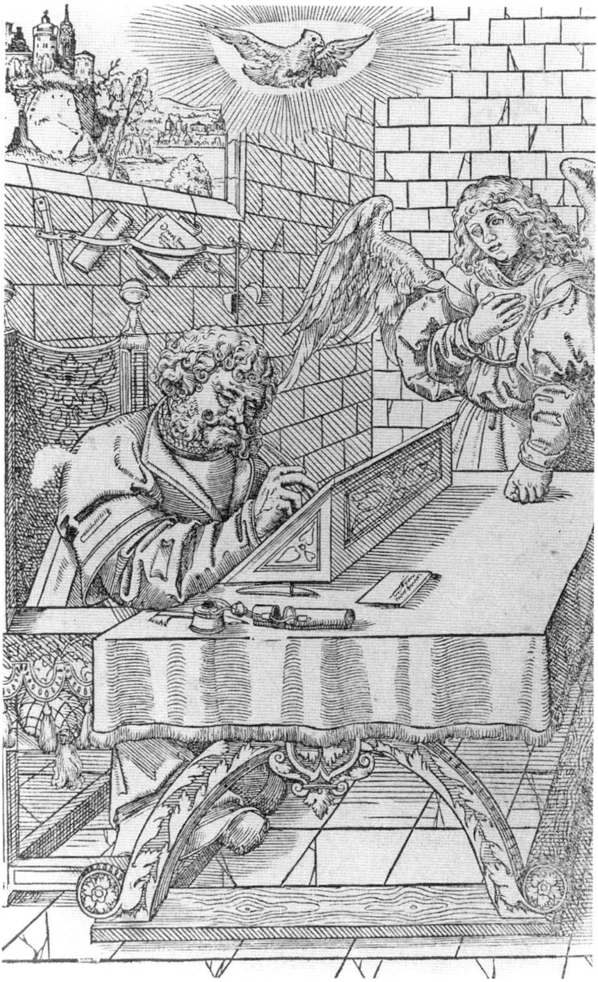

St Matthew, from the series:
'The Four Apostles and St Paul', 1540.
Woodcut, 25.2 x 15.7 cm.
Gotha, Stiftung Schloss Friedenstein.

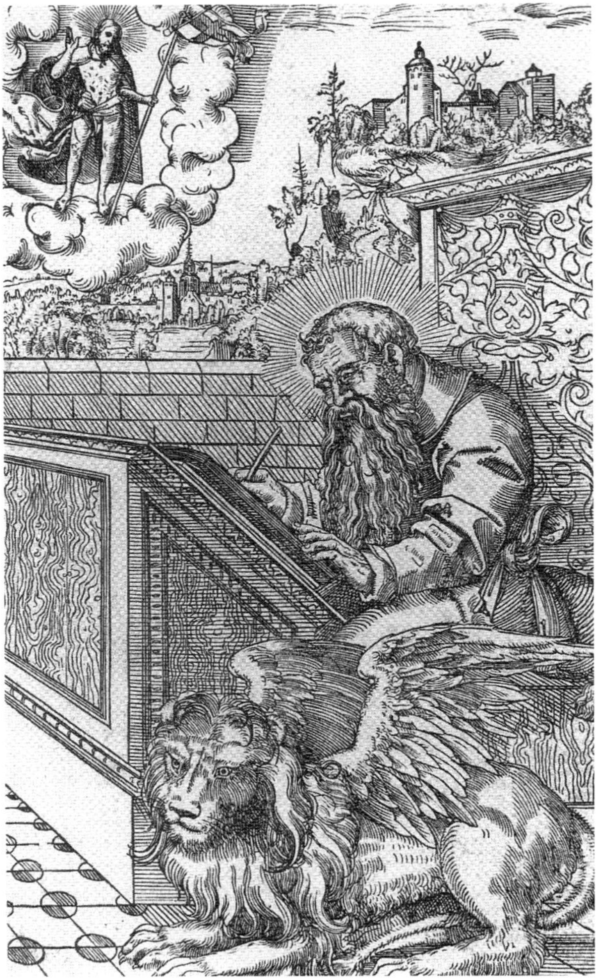

St Mark, from the series:
'The Four Apostles and St Paul', 1540.
Woodcut, 25.8 x 15.7 cm.
Gotha, Stiftung Schloss Friedenstein.

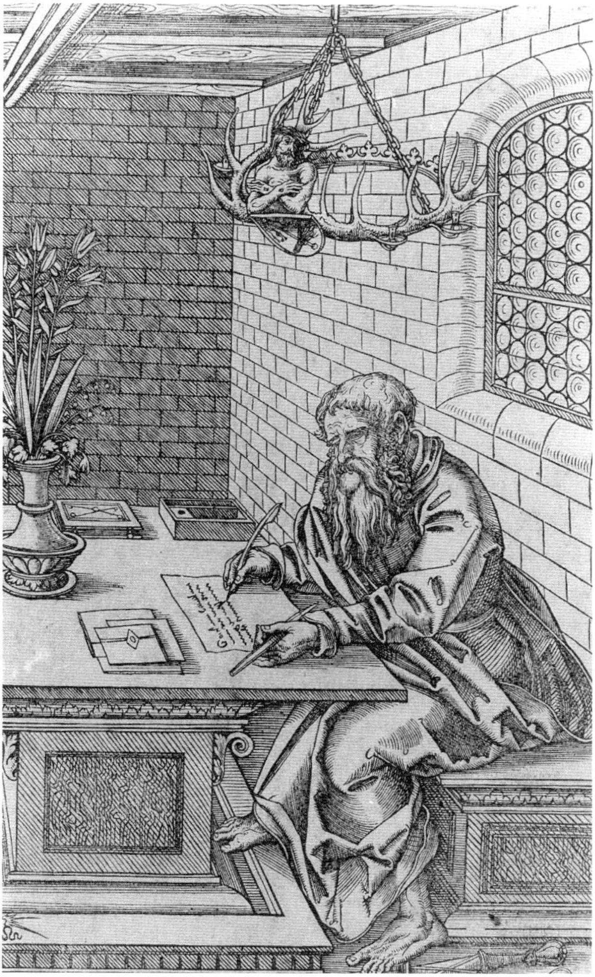

St Paul, from the series:
'The Four Apostles and St Paul', 1540.
Woodcut, 25.9 x 15.7 cm.
Gotha, Stiftung Schloss Friedenstein.

1541

☐ On 20.02.1541, the 26-year-old painter Lucas Cranach the Younger married Barbara (+1550), the 23-year-old daughter of the approximately 56-year-old former Chancellor of the Electorate of Saxony, Gregor Brück. The marriage produced four children: Lucas, Barbara, Johann and Christian.

☐ Duke Maurice of Saxony married the 13-year-old Agnes (*31.05.1527), daughter of Philipp I, Landgrave of Hesse, and his first wife, Christina, daughter of Duke George of Saxony, on 09.01.1541 in Marburg. The marriage took place against the wishes of the 20-year-old Duke's parents as Philipp I of Hesse was living in a state of open bigamy. The marriage produced two children: Anna (1544–77) and Albrecht (1545–46).

☐ Henry the Pious, Duke of Saxony and son of Albert III, the founder of the Albertine line of the House of Wettin, died at the age of 68 on 18.08.1541 in Dresden. He had surrendered his title on 07.08.1541 to his son, the 20-year-old Maurice of Saxony (*21.03.1521, Freiberg, +11.07.1553 near Sievershausen).

☐ Andreas Karlstadt died on 24.12.1541, probably at the age of 61, in Basel. Karlstadt had joined with Luther in 1517 and had withstood the Leipzig Disputation of 1519 with him. He had split with Luther due to a difference of opinions regarding the Eucharist.

☐ At the Diet of Regensburg (which started on 05.04.1541), Emperor Charles V was forced to acknowledge that his peaceful mediation had failed. The hasty Regensburg Decree once again extended the religious Peace of Nuremberg of 1532 and prohibited the expansion of the Schmalkaldic League.

By means of a secret pact with the Emperor, Philipp I, Landgrave of Hesse, significantly weakened the position of the Schmalkaldic League (13.06.1541). He agreed to not enter into any alliance with a foreign power, to support the Emperor's demands for financial support and to prevent Cleves being accepted into the Schmalkaldic League. Due to this treachery, the power of the Protestant alliance was paralysed and the starting point was reached for military action on the part of Emperor Charles V.

1542

□ A campaign started by the Schmalkaldic League against the Dukedom of Brunswick-Wolfenbüttel. The artillery attack on the city of Wolfsbüttel was portrayed by Lucas Cranach in a woodcut with eight blocks (total format of 67 x 110 cm.).

The Electorate of Saxony and Hesse drove out Henry II the Younger, Duke of Brunswick, the most influential follower of the Emperor, from Wolfenbüttel and reformed the state of Brunswick. The Reformation was also brought to the Saxon bishoprics of Naumburg and Merseberg.

□ A year later, Cranach sent a bill to the court of the Elector of Saxony for 45 thaler and almost 100 florins for military equipment, including the varnishing of 50 halberds as well as the delivery of 25 standard bearer's flags and 1,900 coloured coats of arms. The allied Landgrave of Hesse received a similar amount of coloured coat-of-arm woodcuts. They were presumably used to identify possession of occupied or commandeered areas and buildings.

1543

□ Dr Christian Brück, the 33-year-old son of the former Chancellor of the Electorate of Saxony Gregor Brück, married Cranach's 23-year-old daughter, Barbara.

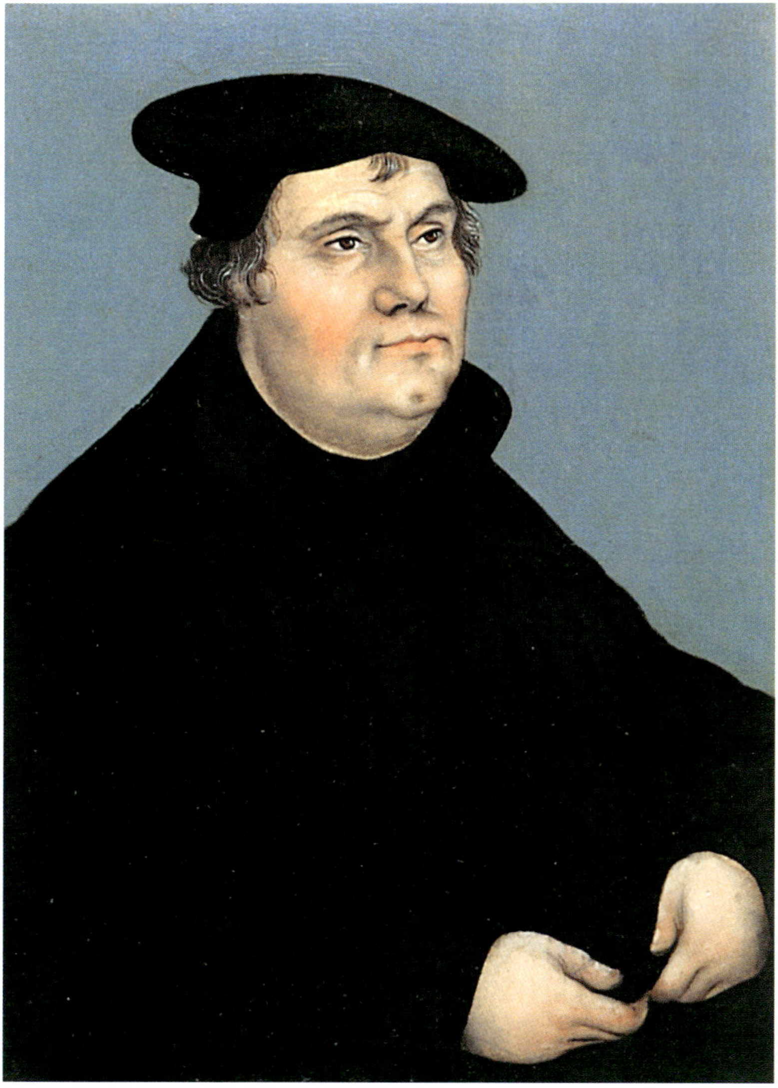

Martin Luther, around 1543.
Oil on oak wood, 20.6 x 15.2 cm.
Private collection.

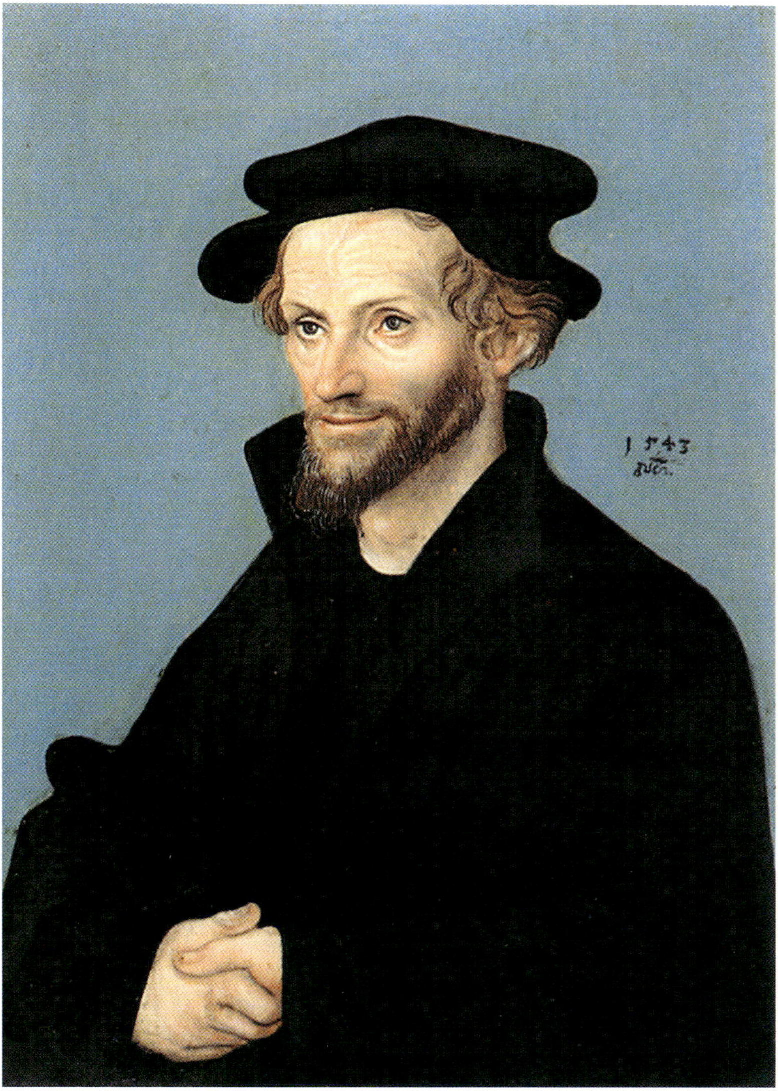

Philipp Melanchthon, 1543.
Oil on oak wood, 20.5 x 15.2 cm.
Private collection.

1544

□ Lucas Cranach handed over his house in Wittenberg to his son Lucas.

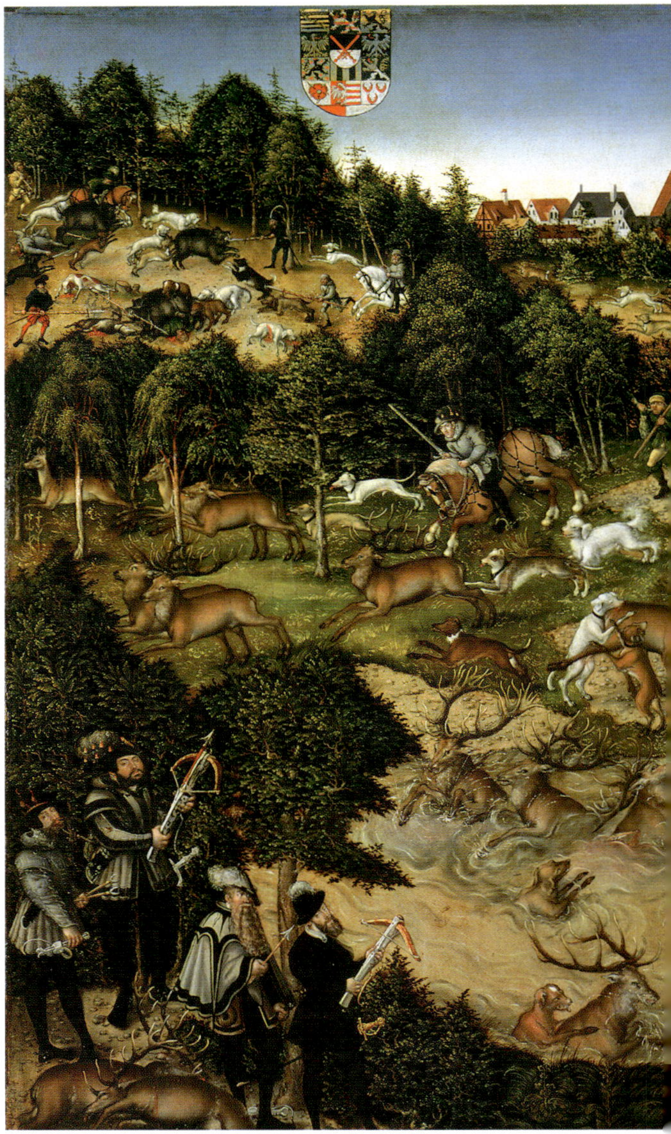

A Stag Hunt in Honour of Emperor Charles V at Hartenfels Castle, 1544. Oil on panel, 114 x 175 cm. Madrid, Museo del Prado.

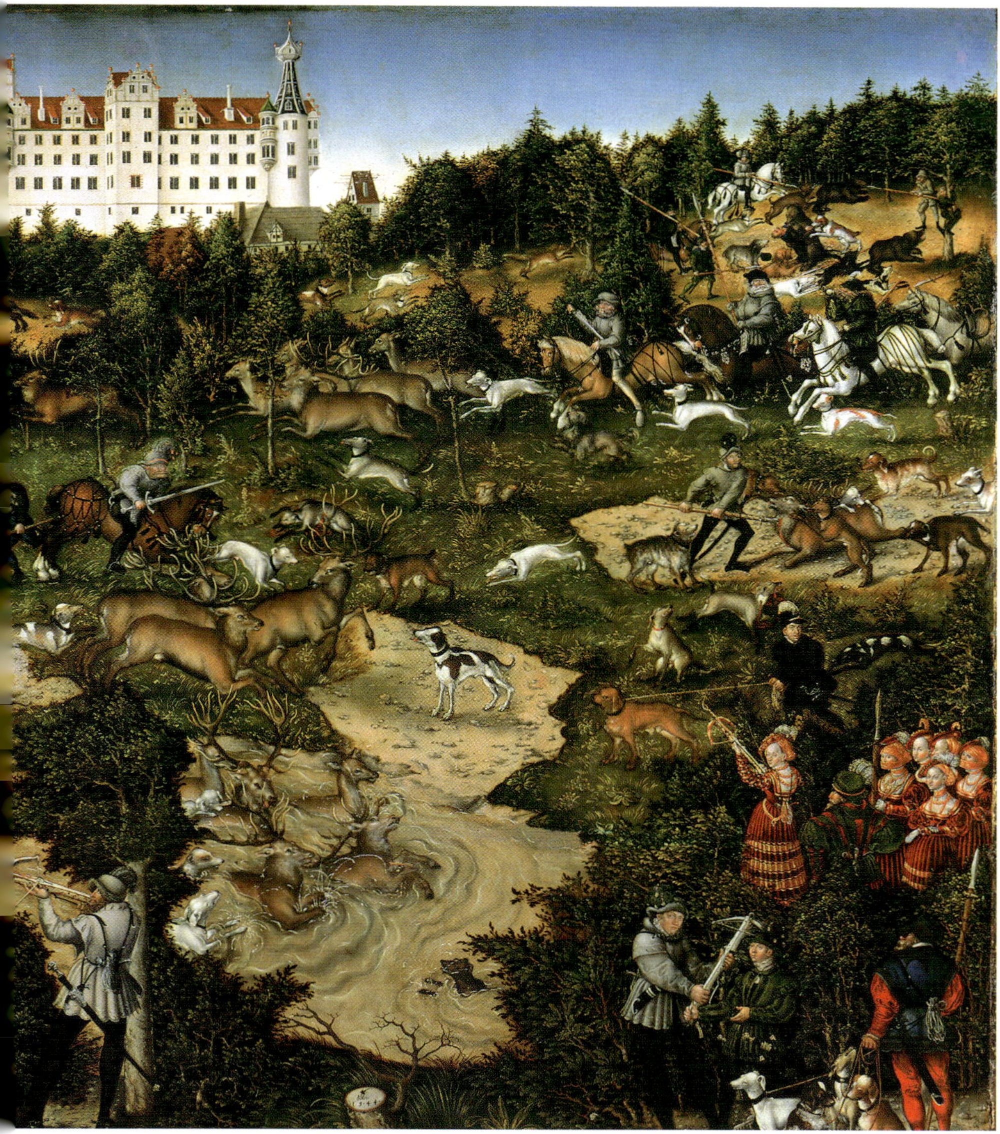

1545

☐ At the end of the legislative period 1544/45, the 73-year-old Lucas Cranach gave up his duties as a councillor of the town of Wittenberg after serving on the council for 26 years.

☐ Cranach worked with six assistants at Hartenberg Castle above Torgau and in Wittenberg he carried out decorative work with his journeymen. Remarking on the work of one of his pupils, he noted that the pupil's picture of the Madonna had turned out successfully, 'I did not help him at all with it; he did it all himself. You can see very well how he has improved'.

☐ Georg Spalatin died on 16.01.1545 in Altenburg at the age of 61.

☐ Albert II, Margrave of Brandenburg, died on 24.09.1545, aged 55, in Mainz. In 1513, he had become the Archbishop of Magdeburg and Administrator of Halberstadt; in 1514, he had also become the Archbishop of Mainz and in 1518, Cardinal. He was the son of Elector Johann Cicero and the brother of the Elector Joachim I of Brandenburg.

☐ On 13.12.1545, Pope Paul III opened the Council of Trent. It lasted until 1563 and was directed against Protestant teachings (justification, etc.). From 1562/63 onwards, it was led by the Jesuits. The Lutherans refused to send representatives to the Council.

1546

☐ In January, despite his weak state of health, Martin Luther travelled to Eisleben via Halle to mediate in a family feud between the counts of Mansfeld. On 18.02.1546, Luther died; he had been suffering from heart problems for a long time and was afflicted with kidney and bladder stones, constipation and other illnesses. He died in his birthplace, to which he had travelled despite the cold weather and flooding at that time. His body was transported to Wittenberg where he was buried in the Castle Church on 22.02.1546.

☐ Charles V, who had always been hesitant throughout the summer of 1546 and who had always appeased the Protestants, finally formally declared war from his seat in Regensburg by implementing the state of outlawry against Hesse and Saxony due to their attack on Brunswick.

☐ The summer of 1546 was characterised by a great military presence on both sides. The Schmalkaldic troops with 57,000 soldiers had taken up positions from the Northern German plains to the edge of the Alps, but they did not attack the Emperor with their overwhelming forces although the former still had to summon his forces from Italy and the Netherlands.

On 13.08.1546, the papal forces came to his aid. Otherwise, it is possible that the inadequate imperial troops would have hardly stood a chance against the quick Schmalkaldic forces.

Two weeks later, close to Ingolstadt, the first engagement took place, which was initiated by heavy artillery fire from the Protestants. They were soon able to meet up with the Dutch forces, who had come across no resistance while crossing the Rhine.

For the further progress of the Danube campaign, the disunity within the Protestant camp played a decisive role. First of all, John Frederick I withdrew his 20,000 soldiers in order to defend the completely unprotected Electorate of Saxony which his Protestant cousin Maurice of Saxony, together with King Ferdinand, had invaded. The leaders of the League did not subsequently risk any serious attacks. In October, Philipp I of Hesse also withdrew northwards into the area between Donauwörth and Nördlingen. The whole of Southern Germany was then in the hands of the Emperor. The Emperor took up re-sidence in Ulm for the winter.

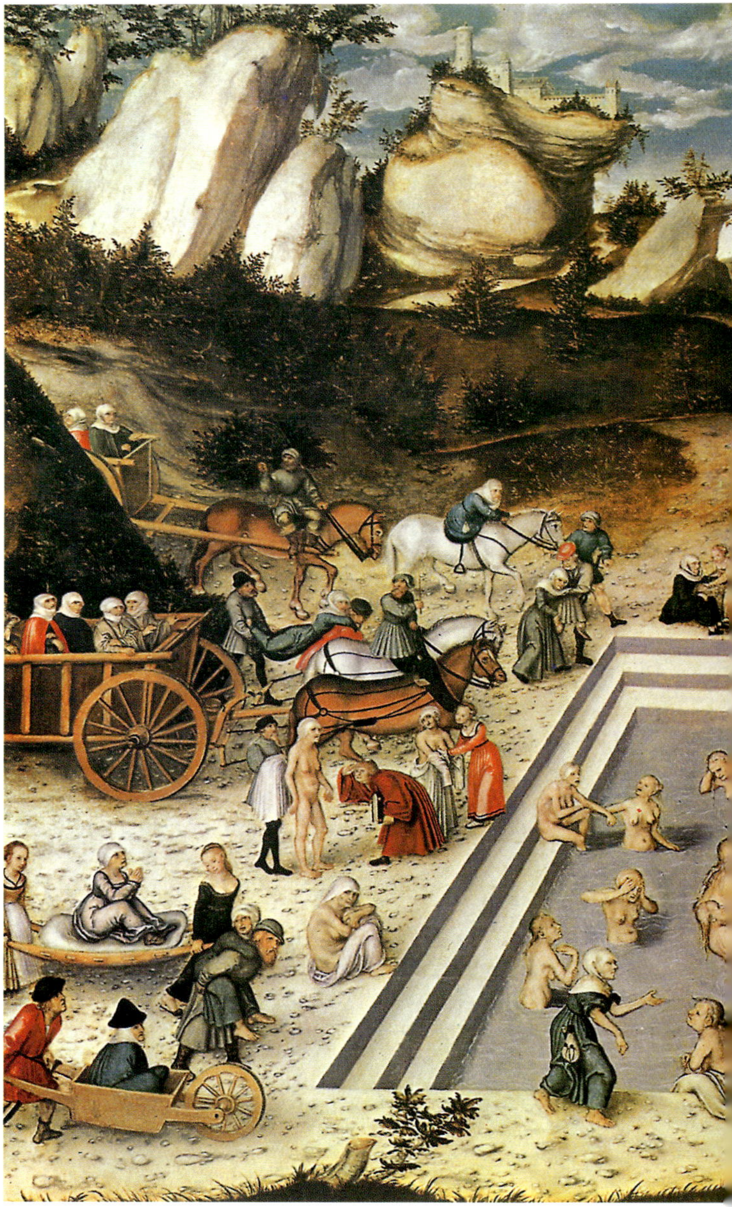

The Fountain of Youth, 1546. Oil on panel, 121 x 184 cm. Berlin, Staatliche Museen.

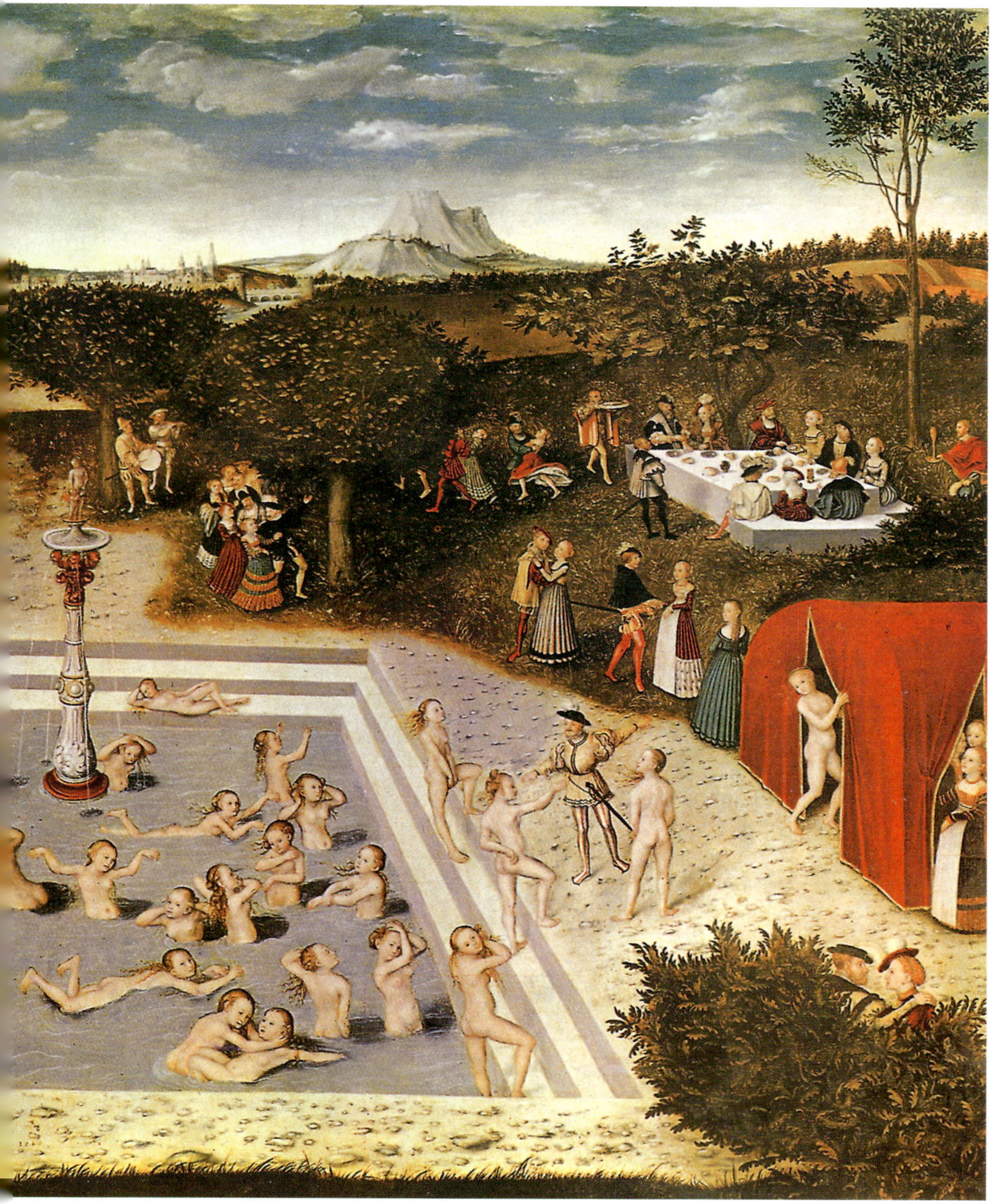

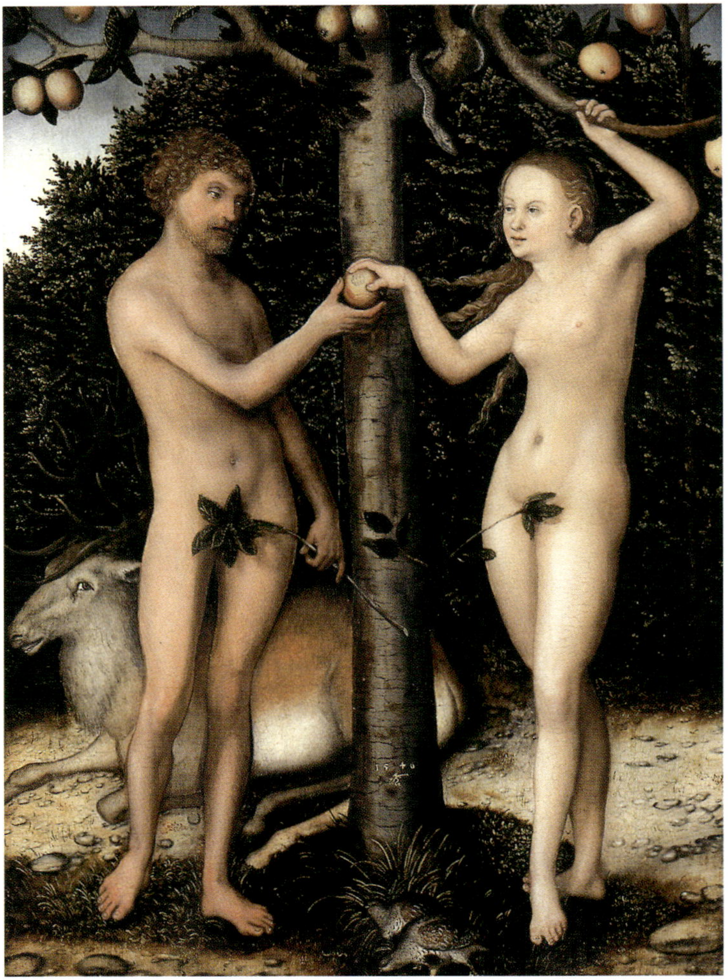

Adam and Eve, 1546.
Oil on panel, 78 x 58 cm.
Private collection.

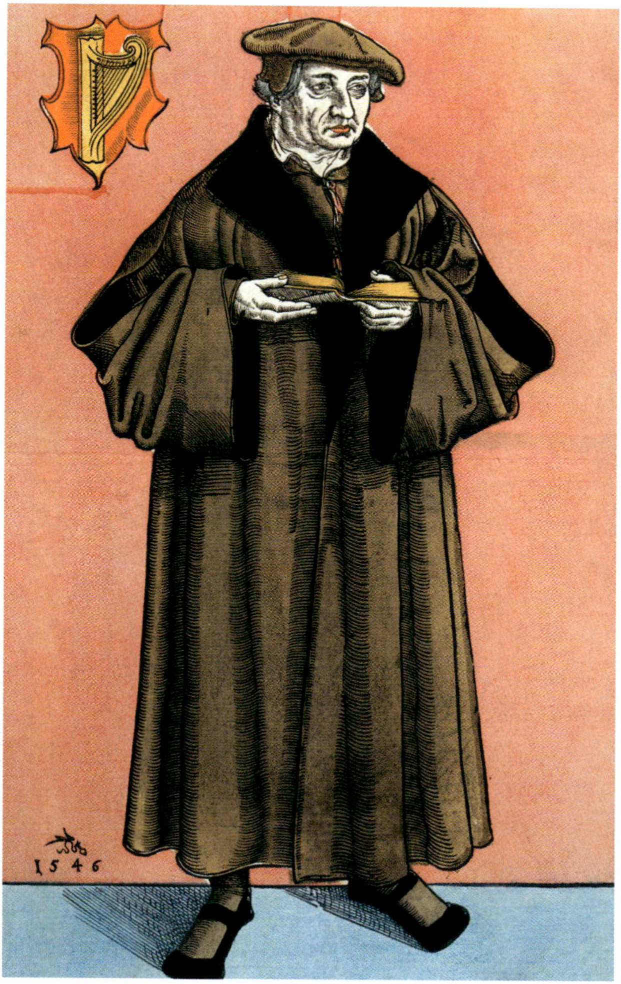

Johann Bugenhagen, 1546.
Woodcut, 33.3 x 21.4 cm.
Gotha, Stiftung Schloss Friedenstein.

1547

□ In February, the Emperor received pleas for aid from his brother Ferdinand and Duke Maurice whose situation in the Electorate of Saxony had become critical. John Frederick I, whose fortifications were holding against the two invaders, turned against Albertine Saxony. The Emperor marched via Eger and Plauen towards the Elector John Frederick I who was moving northwards in the direction of Mühlberg on the River Elbe.

The town (which had had this status since 1295) of Mühlberg lies on the River Elbe, in the administrative district of Bad Liebenwerda, in the region of Cottbus, 20 kilometres south-west of Torgau and 60 kilometres northeast of Leipzig.

John Frederick I believed that the river, over which the opposing sappers first had to build a bridge, would offer him enough protection. The Emperor, however, used a ford and crossed the Elbe on Sunday 24.04.1547 very early in the morning under the cover of the dense early morning mist. In the ensuing battle on the Lochau Heath close to Mühlberg, John Frederick I was defeated by the allied forces of Albertine Saxony and the Italian-Spanish contingent of the Emperor and was arrested while taking flight.

In the Wittenberg Capitulation of 19.05.1547, John Frederick I renounced the title of Elector, which, as the Emperor had promised, was handed over in a document of 04.06.1547 to Duke Maurice of Saxony from the Albertine line. Thus, the political head of German Protestantism was shamefully degraded. The agreement also meant the loss of approximately two thirds of the Ernestine territories.

□ 'Spanish and other Southern European warriors' destroyed works by Cranach in Hartenfels Castle above Torgau.

□ Charles V invited Lucas Cranach to his military camp. The Emperor was encamped to the west of Wittenberg (Piesteritz). The two of them, according to the chronicles, discussed art. The painter then went down on his knees at the end of the audience to beg for imperial mercy to be shown to his imprisoned duke.

☐ Landgrave Philipp I of Hesse was arrested in Halle on 19.06.1547 and was also imprisoned.

☐ Charles V moved to Augsburg with the captured leaders of the Schmalkaldic League where he opened the Diet (the *geharnischter* Diet, as it is known) on 01.09.1547.

☐ The imprisoned John Frederick I asked Cranach in a letter of 02.08.1547 to come to Augsburg. The almost 74-year-old painter explained his refusal to come on 14.08.1547 as being due to illness: 'I cannot travel at the moment as I have a feeling of dizziness in my head and often cannot leave the house for fourteen days at a time'. In response to his refusal, Cranach's yearly payment of 100 florins was initially cancelled. He was temporarily relieved of his position as court painter.

☐ Lucas Cranach asked John Frederick I to return the 5,000 florins he had given him as an advance (presumably before the war started). His share, together with that of the Chamberlain of the Electorate of Saxony, Hans von Ponickhans, was 3,942 florins. The remainder came from five other people, amongst them Gregor Brück.

☐ More as a hostage than as a prisoner, John Frederick I was taken away in the *baggage train* of the victor. He was held until 1550 in the Netherlands (Antwerp, Mecheln, Ghent and Brussels) and then eventually brought back to Augsburg via Cologne. There is evidence of him being in Augsburg from 23.07.1550 onwards, then possibly from February 1551 in Innsbruck before being imprisoned again in Augsburg.

☐ The large, stone portrait of the imprisoned Elector was moved at the end of September from the Castle Church in Wittenberg to Cranach's house.

1548

☐ On 30.06.1548, the Augsburg Interim was passed. This is the term for an imperial law by which the religious question in the Empire was temporarily resolved at the Diet of Augsburg after the Schmalkaldic War (1547). Some concessions were made to the Protestant estates of the Empire (Holy Communion being administered to the laity, the marriage of priests); claims were also not made for the restitution of stolen church property. In exchange, the Catholic ceremonies were by and large to be re-introduced.

☐ The two sons of the imprisoned Elector, John Frederick II (aged 19) and Johann Wilhelm (18) asked Lucas Cranach to send the canvas painting from Lichtenburg and Dürer's work, *The Martyrdom of the Ten Thousand*, which he had taken into his safekeeping, to Marcus Bucher in Leipzig (02.08.1548).

☐ The sons informed their father that Dürer's *The Martyrdom of the Ten Thousand* had been sent to Antwerp via Frankfurt am Main. Beforehand, the sons had received directions to send the picture to a branch of the Fugger bank in Antwerp; it remains unclear whether this was a place where it was to be stored or sold or whether the painting was to serve as security for a loan.

It is reported that Cranach sent the following canvases: *John Frederick With His Councillors* from Lichtenberg, *The Hares Catch the Hunters*, *Lot and his Daughters* and *The Parable of the Wicked Husbandmen.* According to the two sons, Cranach still had many paintings in his safekeeping.

This must have been a large-scale, secret plan to rescue the Elector's art treasures from Wittenberg.

In the following year, Dürer's painting *The Martyrdom of the Ten Thousand* (99 x 87 cm.) was sent as a present from the imprisoned Elector to the 63-year-old Imperial Chancellor Nicolas Perrenot de Granvelle (+1550, Augsburg).

1549

☐ The 46-year-old imprisoned Elector wrote from Antwerp on 08.02.1549 to his sons in Weimar. The letter dealt with Dürer's painting and with Lucas Cranach's work in the hunting castle in Trockenborn-Wolfersdorf, 35 kilometres southeast of Weimar.

John Frederick I had already commissioned a hunting castle to be built in Trockenborn-Wolfersdorf in 1546. The moated castle was built from 1547–51 in the Renaissance style in a low-lying location by the name of Schlüsselgrund.

1550

☐ Barbara Brück, the wife of the 35-year-old Lucas Cranach the Younger, died on 10.02.1550 at the age of 32 in Wittenberg.

☐ Lucas Cranach made his will and handed over his workshop to his son, Lucas.

☐ Three years after his refusal to join the Elector in imprisonment, the artist decided to take this step after all. Cranach's son-in-law Dr Christian Brück informed the authorities in Augsburg of this decision around Easter 1550. In summer, Cranach arrived in Weimar where he met his son-in-law. Together, they travelled on to Augsburg, arriving there on 23.07.1550.

From this day on, the painter was guaranteed a payment of 100 florins annually for the rest of his life. The imperial city offered a painter of Cranach's stature commissions and contacts. He painted portraits not only of his Elector, whose portraits were given as presents to friend and foe alike, but he also painted on his own account.

He met Tizian, who was painting a portrait of John Frederick I.

☐ It is possible that the self-portrait at the age of 77, which is occasionally also attributed to his son, was painted at this time. The Latin inscription reads: 'Aetatis Suae LXXVII, 1550'. Above one shoulder, there is his coat of arms, the winged serpent. In 1676, the Dresden alderman and mayor Gabriel Tzschimmer gave the self-portrait as a present to the Elector of Saxony, John George II (+1680), with the information that this was 'the old Lucas Cranach's half-length portrait on which he himself was supposed to have painted the year 1550 and Aetatis 70'. After 1707, August II the Brave (1670–1733) is said to have given it as a present to the Grand Duke of Tuscany.

☐ In December, Anna, Cranach's daughter, married Caspar Pfreundt, the 'servant' of her father in his apothecary.

Emperor Charles V, 1550.
Oil on panel, 21 x 18 cm.
Eisenach, Wartburg-Stiftung.

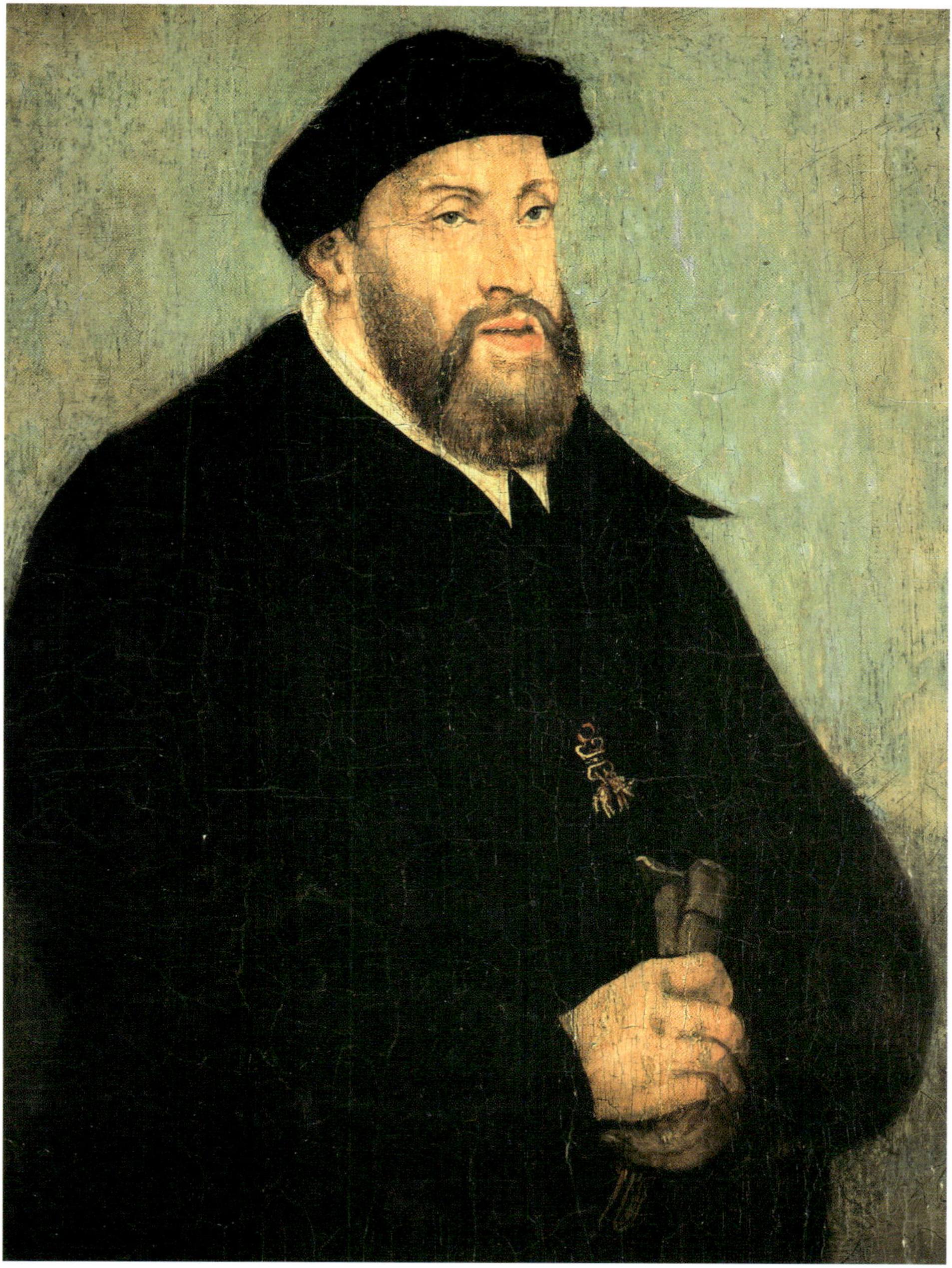

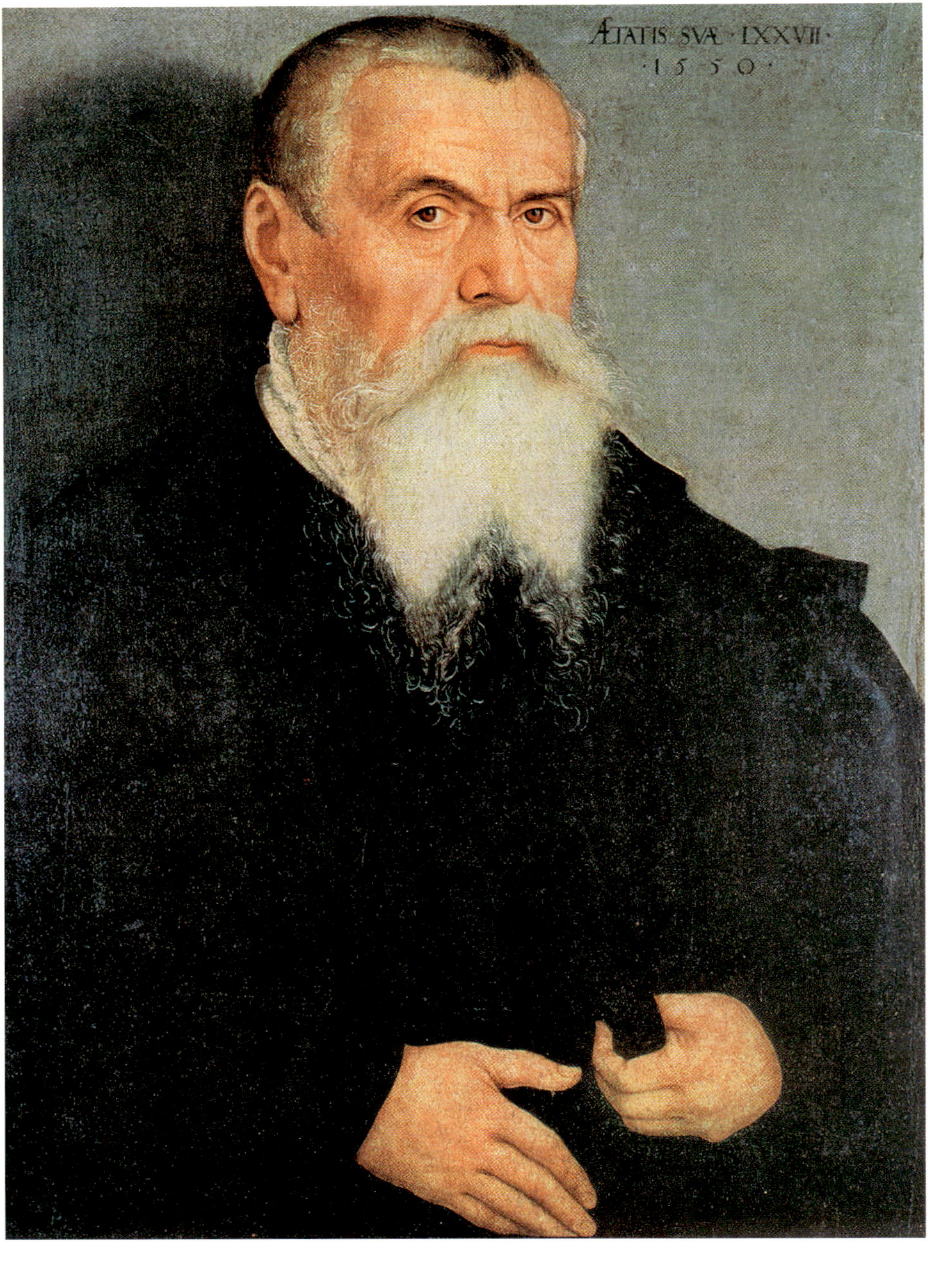
ÆTATIS SVÆ LXXVII
·1550·

1551

☐ The imprisoned Elector in Augsburg promised his wife to have a depiction of the seven virtues painted by Cranach (10.01.1551). There is copious correspondence with his family in the course of this year.

☐ Between 12.04.1551 and 24.05.1551, Lucas Cranach the Younger (36) married his second wife, the 20-year-old Magdalena Schurff (+1606), the daughter of the Saxon personal physician Professor Dr Augustin Schurff, and the niece of Melanchthon. The marriage produced five children.

☐ Elector Maurice of Saxony became the leader of the alliance of Electors from Mecklenburg, Prussia, Küstrin and Hesse against the Emperor. In an alliance brokered by councillors from Hesse, Maurice of Saxony joined with King Henry II of France (03.10.1551) who, as a child, had been imprisoned with his father, Francis I, by Charles V. The treaty was ratified on 15.02.1552 in Chambord on the River Loire.

Self-Portrait with the Inscription "Aetatis suae – LXXVII – 1550",
1550.
Oil on panel, 67 x 49 cm.
Florence, Uffizi.

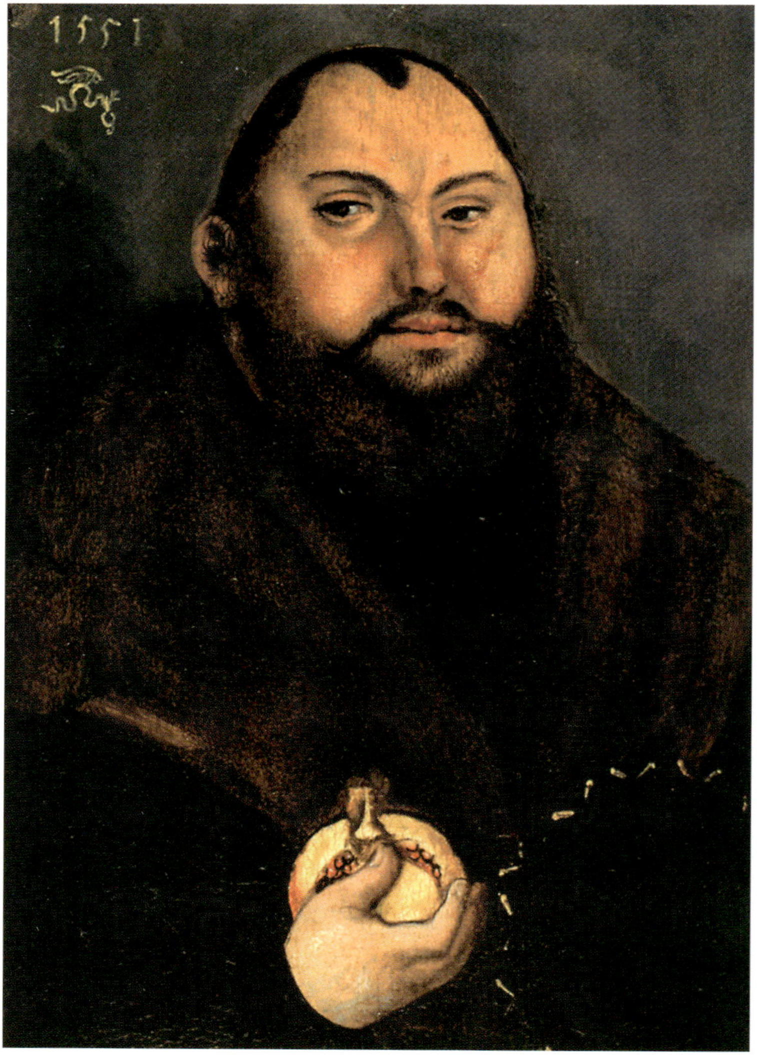

Elector John Frederick the Magnanimous, 1551.
Oil on panel, 20.5 x 14.7 cm.
Private collection.

1552

☐ In March 1552, the warring Electors of Saxony, Hesse and Kulmbach marched with their troops gathered from Franconia towards Augsburg, to 'protect the Electoral liberty', to free the two prisoners who had been incarcerated since 1547 and to secure the permanence of religious peace. The Emperor, who had stubbornly refused to credit all the warnings he had been given, fled in haste and, without his soldiers, rescued himself from Augsburg by fleeing to Villach via Innsbruck and Linz. Maurice of Saxony entered Augsburg with his forces on 04.04.1552 and Innsbruck on 18.05.1552. The negotiations for settlement were conducted by his brother Ferdinand in Linz and Passau.

The two prisoners, John Frederick I of Saxony and Philipp I of Hesse, were released.

☐ In the Treaty of Passau, which was negotiated between King Ferdinand I and the Elector Maurice of Saxony, the conspiracy of the Electors was ended, the Augsburg Interim was repealed and the followers of the Augsburg Confession were guaranteed freedom to practice their religion and possess the secularised church possessions until the next Diet (02.08.1552).

☐ John Frederick I left the city of Augsburg together with his painter on 01.09.1552 ('after cordially taking leave from the Emperor') and travelled via Nuremberg, Bamberg, Coburg and Jena to his future residence in Weimar.

On 07.09.1552, he visited his 31-year-old half-brother John Ernst I, Duke of Saxe-Coburg (+1553) in Coburg. His consort and two sons as well as several important councillors had come to Coburg to meet the two released men en route.

On their way from Coburg via Saalfeld and Rudolstadt to Jena, the party also visited the newly built Renaissance hunting castle in Trockenborn-Wolfersdorf, 20 kilometres southeast of Jena. Since then, the moated castle has borne the name 'Fröhliche Wiederkunft' ('Happy Return'). In this area which is rich in forest, game and water, the former Elector already owned the hunting lodge Hummelshain which was five kilometres west of Trockenborn-Wolfersdorf and which he used as a summer residence.

☐ On 26.09.1552, Cranach arrived at the new residence in Weimar, taking up rooms in the house of his son-in-law Dr Christian Brück and his daughter Barbara on the market place (at number 11). The house had been built between 1547 and 1549. It was here that he saw his family again, his son Lucas and new

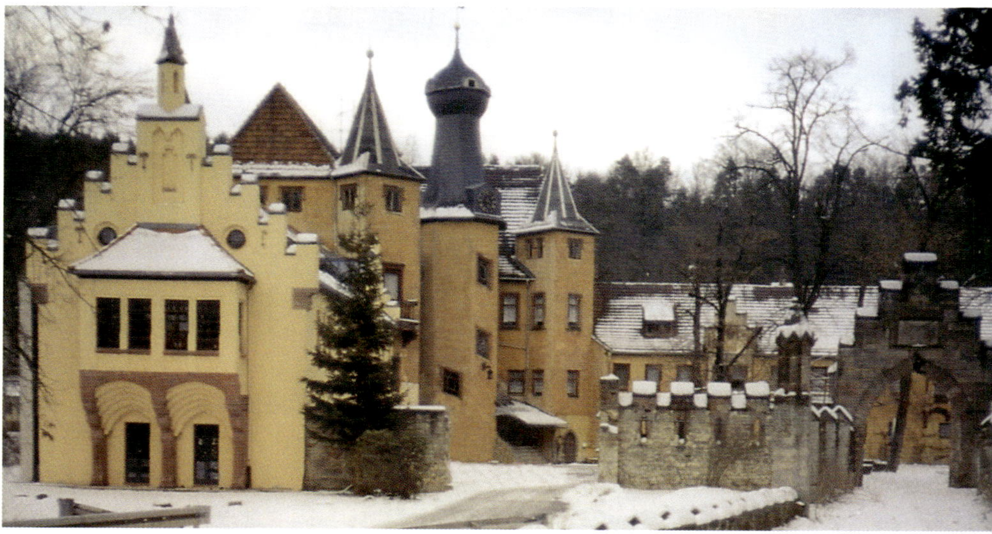

The Moated Castle and Hunting Lodge 'Zur fröhlichen Wiederkunft' in Trockenborn-Wolfersdorf.

daughter-in-law Magdalena Schurff, who had temporarily fled from Wittenberg to Weimar because of the plague.

☐ Lucas Cranach the Elder received back his position as court painter on the condition that he would serve only John Frederick I and his sons. He was promised a yearly sum of 100 florins, winter and summer apparel and food from the court (02.11.1552).

☐ Katharina von Bora, Luther's wife, died on 20.12.1552 at the age of 53 in Torgau. Her grave can be found in the Church of St Mary.

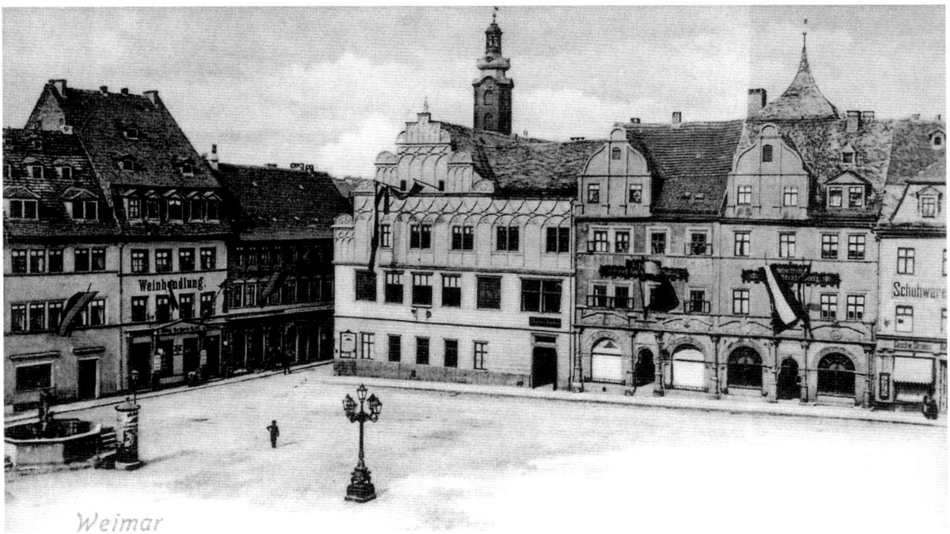

Weimar, Townhouse and Lucas Cranach House on the Market Square.
Photograph from around 1900.
Weimar, Stadtarchiv.

1553

□ As Margrave Albert Alcibiades of Brandenburg-Kulmbach did not abide by the Emperor's peace and, in the manner of a robber baron, carried on the war independently, Maurice of Saxony went up against him with his army. After an acrimonious battle on horseback (09.07.1553), the Margrave was defeated.

However, Maurice was hit by a bullet and died of the wound on 11.07.1553 close to Sievershausen, 8 kilometres north-west of Peine, at the early age of 31. It was the bloodiest battle of the whole Reformation.

Maurice had been married since 1541 to Agnes, the daughter of Landgrave Philipp I of Hesse. Barely two years after this event, the 26-year-old widow celebrated her marriage to the 26-year-old Duke John Frederick II of Saxony (1529–65) on 26.05.1555 in Weimar.

Agnes died on 04.11.1555; her grave can be found in the Town Church in Weimar.

□ Lucas Cranach died in Weimar on 16.10.1553 at the age of 81. He was buried in St James' graveyard, which had been used as Weimar's burial ground since the graveyard at the Town Church closed in 1530.

The three sons of his last patron are said to have provided the gravestone, which is still in existence today. It depicts the deceased in a flattened relief with a circular palette in his hand; at his feet is the Cranach coat of arms in the version of 1537 with a complete helmet decoration. The surrounding Latin inscription reads in translation: 'In the year of our Lord 1553, on 16.10., Lucas Cranach I died at the age of 81 in piety, the swiftest of painters and councillor of Wittenberg who, through his virtue, was held in high esteem by three Electors of Saxony.' The inscription on the grave honours him as *pictor celerrimus*; he had always amazed his contemporaries with his extraordinary speed and dexterity.

His gravestone has stood on the north chancel wall of the Town Church in Weimar since 1859. A copy can be found in the graveyard of St James' Church. He was posthumously honoured by his portrait on the altar painting in the Town Church, which was painted in 1555 by his son Lucas Cranach the Younger as an epitaph for the Elector.

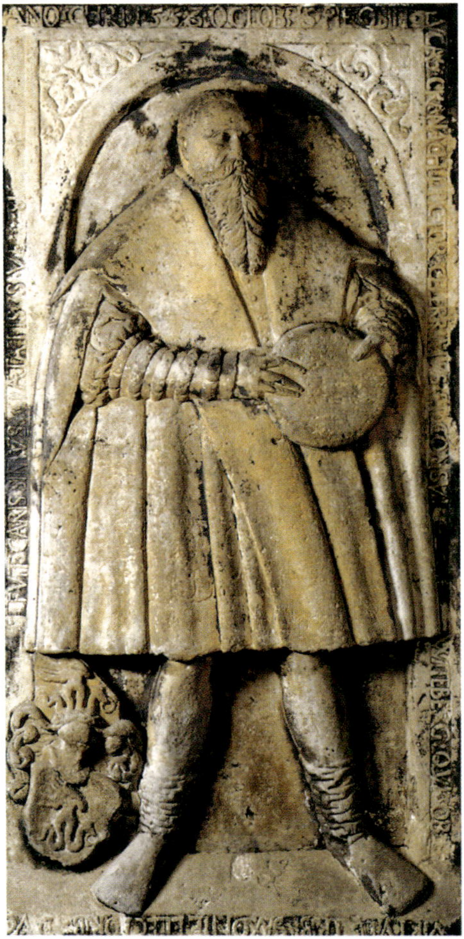

Lucas Cranach's gravestone.
Weimar, Stadtkirche St. Peter und Paul (Herderkirche).

1554

□ Sibyl of Cleves (*17.07.1512, Düsseldorf), Electress of Saxony and consort of John Frederick I died at the age of 42 on 21.02.1554 in Weimar.

□ The Treaty of Naumburg on 24.02.1554 reached a settlement with Maurice of Saxony: John Frederick was given back Altenburg and other territories. From this point on, he was allowed to officially call himself the 'Elector by birth'.

□ Sibyl's husband, John Frederick I the Magnanimous (*30.06.1503, Torgau), Elector of Saxony, died on 03.03.1553 at the age of 51 in Weimar. Both are buried in the Town Church in Weimar.

□ Elector August of Saxony (1526–86) renewed the privileges of an apothecary to Cranach's son-in-law, Caspar Pfreundt, who had inherited the apothecary's in Wittenberg.

1555

□ At the Diet of Augsburg, the adversaries agreed upon the religious Peace of Augsburg, 34 years after the Edict of Worms. This compromise had disastrous consequences for the religious freedom of the citizens: every ruler determined in future which religion was valid for his region according to the motto *cuinus regio, eius religio* (whoever has the land determines the religion). The Diet thus confirmed the division of Germany according to the religious faiths.

□ The Cranach altar for Weimar's Town Church was completed. It is still a matter of debate as to how much Lucas Cranach the Elder was able to work on his last altarpiece. It depicts him and Martin Luther on the middle section of the altar. The stream of blood flowing from Jesus' side lands on the head of the bearded Cranach who was added to the picture at a later date to stand between Martin Luther and John the Baptist.

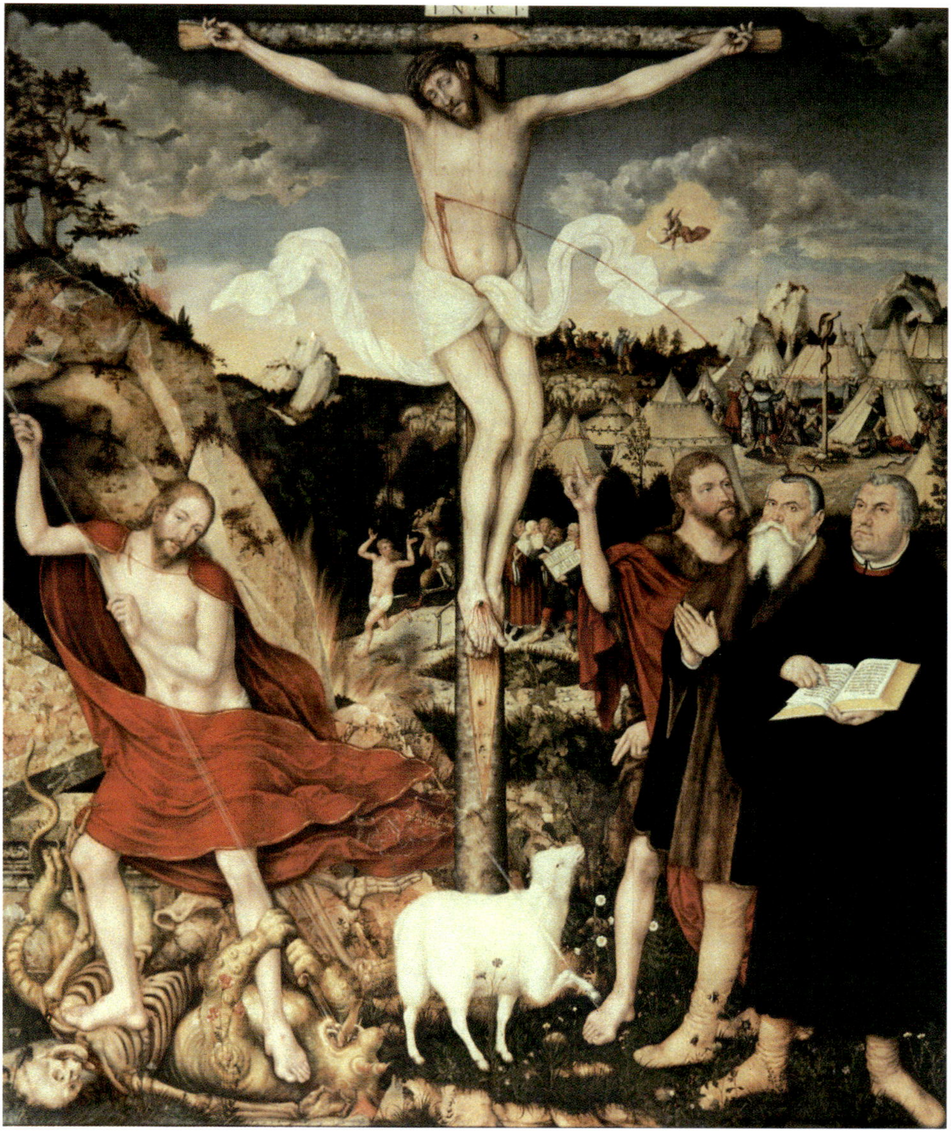

Lucas Cranach, Centre section of the Cranach altar, 1555.
Oil on panel, 360 x 311 cm.
Weimar, Stadtkirche St. Peter und Paul (Herderkirche).

1556

☐ Dr Christian Brück, who was married to Cranach's daughter Barbara, was appointed Chancellor. He held this office until 1567.

☐ Emperor Charles V abdicated in favour of his brother Ferdinand I (1503–64).

1557

☐ The University of Jena was founded.

1558

☐ Johannes Bugenhagen died at the age of 73 on 19.04.1558 in Wittenberg.

☐ Emperor Charles V died at the age of 58 on 21.09.1558 in a monastery in the Estremadura, Spain.

1560

☐ Philipp Melanchthon died at the age of 63 on 19.04.1560 in Wittenberg.

1563

☐ The Council of Trent came to an end. The Huguenot Wars of Religion started in France and, from 1566 onwards, the Dutch struggle for independence.

1564

☐ Emperor Ferdinand I died at the age of 61 on 25.07.1564 in Vienna.

1565

☐ Lucas Cranach the Younger became mayor of Wittenberg (he had been the Chamberlain of the town since 1555).

1567

☐ Philipp I the Magnanimous, Landgrave of Hesse, died at the age of 63 on 31.03.1567 in Kassel.

☐ Dr Christian Brück was executed due to his involvement in the uprisings led by Grumbach against the Electorate.

1586

☐ Lucas Cranach the Younger died at the age of 71 on 25.01.1586 in Weimar.

The Woodcut

The woodcut, first employed in China, is the oldest method of reproduction in relief printing.

As a precondition for woodcutting, it was important to know about the production of paper. The Chinese kept this art a closely guarded secret for a long time. The first European paper mill was founded in Fabriano (in the province of Ancona) in Italy in 1276.

Germany's first paper mill was built by the Nuremberg merchant and chronicler Ulman Stromer (1329–1407) in the Hadermühle, which started production in the winter of 1390/91. It was located at the Wöhrder Gate, north and south of the left branch of the River Pegnitz. By 1499, a further four paper mills had been established within the city of Nuremberg (Schniegling, Lauf, Röthenbach and Tullnau).

The earliest European woodcuts originate from the end of the 14th century. They were prints of individual plates, as they are known; that is, prints which were produced as individual sheets (for example, images of saints, playing cards and pamphlets). Between 1430 and 1470, woodcuts were used for printing block books. In these prints, pictures and texts were cut together into a sheet or printing plate. From the mid-15th century onwards, the woodcut was employed many times in books printed with moveable type (invented by Johannes Gutenberg around 1450). Even after this invention, the woodcut remained closely linked with book printing: the same results could not be obtained with the metal plates which were used in copperplate engraving after 1420.

The woodcut represents an exceptional technique for every artist employing expressive forms of creation; an ideal medium which matches every temperament.

A vital aspect is the choice of wood. Wood is an organic material and it requires a motif that fits to it. No piece of wood is like any other. Every piece has been subject to different conditions while it was growing. Every piece carries within it the special characteristics of the type of tree from which it was cut. Nearly every kind of wood can be used for woodcuts.

A burin, a parting tool, a rounded gouge, a flat-bladed chisel and contour knife belong to the basic equipment of a woodcutter. He uses special knives with certain profiles to cut out those parts which are not to be used for printing.

There are not many ways to transfer the sketch for the cut onto the surface of the wood: either direct, freehand drawing or by using tracing. In producing a woodcut, the parts of the drawing which are not to be printed are cut from the relief plate with a knife in a mirror image (the wrong way round). Gouging (cutting away the non-printed lines and surfaces) is possible in all directions irrespective of the grain.

For the printing of the woodcut, the relief plate is coated with paint. A piece of paper is laid on the coated plate; it is then pressed or brushed flat and printed on in the printing press. Prints made by hand or block prints can be made without a printing press.

The Copperplate Engraving

The technique of copperplate engraving was first employed around 1420. For this art, a copper plate is used which is not too thick and which must be completely flat with an even structure.

In the case of all the early engravings, the proximity in this craft to the contemporary art of the goldsmith is apparent. Indeed, many early copperplate engravers came from the ranks of the goldsmiths.

The copperplate engraving is similar in its technical process to that of wood engraving. In the case of this graphic art, the designer of the images and the engraver are usually one and the same person. The artist transfers the drawing onto the plate whereby he must take into account the fact that the finished print will appear as a mirror image.

The drawing is engraved or etched into the shiny, polished copper plate by means of a burin or other type of chisel. The burin has a wide, rounded end, which must fit well into the engraver's hand, and a diversely sharpened metal point.

The resulting burrs and shavings are then removed with a scraper. In contrast to the use of a writing implement, the burin is not moved from left to right, but is pushed with the right hand against the copper plate, which is held in the left hand, so that the diamond-shaped point at the tip cuts into the copper in the manner of a plough share.

The engraver counters the resistance of the soft, yet resilient metal with an engraving movement of the hand away from his body. So that the course of the engraved lines can be finely differentiated, the plate is manipulated on a leather cushion filled with sand, which enables more precise guidance by the artist. The sharply defined lines run to a fine point. Depending on the pressure applied by the engraver's hand, the lines swell and taper, which determines the *Taille*, as it is known, of the copperplate engraving.

In order to make the print, the plate is gently warmed and coated or rolled in coloured printing ink. As a result of warming, the printing ink becomes softer and thus finds its way into the finest of furrows. This is why copperplate engravings can appear very delicate. Finally, the plate is wiped in such a way that the areas that have not been engraved seem polished, but, in the engraved, recessed lines and points, the printing ink remains.

For printing, absorbent paper and a special press were needed, with the press having two rollers which pushed against each other. This was necessary because the paper, which was moistened before printing, has to be pressed very tightly against the plate. Otherwise it would not be possible to remove the ink which was only in the depressions.

Printing copperplate engravings requires particular technical knowledge and equipment. The correct contact pressure of the two rollers is alone of great importance. If they are too slack, the paper does not take up the printing ink; if they are too tight, there is a danger that the soft copper plates are damaged or at least prematurely worn out. Copperplate engravings are produced in intaglio printing (the opposite of relief painting, with the ink forming the design being printed only from recessed areas of the plate).

Index of People

An underlined date refers to a painting in the book.

Baldung, Hans, known as Grien (1484/5–1545), German painter, artist, master woodcutter and copper engraver
1515

Barbari, Jacopo de (1440/50–before 1516), Italian painter and copper engraver
1505

Brengbier, Jobst (dates unknown), Councillor of Gotha and Cranach's father-in-law
1477, 1511
□ Katharina, née Jahn (dates unknown)
□ Barbara (1477–1540)

Brück, Christian, Dr (1510–67), Chancellor in Wittenberg and Weimar 1556–67
1543, 1550, 1552, 1556, 1567
□ Barbara, née Cranach (1520–1601), wife from 1543 onwards
1515, 1520, 1543, 1552, 1556

Brück, Gregor, Dr (1485–1557), Chancellor of the Electorate of Saxony 1520–29
1533, 1541, 1543, 1547

Bugenhagen, Johannes (1485–1558), German Reformer and town priest in Wittenberg
1521, 1525, 1526, 1532, 1546, 1558

Burgkmair, Hans (1473–1531), German painter, artist and woodcutter
1515

Eck, Johannes (1486–1543), supporter of the Catholic theology of controvery, Professor of Theology
1519

Ernst of Saxony (1441–86), founder of the Ernestine line, Elector from 1464 onwards
1485, 1486, 1506
□ Elisabeth (1443–84), wife from 1460 onwards, daughter of the Duke of Bavaria
□ Christina (1461–1521); Frederick III; German: *Friedrich III* (1463–1525); Ernst (1464–1513) Archbishop of Magdeburg; Albert; German: *Albrecht* (1467–84) Administrator of Mainz; John; German: *Johann* (1468–1532); Margareta (1469–1528); Wolfgang (1473–78)

Ernst (1464–1513), Archbishop of Magdeburg and Bishop of Halberstadt, brother of Elector Frederick III the Wise (German: *Friedrich III der Weise*) and John the Steadfast (German: *Johann der Beständige*)
1513

Ferdinand I (1503–64), German Emperor from 1556 onwards
1532, 1546, 1547, 1552, 1556, 1564

Ferdinand II the Catholic (1452–1516), King of Sicily from 1468 onwards, of Castilian-Leon from 1474, of Aragon from 1479 and of Naples from 1504 onwards

Francis I (1494–1547), King of France from 1515 onwards
1519, 1551

Henry V the Devout; German: *Heinrich V der Fromme* (1473–1541), Duke of Saxony from 1539 onwards
1514, 1539, 1541
□ Katharina (1487–1561), wife from 1512 onwards, daughter of the Duke of Mecklenburg
1514
□ Moritz (1521–53); Severinus (1522–33); August (1526–86)

Henry II the Younger; German: *Heinrich II der Jüngere* (1489–1568), Duke of Brunswick-Wolfenbüttel from 1514 onwards
1542

Henry II (1519–59), King of France from 1547 onwards
1551

Joachim I (1484–1535), Elector of Brandenburg from 1499 onwards
1499, 1502, 1514, 1528, 1529, 1531, 1535, 1545
□ Elisabeth (1485–1555), wife from 1502 onwards, daughter of King Johann I of Denmark
1502, 1528
□ Joachim II (*1505); Anna (*1507); Elisabeth (*1510); Johann (*1513)

Johann Cicero (1455–99), Elector of Brandenburg from 1486 onwards
1499, 1514, 1545

John the Steadfast; German: *Johann der Beständige* (1468–1532), Duke of Saxony from 1486, Elector of Saxony from 1525 onwards
1486, 1500, 1503, 1506, 1509, 1510, 1513, 1515, 1521, 1525, 1526, 1532, 1535, 1536
□ Sophie of Mecklenburg (1481–1503), 1st wife from 1500 onwards
1500, 1503, 1513
□ John Frederick I (German: *Johann Friedrich I*)
□ Margarethe of Anhalt-Zerbst (1494–1521), 2nd wife from 1513 onwards
□ Marie (+1536); Margarethe (+1535); John II; German: *Johann II* (dates unknown, died shortly after his birth); John Ernst I; German: *Johann Ernst I* (1521–53)

John Ernst I; German: *Johann Ernst I* (1521–53), son of Elector John the Steadfast (German: *Johann der Beständige*), Duke of Saxe-Coburg
1513, 1521, 1552

John Frederick I the Magnanimous; German: *Johann Friedrich I der Großmütige* (1503–54), Elector of Saxony 1532–47
1500, 1503, 1506, 1506, 1509, 1512, 1513, 1526, 1526, 1527, 1528, 1530, 1531, 1532, 1532, 1533 (2), 1534, 1537, 1546, 1547, 1548, 1549, 1550, 1551, 1552, 1554
□ Sibyl of Cleves (1512–54), wife from 1526 onwards
1526, 1526, 1527, 1531, 1533 (2), 1554
□ John Frederick II; German: *Johann Friedrich II* (1529–95); Johann Wilhelm (1530–73); John Ernst II; German: *Johann Ernst II* (*+1535); John Frederick III; German: *Johann Friedrich III* (1538–65)

Luther, Hans (1459–1530), miner and master smelter
1483, 1527 (2)
□ Margarethe, née Lindemann (+1531), wife from around 1483 onwards
1483, 1527
□ Martin (1483–1546) and eight other children

Luther, Martin, Dr (1483–1546), German Reformer
1483, 1505, 1507, 1510, 1512, 1514, 1517, 1518, 1519, 1520, 1521 (2), 1522, 1523, 1524, 1525, 1526, 1527, 1528, 1529, 1530, 1531, 1532 (2), 1537, 1540, 1541, 1543, 1545, 1546, 1552, 1555
□ Katharina von Bora (1499–1552), wife from 1525 onwards
1523, 1525, 1526, 1552
□ Johannes (1526–75), Chancellor to Duke Albert of Prussia (German: *Albrecht von Preußen*); Elisabeth (1527–28); Magdalena (1529–42); Martin (1531–65), theologian; Paul (1533–93), physician to the court of the Elector of Saxony; Margarete (1534–70)

Maler, Hans (1448 (?) – before 1528), painter
1472
□ (Barbara ?), née Hübner (1451–91/92 (?), + vor 1528), wife from around 1472 onwards
1472
□ Lucas (1472–1553); daughter (name unknown) (1474–75); Margarete (1476–1530); son (name unknown) (1479–83); daughter (name unknown) (1482–85); Anna (1485–1577); Kuni (1488–1555); Ennlein/Agnes (*1489); Mathias (um 1490–1553)

Philipp I the Magnanimous; German: *Philipp I der Großmütige* (1504–67), Landgrave of Hesse from 1509 onwards
1523, 1531, 1540, 1541, 1546, 1547, 1552, 1553, 1567
□ Christine (1505–49), 1st wife from 1523 onwards, daughter of Duke George of Saxony; German: *Georg*
□ Agnes (*1527); Anna (*1529); Wilhelm IV (*1532); Barbara (*1536); Ludwig IV (*1537); Elisabeth (*1539); Philipp II (*1541); Christine (*1543); Georg I (*1547)
□ Margarete von der Saale (1522–66), 2nd wife from 1540 onwards, daughter of Hans von der Saale
□ Philipp (*1541); Hermann (*1542); Christoph (*1543); Margarethe (*1544); Albert (*1546); Philipp (*1547); Maurice; German: Moritz (*1553); Ernst (*1554)

Ponickaus, Hans, von (dates unknown), Chamberlain of the Electorate of Saxony
1547

Scheurl, Christoph (1481–1542), German Humanist
1507, 1509, 1519

Scheyring, Johannes, Dr (approx. 1454–1516), Rector of the University of Leipzig and Canon of Magdeburg
<u>1529</u>

Schurff, Augustin, Dr (+1548), Professor of Medicine
<u>1551</u>

Solms, Graf Philipp of (1486–1544), councillor to the Elector
1520, <u>1520</u>

Spalatin, Georg (1484–1545), German theologian
1512, 1518, 1520, 1530, 1545

Staupitz, Johannes von (1468/9–1524), German theologian
1512

Tizian; real name: Tiziano Vecellio (approx. 1477–1576), Italian painter
1550

Wichmann (1152–92), Archbishop of Magdeburg
1506

Winterburger, Johannes (approx. 1460–1519), German printer and publisher
1503

Zwingli, Ulrich (1484–1531), Swiss Reformer
1522

Index of Place Names

An underlined date refers to a painting in the book.

Darmstadt	1525
Dessau	1510 (2)
Dresden	1485, 1500, 1506 (3), 1509 (2), 1514 (2), 1515 (2), 1517, 1522, 1523, 1525 (7), 1534, 1539, 1541
Eisenach	1520 (2), 1521, 1527 (2), 1533, 1550
Eisleben	1483, 1546
Emden	1485, 1500
Erfurt	1503, 1505, 1507, 1510, 1512, 1524
Florence	1510, 1514, 1550
Frankenhausen	1525
Frankfurt a.M.	1509, 1515, 1519, 1521, 1524, 1532, 1539, 1548
Freiberg	1541
Geldern	1541
Ghent	1519, 1547
Gotha	1506 (4), 1508, 1509 (4), 1510 (4), 1511, 1512 (4), 1514, 1515 (2), 1516, 1518, 1521, 1523, 1525, 1526, 1528, 1531 (2), 1533 (2), 1537 (2), 1540, 1546
Gottorf	1525
Grimma	1485, 1525, 1531
Halle	1525, 1546, 1547
Hamburg	1532
Hummelshain	1552
Innsbruck	1547, 1552
Jena	1552, 1557

Genealogical Table of the House of Wettin

- Frederick II the Gentle
  1412–64, Elector
  oo 1431 Margarethe, daughter of
  Duke Ernst of Austria
  - Anna, 1437–1512
    oo 1458 Albert Achilles, Elector of
    Brandenburg
  - Ernst, 1441–86, founder of the
    Ernestine line, Elector
    oo 1460 Elisabeth, daughter of
    Duke Albert III of Bavaria
    - Christine,
      1461–1521
      oo 1478 John,
      King of Denmark
    - Frederick the Wise
      1463–1525, Elector
    - Ernst, 1463–1513
      Archbishop of
      Magdeburg and
      Bishop of
      Halberstadt
    - John the Steadfast
      1468–1532, Elector
      oo 1500 Sophie,
      daughter of Duke
      Magnus II of
      Mecklenburg;
      oo 1513 Margarethe,
      daughter of Prince
      Waldemar VI of Anhalt
      - John Frederick I, 1503–54
        Elector
        oo 1526 Sibyl, daughter of
        Duke John III of Jülich-Cleve-Berg
      - John Ernst, 1521–63
        oo 1542 Katharina, daughter of
        Duke Philipp I of Brunswick-
        Grubenhagen

- John, 1498–1537
  oo 1516 Elisabeth, daughter of
  Landgrave Wilhelm II of Hesse
- Frederick, 1504–39
  oo 1539 Elisabeth, daughter of
  Duke Ernst II of Mansfeld

Frederick I the Warlike
1370–1428, Elector of Saxony
oo 1402 Katharina, daughter of Duke
Henry of Brunswick-Lüneburg

Wilhelm III the Brave
1425–82, granted Thuringia
oo 1446 Anna, daughter of
King Albert II;
oo 1463 Katharina, daughter of
Eberhard of Brandenstein

Margarethe, 1449–1501
oo 1476 Johann Cicero,
Elector of Brandenburg

Albert the Courageous
1443–1500, founder of the Albertine line,
granted Meissen
oo 1459 Sidonie, daughter of
King George Podiebrad of Bohemia

Georg, 1471–1539
oo 1496 Barbara, daughter of
King Kasimir IV of Poland

Henry V the Devout
1473–1541
oo 1512 Katharina, daughter of
Duke Magnus II of Mecklenburg

Friedrich, 1474–1510
Grand Master of the Teutonic
Order in Prussia

Maurice, 1521–53
oo 1541 Agnes, daughter of
Landgrave Philipp I of Hesse

Severinus, 1522–33

August, 1526–86
oo 1548 Anna, daughter of
King Christian III of Denmark;
oo 1586 Agnes Hedwig,
daughter of Prince Joachim
Ernst of Anhalt

Christine, 1505–49
oo 1523 Landgrave Philipp I of
Hesse

Magdalene, 1507–34
oo 1524 Joachim II, Elector of
Brandenburg

Genealogical Table of the House of Brandenburg (Hohenzollern)

Johann Cicero
1455–99, Kurfürst
oo 1476 Margarethe, daughter of
Duke Wilhelm of Saxony

Kasimir, 1481–1527
Margrave of Kulmbach
oo 1518 Susanna, daughter of
Duke Albrecht of Bavaria

George, 1484–1543
Margrave of Ansbach
oo 1533 Emilie, daughter of
Duke Henry of Saxony

Joachim I, 1484–1535
oo 1502 Elisabeth, daughter of King John I of
Denmark

Ursula, 1488–1510
oo 1507 Henry V the Peaceful,
Duke of Mecklenburg-Schwerin

Joachim II, 1505–71
1535 Elector;
1539 converted to Lutheranism
oo 1524 Magdalene, daughter of
Duke George of Saxe-Meissen

Anna, 1507–67
oo 1524 Duke Albert VII of
Mecklenburg-Schwerin

Albert Achilles
1414–86, Elector
oo 1446 Margarethe, daughter of
Margrave Jakob I of Baden;
oo 1458 Anna, daughter of Frederick II,
Elector of Saxony

Frederick V, 1460–1536, Margrave
oo Sophie, daughter of
King Kasimir IV of Poland

Sibyl, 1467–1524
oo 1481 Wilhelm IV Duke of
Jülich and Berg

Albrecht, 1490–1568
1511 Grand Master of the Teutonic Order in
Prussia;
1525 Duke of Prussia
oo 1526 Dorothea, daughter of
King Frederick I of Denmark

John, 1493–1525, Margrave
oo 1519 Germaine, widow of
King Ferdinand the Catholic of Spain

Albrecht, 1490–1545
1509 Canon of Mainz; 1513 Archbishop of
Magdeburg and Administrator of the
bishopric of Halberstadt; 1518 Cardinal Archbishop of
Mainz (= Elector)

Johann (Hans), 1513–71
Margrave of Brandenburg-Küstrin
1552 Councillor to Emperor Charles V
oo 1531 Katharina, daughter of
Henry II of Brunswick-Wolfenbüttel

Map

Saxon-Thuringian Territories around 1500

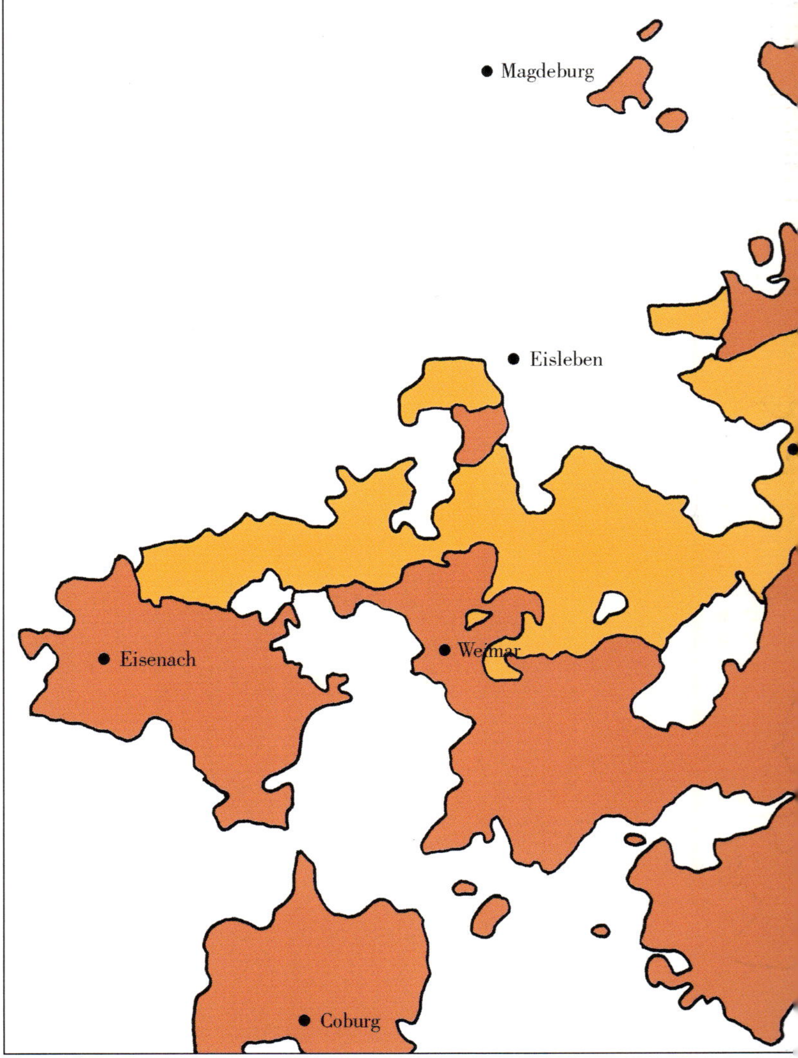

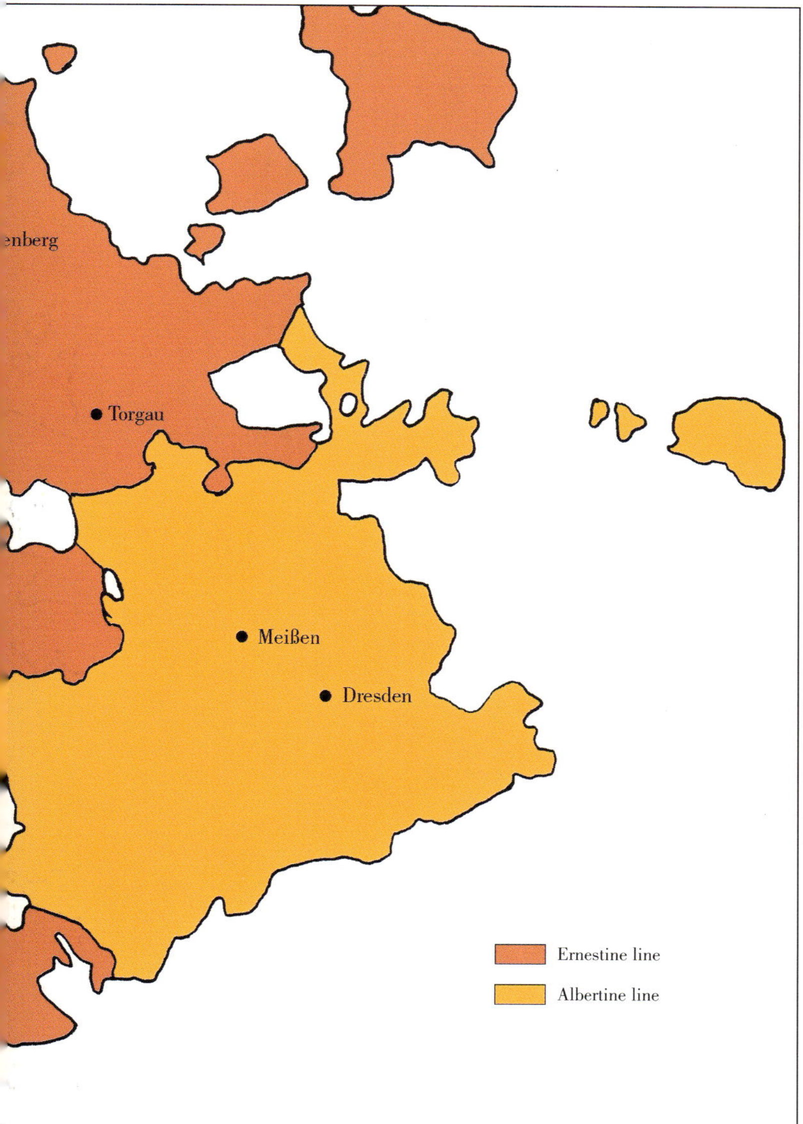

enberg
Torgau
Meißen
Dresden
Ernestine line
Albertine line